The Birth of Lean

Conversations with **Taiichi Ohno**, **Eiji Toyoda**, and other figures who shaped Toyota management

Koichi Shimokawa *and* Takahiro Fujimoto, *Editors*

Translated by Brian Miller with John Shook

The Lean Enterprise Institute

Cambridge, Massachussetts

lean.org

Version 1.0

March 2009

ISBN: 978-1-934109-22-9
Cover design by Lapisworks
March 2009

The Lean Enterprise Institute, Inc.
One Cambridge Center, Cambridge, MA 02142 USA
Tel: 617-871-2900 • Fax: 617-871-2999 • lean.org

Acknowledgments

The publisher expresses heartfelt gratitude to...

Koichi Shimokawa and Takahiro Fujimoto, the editors of the original, Japanese edition of this book, for their cooperation in making this English-language edition possible;

Kenichi Kuwashima, Takashi Matsuo, Nobuya Orihashi, Hiroaki Satake, and Yasuo Sugiyama for their contributions as interviewers and editors in preparing the Japanese edition;

Bunshindo, the publisher of the Japanese edition, for permission to publish this English-language edition; and

Daihatsu Motor, Hashida Giken, the Toyota Commemorative Museum of Industry and Technology, and Toyota Motor Corporation for furnishing the photographs that appear in this book, as detailed below:

Daihatsu Motor

pp. 22 (upper), 25, 28

Hashida Giken

p. 22 (lower)

Toyota Commemorative Museum of Industry and Technology

pp. 3, 4, 5 (upper), 7, 12, 17, 78, 114, 137, 178, 227

Toyota Motor Corporation

pp. 5 (lower), 6, 9, 26, 77, 103, 110, 112, 113, 115, 141, 144, 175, 218, 230, 242, 245, 251, 261

Note: **English translations of divisional names**

The translators have rendered the names of most divisions, departments, and other organizational units in lower case. That is because several of the names have changed over the years and because some of the units did not originally have official English names. However, the translators have capitalized divisional names that are of historical interest in their own right: the names of Toyota's Operations Management Consulting Division, of that division's previous incarnations, and of Toyota's Auditing and Improvement Department.

Foreword

From the Chairman of the Lean Enterprise Institute
Jim Womack

Since the beginning of the Lean Enterprise Institute, we have been interested in the origins of lean. Scholars have written widely on this topic, and we have identified a number of volumes, including Takahiro Fujimoto's *The Evolution of a Manufacturing System at Toyota,* to recommend to members of the lean community. But we had not heard from the actual creators—those present at the birth of lean in the 1940s, 1950s, and 1960s—in their own words about just what they did and why they did it.

Fortunately, in *The Birth of Lean,* Fujimoto and Koichi Shimokawa have rectified this shortcoming. They have presented the insights of these Toyota pioneers through extensive interviews and annotated talks. This kind of personal commentary has never been available outside Japan. It comes to us through the editorial and translation efforts of longtime Toyota observer Brian Miller and Toyota veteran John Shook.

Although I have read practically all of the literature available in English on Toyota, I found the interviews, talks, and commentary in this volume enormously helpful in clarifying what actually happened and invaluable for those planning the path to lean transformation in their organizations. At a time when all of us are struggling to implement lean production and lean management, often with complex programs on an organization-wide basis, it is helpful to learn that the creators of lean had no grand plan and no company-wide program to install it. Instead, they were an army of line-manager experimenters trying to solve pressing business problems, in particular a lack of financial resources, to grow rapidly without accumulating large inventories.

Taiichi Ohno, Eiji Toyoda, Kikuo Suzumura, Masao Nemoto, and others you hear from here in their own words knew they could not solve their problems by employing the standard practices of large mass production organizations, as typified by General Motors. So they tried experiment after experiment, keeping careful notes on the results and spreading methods that worked.

Remarkably, they only came up with a name for what they discovered—the fabled Toyota Production System—in 1970 after they had invented and deployed all of the elements. And they only created a program office—now the Operations Management Consulting Division—at about the same time, after the Toyota Production System had already taken hold throughout Toyota's operations.

I found Toyota's approach heartening for those of us who have discovered the hard way that big, top-down lean programs rarely achieve the desired results. And I was inspired to hear the stories of line-manager experimenters who pushed steadily ahead without a grand plan but in a consistent direction, often over intense opposition.

Surely we can all make progress using Toyota's approach if we clearly define our business problems and go to the *gemba*—the workplace—to experiment. I hope that you, too, will be enlightened and inspired by this volume as we all continue on our hard but rewarding lean journeys.

Cambridge, Massachusetts

March 2009

Contents

Preface

Adapted from the Preface to the Japanese Edition
Koichi Shimokawa *and* **Takahiro Fujimoto**

Toyota established a globally influential corporate model in the latter half of the 20th century. The model is most familiar as the Toyota Production System, though Toyota-style manufacturing encompasses more than the elements narrowly associated with that system. Most notably, Toyota's prodigious success has benefited crucially from total quality control (TQC).

Companies worldwide have adopted the Toyota Production System under the name of lean manufacturing. And TQC, which Toyota and other Japanese manufacturers built from American concepts, has taken hold worldwide under the name total quality management.

Numerous commentators have described in detail the structure and functions of the Toyota Production System and of TQC. Likewise, descriptions of the development of both systems appear in official corporate histories and in works by industrial historians. Nearly all of those descriptions, however, are after-the-fact accounts that focus to a fault on the rationalization and the competitiveness that the systems engendered.

The standard histories have largely overlooked the serendipitous process of creation, the trial and error, and the multiplicity of inputs that shaped both the Toyota Production System and TQC. That has encouraged mistaken notions that the development of the systems proceeded in line with some sort of master plan. We should bear in mind, incidentally, that the management, manufacturing, and marketing methodologies based on the "scientific management" of Frederick Taylor and on the conveyor line production of Henry Ford also evolved in a less-systematic manner than historical oversimplification frequently suggests.

Toyota has unquestionably displayed a tenacious consistency over 70 years in building competitiveness and in honing the fundamental capabilities that underlie that competitiveness. That consistency, however, has masked a stunning array of happenstance, confrontation, confusion, wrong turns, and occasional crisis. The ability to nurture a capacity for perseverant organizational learning amid that chaos is arguably Toyota's most essential core competence. On the following pages, individuals who were "present at the creation" offer a wealth of insight into that competence.

Individuals who shaped Toyota manufacturing definitively from the 1940s to the 1970s appear here through talks and interviews. The remembrances presented touch on dead ends, disputes, and differing interpretations that do not appear in the official histories. Sometimes highly subjective, they furnish an invaluable contribution to the historical record. Additional commentary by the editors rounds out the first-person accounts.

Maximizing the value of these recollections is the combination of voices. Here are first-person accounts from complementary perspectives: Taiichi Ohno, the Toyota executive who was the theorist behind the Toyota Production System; Michikazu Tanaka, a manufacturing executive at the Toyota affiliate (now subsidiary) Daihatsu Motor who was close to Ohno; Kikuo Suzumura, the Toyota manager who was most influential in implementing Ohno's ideas in the workplace; Kaneyoshi Kusunoki, a Toyota executive who collaborated and occasionally sparred with Ohno from the standpoint of production engineering; Masao Nemoto, the Toyota executive who led the company's adoption of TQC; and Eiji Toyoda, the leader who oversaw the development of the Toyota Production System and the introduction of TQC while steering the company's impressive growth.

Something that emerges convincingly in these talks and interviews is the continuing relevance of the basic principles of the Toyota Production

System and TQC. That lasting pertinence is astounding in view of the forces that have reshaped manufacturing in the past half century: information
technology, globalization, flexible manufacturing, and shareholder activ-
ism, just to name a few prominent examples. Those forces have spawned
innumerable management fads, and the proponents of each new theory
have proclaimed a de facto standard for generating corporate value. Amid
the ephemera of management fashions, Toyota's system remains the singularly enduring gold standard for global manufacturing.

Tokyo

January 2001 (revised in March 2009)

Introduction

Adapted from the Introduction to the Japanese Edition
Koichi Shimokawa

Factories that use the Toyota Production System bear a deceptive resemblance to those that use Henry Ford's system of flow-based mass production. Both kinds of factories center on conveyor lines that operate in smooth synchrony. That apparent similarity, however, masks a profound difference born of an epochal paradigm shift.

The Toyota Production System defies easy characterization, but its most definitive element is unquestionably the principle of just-in-time manufacturing. That principle marked a historic departure from the Ford system's high-volume, high-speed, make-to-sell production. Just-in-time manufacturing was a rejection of the wide-ranging loss inherent in Ford's approach: vast accumulations of part and product inventories, unnecessarily long changeover times for tools and dies, inefficiencies in the deployment of human resources associated with narrow skill sets and a resultant inflexibility in accommodating changing ranges of work, and immense waste caused by product defects.

Just-in-time manufacturing reduced waste by replacing the "push" dynamic of make-to-sell production with the "pull" dynamic of make-to-order production. In traditional manufacturing, processes throughout the production sequence operated with little regard for the pace of production elsewhere in the sequence and foisted their output onto the following processes—a practice that culminated in foisting make-to-sell accumulations of products onto the marketplace. In just-in-time manufacturing, each process withdrew material from the previous process only to replace material it had actually used, and each process generated additional output only to replace material that the following process had withdrawn. Thus did the system provide for making only what is needed, only when it is needed, and only in the amount needed.

Practitioners of traditional manufacturing had countenanced large inventories throughout the production sequence as a necessary evil—necessary to keep things moving smoothly. In just-in-time manufacturing, any inventory in excess of a minimal "standard in-process stock" became absolutely unacceptable. Production of a limited range of products in large volumes gave way, meanwhile, to producing a large range of products in generally small volumes. That meant a shift in emphasis from maximizing equipment capacity and utilization rates to maximizing flexibility in responding nimbly to trends in demand. Factories shifted to processing in increasingly smaller lots. People found ways to shorten changeover times and streamline layouts to minimize the adverse effect of frequent changeovers on capacity utilization rates.

The paradigm shift embodied in the Toyota Production System established a framework for ensuring high productivity and—by building quality assurance into each process—consistently high quality. The flexibility of the Toyota Production System proved responsive to ever-changing markets and supportive of advances in product technology and of evolving approaches to product development and design. Equally important, the system proved applicable beyond Toyota's factories. It took hold at suppliers' factories, in purchasing organizations, and in logistics networks, and the synergies among the growing range of participants in the system maximized the benefits for all.

Revolution, an overused term, is a perfectly apt description for the change wrought by the Toyota Production System. The system was largely responsible for the surging international competitiveness of Japan's automobile industry in the 1980s, as documented by the Massachusetts

Institute of Technology–based International Motor Vehicle Program. Japanese manufacturers of electronic equipment and of other assembly manufacturing products also employed elements of Toyota's system in asserting international competitiveness.

Japanese automakers and parts makers transplanted the Toyota Production System abroad when they began building large numbers of factories overseas in the late 1980s. Elements of the system soon started appearing in the factories of U.S. and European automakers: slimmed-down inventories, smaller processing lots and shortened changeover times, bar-coded kanban cards, "idiot-proof" features on equipment, lighted *andon* display panels above factory workplaces to indicate where problems were occurring, and sequenced withdrawal of parts and materials in accordance with the "pull" precepts of just-in-time manufacturing.

People at the overseas companies that emulated the Toyota Production System generally had an incomplete understanding of the philosophy behind the system. Worker participation, meanwhile, tended to be less thorough than in Japan, partly because of union rules and different labor practices. On the other hand, the growing application of information technology in factory operations, especially in the United States, favored the Toyota Production System. Database management furnished a new basis for evaluating manufacturing methods objectively and for retaining know-how of demonstrated value. It verified the effectiveness of elements of the Toyota Production System, and managements moved to adopt those elements in their operations.

Employee participation in the Toyota Production System in Japan has unfolded primarily in the context of tacit knowledge. Promoting similar participation in other nations has required companies to translate that tacit knowledge into explicit knowledge. Several business models have emerged for that purpose, and some of them cover far more than individual production processes. Companies have borrowed concepts and methods from the Toyota Production System to foster just-in-time linkage all the way from product development through purchasing, manufacturing, and logistics to sales and service. They have used that linkage to focus activity throughout the value chain on earning and retaining customer satisfaction.

Manufacturers today face challenges of unprecedented severity. Automakers, especially, are struggling to survive. Toyota, too, was struggling to survive when Taiichi Ohno began experimenting with the methods that became the Toyota Production System. This is therefore an opportune time to examine carefully the convergence of factors that engendered the success of Ohno's experiments. Foremost among those factors was an unwavering focus on the *gemba*: the workplace.

The managers who worked under Ohno strove untiringly to explain his ideas to the workplace supervisors and to secure *gemba* participation in implementing those ideas. Toyota's continuing vitality is testimony to the vibrant workplace that the company has carefully fostered. It is also testimony to the company's continuing readiness to encourage the interplay of frequently conflicting ideas. Here, in the words of Taiichi Ohno, Eiji Toyoda, and four other remarkable individuals, is the story of how that interplay perpetrated a revolution in global manufacturing.

Chapter I

How It All Began

An interview with **Taiichi Ohno**

As conducted and edited by **Koichi Shimokawa** *and*
Takahiro Fujimoto

The Interview

1. Lessons from Toyoda Boshoku

When I was a student, people simply assumed that Japan was no place to make cars. That was around 1930. The United States had high efficiency and high wages. In Japan, efficiency was low, and so were wages. But the pursuit of higher efficiency ended in the United States in the early 1930s, and only wages kept rising after that, as we figured out later.

About the Interview

This chapter is the distillation of a three-hour interview with Taiichi Ohno. Koichi Shimokawa and Takahiro Fujimoto conducted the interview on July 16, 1984. The interview took place at the headquarters of Toyoda Gosei, a Toyota Group manufacturer of weatherstrip, interior and exterior trim, airbags, and other automotive components based mainly on plastic and rubber technologies. Ohno was serving as an adviser to Toyoda Gosei at the time of the interview.

Shimokawa asked most of the questions, and Fujimoto took detailed notes of Ohno's responses. The text is a reconstruction based entirely on Fujimoto's notes because the interviewers refrained from using a tape recorder. It is therefore less precise in regard to the speaker's exact phrasing than the other texts presented in this volume. All of the technical terms that appear here are faithful, however, to Ohno's word selection.

I worked as a production supervisor at Toyoda Boshoku (Toyoda Spinning and Weaving) up to and into World War II. The productivity there wasn't bad. But Dainippon Spinners [now Unitika] and some of our other competitors used completely different production systems, and their productivity was even higher.

A Comparison of Toyoda Boshoku and Dainippon Spinners

	Plant layout	Thread conveyance	Skills deployment	Quality control
Toyoda Boshoku	Processes in separate buildings	Large lots conveyed by trolleys, heavy labor performed by male workers	New workers load and unload spindles, veteran workers (3 to 5 years of experience) operate machines	Reliance on skilled workers to reconnect broken threads, emphasis on corrective action in following process
Dainippon Spinners	Processes in same building, integrated production	Small lots conveyed by female workers, less expensive than conveying large lots	New workers operate machines, veteran workers load and unload spindles	Emphasis on making quality threads in preceding process to eliminate need for corrective action in following process

Ohno's comments are in response to questions that focused on the following subjects:

1. What Ohno learned at the Toyota Group company Toyoda Boshoku (Toyoda Spinning and Weaving), where he worked before joining Toyota Motor and how that figured in his subsequent activities

2. Ohno's initial experiences at Toyota Motor after moving to that company in the midst of World War II

3. How Ohno and Toyota worked to raise productivity while rebuilding the company's automotive operations after the war, what lessons he and the company learned from the labor dispute of 1950, and how they applied those lessons in devising their production system

4. How Toyota established standardized work procedures in the early years and how flow-based production and leveled production took shape

We learned a lot by comparing the production systems used by different companies. Especially interesting was the concept of making sure the front-end processes delivered consistently high-quality work to the following processes. That concept is the basis of total quality control

A reenactment of the work of loading spindles on an automatic loom

(TQC). The Toyota Production System is one and the same with TQC and with its principle of zero defects. They're simply different names for the same basic approach.

Another lesson we learned at Toyoda Boshoku was the importance of not relying on craftsmen. We learned to design systems that could be operated by anyone—amateurs—with a minimum of training. That's what standardized work is all about.

5. The origins of multiskilled workers and multiprocess handling and Toyota's response to the surge in demand that accompanied the Korean War

6. The history of kanban, including the reasons for adopting the kanban system, issues that Ohno encountered in deploying the system, and how he resolved those issues

7. How the kanban system was superior to the production systems employed by other Japanese automakers

8. The relationship between the kanban system and quality control

9. How and why Ohno employed the *jidoka* principle of intelligent automation

The interviewers gave Ohno every opportunity to recall and relate pertinent episodes from his trial-and-error experience in implementing Kiichiro Toyoda's just-in-time concepts. He responded in detail to the questions, offering concrete examples and touching on related contemporary issues that came to

A prewar factory scene at Toyoda Boshoku

The Toyota Production System rests on two pillars. One is Sakichi Toyoda's *jidoka*: Turning out defective work is not what we're here for. The other is Kiichiro Toyoda's just in time. This is not the Ohno Production System. It's the Toyota Production System.

2. Wartime Production

Textile work dried up in 1943, so I moved over to the automobile company, where I became a factory manager. We had reached a point in textile spinning production where further gains in productivity were hard to come by. But in vehicle production, just about anything we might try seemed likely to raise productivity three- or even five-fold. We figured that

mind. The interview ended up running an hour longer than the two hours originally scheduled. Especially poignant are Ohno's descriptions of creating a new approach to manufacturing amid the privations of the immediate postwar years. Readers can and by all means should review his account of lean production in his classic, *Toyota Production System: Beyond Large-Scale Production* (New York: Productivity Press, 1988).

we could make vehicles with the production system that we had developed for spinning work.

Toyota's Koromo (now Honsha [Headquarters]) Plant shortly after its completion in 1938

Japan was at war, and we converted our factories to military applications. One produced aircraft oil coolers. Another made exhaust manifolds for aircraft. Our job in production was to increase output in support of the war effort, and we concentrated on simply producing the target volumes. I shifted to Toyota Motor's Koromo [now Honsha (Headquarters)] Plant in February 1945, and that's where I was when the war ended.

About the Speaker

Taiichi Ohno (February 29, 1912–May 28, 1990) is renowned as the father of the Toyota Production System. Born in Japanese-occupied Dalian, China, he joined Toyoda Boshoku (Toyoda Spinning and Weaving) on graduating from what is now the Nagoya Institute of Technology in 1932. He moved in 1943 to Toyota Motor.

At Toyota, Ohno went to work on the problem-solving innovations that became the framework of the Toyota Production System. He became the manager of a

Taiichi Ohno in the 1970s

3. Postwar Productivity Growth

After the war, I became responsible for vehicle assembly at Toyota's Koromo (Honsha) Plant. A lot of people in the company thought that we should outsource small-volume parts to low-cost contractors and make the large-volume parts on our own, like bicycle manufacturers did. They figured that we could build an export business by getting the contractors to supply parts on a just-in-time basis and by assembling vehicles from those parts and from the parts that we made in-house.

I argued for taking the opposite approach. I insisted that we should produce low-volume items in-house and buy large-volume parts—stuff that anyone could make inexpensively—from outside suppliers. Making the low-volume parts in-house would mean high unit costs, and that would pressure us to tackle kaizen improvements and cost reductions. Refining just-in-time efficiency was every bit as important in our in-house operations as it was in our dealings with suppliers.

Taiichi Ohno in his natural environment—the manufacturing workplace

machining shop in 1946, and that shop became the laboratory for the invention of the kanban and the development of flow-based production.

Ohno became a director at Toyota in 1954, a managing director in 1964, a senior managing director in 1970, and an executive vice president in 1975. He retired from Toyota in 1978 but remained active in consulting. In addition, he served as an adviser at Toyoda Gosei and as the chairman of Toyoda Boshoku after leaving Toyota.

Kiichiro Toyoda issued a call right after the war for catching up with the U.S. automakers in productivity within three years. In the spinning industry, we had reckoned in 1935 that productivity was 3 times higher in Germany than in Japan and 3 times higher still in the United States. So I figured that automakers were probably about 10 times more productive in the United States than in Japan.

Kiichiro Toyoda (1894–1952)

The productivity differential between the United States and Japan was too big to blame on differences in production equipment. I could see that different ways of managing production were a bigger factor than equipment. So I went to work on modifying our production system: leveling production, standardizing work, and optimizing factory layouts.

4. Production Restraints Precipitated by a Financial Crisis

We devoted ourselves to raising efficiency in every way possible in the first five years after the war. We raised productivity five- or six-fold and positioned ourselves to turn out 1,000 trucks a month. Unfortunately, we couldn't sell all those trucks, and we ended up with a heap of unsold vehicles. The company was on the verge of collapse.

Management announced a restructuring plan in 1950 that included job cuts, which triggered a huge labor dispute. That was an extremely tough time for Toyota. But it wasn't the first time that Toyota had gotten into serious trouble with excess inventory. The company had let unsold trucks pile up once before the war. Only a helping hand from the military had kept Toyota afloat that time.

The lesson we learned from the postwar crisis was that simply raising productivity is no cure-all. We discovered the importance of raising productivity and reducing costs while limiting production to the kinds of products sold, in the amounts they are sold, and at the time they are sold. In other words, we learned that imitating American-style mass production would be fatal in Japan.

I lobbied aggressively for leveling production in the front-end processes while I was supervising final assembly at the Honsha Plant. People got so tired of hearing me rant that they gave me a machining shop to try out my ideas. It was a shop that produced transmission gears and suspension components. That was in 1946.

We were able to keep raising productivity pretty easily in the latter half of the 1940s by doing basic kaizen. For example, Toyota had assigned three or four operators to each machine in the main processes before the war. We raised labor productivity three- or four-fold by modifying the work procedures to allow for operating each machine with a single operator. Our moves ran into resistance from the old-school craftsmen among the workers, but we had a high worker turnover rate at the time, so measures for reducing manpower requirements went fairly smoothly.

5. Standardized Work

My first move as the manager of the machining shop was to introduce standardized work. The production workplace at the time was under the sway of the craftsmen responsible for the different processes. Neither the shop manager nor the production general manager above him could assert much control over a shop. All that they could do was make excuses for the production delays, and you can be sure that they got a lot of practice.

We took control of the machining shop by defining standardized work for each job, by detailing the work in a manual, and by posting the standardized work procedures in plain view at each workstation. The panels that displayed the standardized work procedures were the forerunners

of kanban. We developed kanban later as a means of making
the flow of work visible. And
the standardized work display
panels served basically the same
purpose: they let the foremen
and supervisors see easily if the
operators were adhering to the
standardized work procedures.
They were just like the sign [kan-

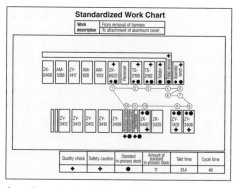

A modern standardized work chart that details the work sequence for a process

ban] outside a retail shop. Anyone could see immediately from the sign
what was likely to be—was supposed to be—going on inside.

I told everyone that they weren't earning their pay if they left the standardized work unchanged for a whole month. The idea was to let people
know that they were responsible for making continual improvements in
the work procedures and for incorporating those improvements in the
standardized work.

Standardized work at Toyota is a framework for kaizen improvements.
We start by adopting some kind—any kind—of work standards for a job.
Then we tackle one improvement after another, trial and error. You could
start by doing motion studies and time studies and whatever and try to
come up with something perfect to start with, but that would never work.
In the workplace, trying something immediately, even something imperfect, is always better than letting things sit while you refine a solution.

Continual improvements are just as important with equipment as they
are with work procedures. Kaizen raises efficiency and improves quality
by imparting a growing accumulation of wisdom to the equipment.

As for the pace of work, we set a pace that an average worker can
maintain for a full day. That means a pace that is maintainable without
undue strain, and the team leader personally verifies the feasibility of

the pace. You mustn't establish a pace based on the hand and foot speed of your most experienced personnel. Taylorism called for setting targets based on the speed of the fastest workers, but that's exploiting labor.

We make sure that everyone can see clearly what our expectations are in regard to the pace of work. Beginners need to improve steadily and gradually become as fast as their team leaders. Until people get up to speed, they receive assistance from more-experienced workers.

6. Leveling

The just-in-time practice of leveling production through the month was a pressing need at Toyota in the 1940s. We were making two truck models. But we spent the first three weeks of each month accumulating the parts we needed to assemble the trucks. When we finally had all the parts, we'd work frantically to assemble a month's worth of trucks in 10 days. So we needed three times more people than we would've needed to assemble the trucks evenly through the month.

Our suppliers produced their parts in huge batches. A supplier might make 10,000 of one part today and 10,000 of another part tomorrow and would bring the parts in when they happened to be ready. We never knew until the parts arrived exactly when we would be able to start putting our trucks together.

The people at our assembly plant did their best to find useful work to do, such as cleaning up the plant. But that didn't change the fact that we had three times as many people as we needed. We desperately needed to find a way to secure the parts we needed, when they were needed, and in the amounts needed.

I was aware of the need for leveling when I was in charge of final assembly in 1945. But we were hardly in a position at that time to tackle the changes that would have been necessary. I finally got the chance to start experimenting with leveling when I took charge of the machining shop in 1946. And we had leveled our purchasing and production pretty much completely by 1950.

7. Flow Production and Multiskilled Workers

Machining shops at Toyota make engines, transmissions, suspension components, and other items. My shop made transmission gears and suspension components. The first change I made was in the layout.

Toyota deployed production equipment in line with the flow of work in machining shops that made big items, like engines. But it deployed the equipment by kind of machine in the machining shops that made transmission and suspension components. So we'd have groups of drills, lathes, milling machines, grinders, and whatnot. The different machine groups produced output in large batches, and they didn't begin operation until a full batch worth of work-in-process had arrived from the previous process. That resulted in huge accumulations of work-in-process between the processes.

I spent two years working out a layout that positioned the equipment in line with the flow of work. That meant increasing the number of machines. For example, we ended up with 200 drills, compared with only 50 before the change in layout. So the capacity utilization rate for individual machines declined. That was a shame, but I had decided not to worry about capacity utilization rates.

The number of operators in my shop did not increase as much as the number of machines did. I minimized the increase by training the operators to handle different kinds of machines. That allowed the operators to move freely to the processes where work needed to be done.

Multiprocess handling and multimachine handling, by the way, are completely different. Multimachine handling means assigning a single operator to run multiple units of the same kind of machine. You stagger the work cycles of the machines, and the operator moves from machine to machine in step with the cycle time. I visited a Volkswagen plant in 1963, and the people there were using multimachine handling with gear-cutting machines.

Multiprocess handling means letting operators move from task to task in step with the flow of work. It means giving higher priority to the utilization rate for our human resources than to the utilization rate for equipment. At Toyota, we prefer multiprocess handling to multimachine handling. We are prepared to accept idle machines—to the minimum extent necessary—in exchange for using our human resources fully.

Multiskilled operators and all-around operators are completely different, too. All-around operators are employees who can step in and go to work anywhere. Multiskilled operators are employees trained to handle the tasks needed across specified stretches of the production sequence. Our emphasis at Toyota is on cultivating multiskilled operators.

8. Productivity Gains after the Korean War

The concept of limiting production to the amount of goods sold took hold after Toyota's financial crisis of 1950. Good production control ensures that processes turn out only as much work as the company is sell-

A Toyota SKB-model truck from the 1950s

ing. Inventory management only becomes an issue when production control isn't working well. So you shouldn't think of linking production to sales as a form of inventory management.

Our restructuring plan called for   maintaining   production capacity for 900 trucks and 60 passenger cars a month. Then the Korean War broke out. Orders for trucks poured in from the U.S. Army Procurement Agency—the APA—and we needed to shift gears and increase our production capacity quickly. The APA was a stickler for quality and for on-time delivery, but it became a huge customer.

We didn't have the financial latitude to invest much in new production equipment. And management was not about to hire more people. Promising guaranteed jobs for Toyota's remaining workers was a decisive concession in resolving the labor dispute of 1950. Neither management nor labor wanted to bring on any more people than we could be sure of supporting over the long term. So we found ways to increase output with the equipment that had survived the war and without increasing our workforce. Incidentally, I understand that Nissan did hire more people at that time.

Our big challenge in 1953 and 1954 was to turn out 3,000 trucks a month. We increased output without increasing our workforce, so productivity rose. But the rise in productivity was less a matter of improvements in our production system than of the growth in volume.

By 1955, our productivity was 10 times higher than it had been 10 years earlier. I visited General Motors and Ford engine plants in 1956. What I saw there suggested that productivity was higher at Toyota's engine plant. That's speaking simply in terms of units produced per person per day, without taking into account the product mix or the percentage of work handled in-house.

I realized for the first time that U.S. productivity had not risen significantly since the early 1930s. Henry Ford's production system had been all about minimizing inventories while streamlining production with a conveyor-based assembly line. But somewhere along the way, attention focused entirely on the conveyor. People had perverted the spirit of the original system. At Toyota, we were carrying on in the spirit of Henry Ford and were building on his ideas. We didn't have the kanban system yet, but we had begun splitting up batches to convey items in small lots.

Rising demand in Japan enabled us to keep increasing production after the Korean War ended, but the focus of demand shifted. It shifted especially sharply in 1957, when Japan slipped into a yearlong economic slump. Demand for large trucks plummeted, and demand for smaller trucks rose. Demand for passenger cars, like the Toyota Corona and Crown, fluctuated repeatedly before, during, and after the slump.

Toyota coped with fluctuating demand by continuing to restrain production in the spirit of making only what was selling, only when it was selling, and only in the amounts sold. People remembered how making more trucks than we could sell nearly drove us to ruin in 1950. So the principle of reining in production had become second nature.

We left the production line for large trucks as it was and expanded production capacity on the line for small trucks. That included moving some people to the small-truck line from the big-truck line.

Our challenge was more than just a matter of making things at the lowest-possible cost. We needed to make a variety of products, all of which were subject to sharp fluctuations in demand. Offering diverse products in small quantities was an unavoidable condition for doing business in Japan at that time. Things were different in the United States. The huge U.S. market supported large and more-stable demand for most kinds of vehicle models. So automakers could focus on a narrower range of models at each plant. Making a variety of products and making multiple products on the same production lines obviously raises costs. Finding ways to offset that tendency is an eternal quest.

9. Kanban

We started using kanban sometime after 1955. We began by using them in processes in our own plant. Once the system was working smoothly, we showed it to people from our suppliers and encouraged them to try it in their operations. I remember showing the system early on to people from a stamping plant and from a machining plant.

The first place in our plant where we used kanban was the body-welding line. That line received its raw material from the stamping line. Stamping is inherently a batch-processing kind of work, and the batch processing in that process exerted a powerful influence on the welding work in the following process. People on the welding line naturally tended to want to handle things in batches.

Further down the line were the assembly people. They were serving a growing range of export markets, and they needed to make all sorts of models and model variations in small lots. The specifications were especially diverse for our four-ton trucks. We had 40 sets of specifications for those big trucks, and we were only making 30 of the trucks a day! So the focus of work on the assembly line was completely different from the batch-processing mentality of the stamping line.

I told people that the kanban were like money and that anyone who withdrew parts without depositing a kanban was a thief. Some people would have liked to turn out as much work as possible "for the good of the company." And when they had built up a pile of "reserve output," they'd have walked up the line to help out with other work. I weaned people from that kind of tendency. I told them to go take a walk if they got ahead in their work. We were better off if they would just twiddle their thumbs. Another thing I did was to establish a fixed size—width and height—for the storage place for parts and to forbid people from putting any more pallets there than would fit easily.

Kanban automated production control. With kanban, people in the workplace issue production instructions automatically. They don't need to think about writing up any special directions or about finding ways to convey those directions. With kanban, you don't need a computer.

Here's an example. Let's say you need to revise your production plan. Working out all the necessary changes on a computer would take a couple of weeks, and you'd fall behind in your production control. Even if the computer could handle all the calculations in an instant, you'd still fall behind because accommodating the changes in the workplace would take time.

With kanban, all you need to do is adjust the number of kanban in circulation in accordance with your needs. When kanban start arriving slower than people had expected, they understand immediately that the company has reduced the production plan. As long as you keep your production leveled, changes in the production plan will take effect the next day.

The name "kanban" came after we had been using the concept for a while. We came up with the name when we were preparing to undergo the audit for the Deming Prize in 1964.

A big reason for adopting kanban was our desire to reduce the administrative burden of running a factory. We were looking for ways to reduce paperwork. The tax office told us in 1949 that we couldn't eliminate the paper trail in our purchasing and production work, and that obliged us to give up the idea of kanban for the time being. But the tax people later became more lenient about paperless processing. That was around 1953 and 1954, when companies started computerizing their operations.

We jumped at the chance to try out the kanban concept. If Toyota had introduced computers two or three years earlier, we might never have developed the kanban system. The company might have just used computers to process incoming deliveries and to prepare production instructions.

Kanban appeared in every workplace that I managed at Toyota, but the system took quite a while to really take hold throughout the company. Once we got the kanban system working on the body-welding line, we started using it in the upstream stamping processes, including work at suppliers' plants. We also started using it in our processes that made oil pans and tappet covers. Toyota adopted the kanban system at the Motomachi Plant when it opened that plant in 1959. Motomachi was the first Toyota plant built especially to pro-

A stamping line at the Honsha Plant in the 1950s

duce passenger cars, and it contained a full range of processes, from machining and stamping to welding, painting, and assembly. I became the plant manager at the Honsha Plant in 1962, and we introduced kanban in the forging and casting work and in the heat-processing work.

Putting kanban to work in casting work was hard. Melting the metal for the castings demands batch processing. Theoretically, we could handle the actual casting work in lots as small as a single item, but people naturally wanted to make as many items as possible before changing the casting mold. Of course, keeping fuel costs down was a high priority in running the furnace, and that encouraged people to boil up a big pot of molten metal and pour out a whole series of castings.

We had just as much trouble putting the kanban to work in the heat-processing work. The heat-treatment process for malleable iron parts took a week to complete. By the conventional wisdom, that was all the more reason to use batch processing. But that meant holding a week's worth of inventory. By my thinking, that was all the more reason to use kanban and to switch to smaller lots. And that's what we did.

As much as possible, we kept inventory only in the form of raw material. Having stocks of semifinished items on hand was convenient and reassuring, but it could result in waste if changes occurred in the production plan. We minimized inventory risk by processing raw material on a strictly just-in-time basis.

Our early kanban served mainly as production instructions and as inventory-withdrawal tags. Most of the kanban were simple cards, but we had some variations. For example, we used triangular kanban with forgings, stampings, and other batch-processing items. We would remove the triangular kanban when we had used a specified portion of a lot, and it would go back to the previous process as a production instruction. We had special "slanted" kanban to allocate work when people came in outside their ordinary shifts to help with overloads. And we had interruption kanban to allow for breaking into the ordinary flow of work to do emergency processing.

Kanban highlighted problems as soon as the problems occurred and promoted kaizen activity. But some suppliers didn't like the discipline that kanban imposed. Some of our independent suppliers even got together once to call on Toyota to stop using kanban. That was when they were struggling with the fallout from the first oil crisis. Ironically, that very same crisis was what brought kanban to the attention of the world at large.

Nissan had its so-called Action Plate Method, which was sort of like the kanban system. And Mitsubishi Motors had something similar. But neither of those companies had worked out their systems with their suppliers. So their systems apparently struck the suppliers as arbitrary and unilateral. We at Toyota and our suppliers had gone through production downturns together in the past. We had built relationships that gave us a good basis for making the kanban system work.

10. Quality Control

The essence of quality control is to make what will sell. If the quality is lousy, the products won't sell. In the old days, a casting that had a bird's nest inside got all the way to a downstream process and caused problems there. We taught our people to think of the following process as the customer and to check things carefully in their own process to avoid passing on defective work.

We also taught our people the difference between quick fixes and solutions. Quick fixes that don't address the underlying causes are simply an invitation for bigger problems later. We need to analyze problems carefully and do kaizen that will really solve the problems and keep them from happening again. Preventive maintenance is also essential, of course, in avoiding problems. And I introduced the practice of deploying maintenance personnel in two shifts a day, rather than just one.

Quality control, to be effective, needs to include measures for calling attention in the workplace to any problems that occur. You need to foster quality awareness. Your team leaders need to set an example. The quality commitment that they demonstrate in their work will spread naturally to their team members.

11. *Jidoka*

We adopted the line-stop system sometime in the late 1960s. We didn't have very good sensors then. So our first system was more a matter of stopping the conveyor line than of having the line stop automatically. We later developed systems where the line would stop automatically when problems occurred.

The American approach to manufacturing had an unhealthy emphasis on keeping the line moving and on having it move as fast as possible. If your production line keeps moving as a result of kaizen, that's great. But keeping the line moving should not be an end in itself. If work is exhausting and a worker gets fatigued, he should stop the line. That calls attention to the problem. Then, we can resolve the problem. Maybe by finding a better posture for the worker. Maybe by improving the job rotation.

On the other hand, some kinds of work do not allow for stopping the line or even for varying the speed of the line. Painting is a good example. Those kinds of work call for other approaches to highlighting problems and promoting kaizen.

Chapter II

What I Learned from Taiichi Ohno

A talk by **Michikazu Tanaka**

As recorded and edited by **Koichi Shimokawa** *and*
Takahiro Fujimoto *with* **Kenichi Kuwashima** *and*
Yasuo Sugiyama

The Talk: Under the Guidance of Taiichi Ohno

Professor [Koichi] Shimokawa has asked me to describe for you my memories of Taiichi Ohno, the father of the kanban. I, like numerous others, owe a huge debt to Ohno-san. And since he has passed on, we who learned from him have a responsibility to convey his teachings to the next

About the Text

The accompanying text is an adaptation of a talk delivered in January 1998 by Michikazu Tanaka, a former executive of Daihatsu Motor. Tanaka gave the talk to a study group convened under the auspices of the Japan Technology Transfer Association and chaired and cochaired by the compilers of this volume, Koichi Shimokawa and Takahiro Fujimoto. The study group comprises automotive production engineers and university researchers and has met regularly since 1991 to develop a vision for production systems in the automobile and automotive parts industries. The adaptation presented here reflects subsequent editing by Tanaka.

generation. I don't know how well I can fulfill that responsibility in the limited time available here today. But I will try at least to describe Ohno-san's basic approach to kaizen, and I will offer some concrete examples.

Daihatsu's headquarters and plant in Ikeda, Osaka, in the 1970s

My first encounter with Ohno-san was in 1967. Daihatsu had entered a strategic alliance with Toyota that year, and Ohno-san visited our headquarters plant, in Ikeda. I was a production manager there, and the first thing he said to me was, "You've got too many parts along the assembly line and too much work-in-process between the processes. You can't get any kaizen done in that mess."

I would hear that repeatedly during Ohno-san's plant tour. But I was a stubborn sort, and I was thinking all along that people have different ways of doing kaizen, that Ohno-san's way was not the only way. I couldn't see

About the Speaker

Michikazu Tanaka spearheaded the transplanting of the Toyota Production System to Daihatsu, a manufacturer of minivehicles. He began receiving guidance from Taiichi Ohno in 1967, the year that Daihatsu entered into a strategic alliance with Toyota. And he demonstrated uncommon creativity and passion in adapting the Toyota Production System to needs and circumstances at his company.

Michikazu Tanaka (*center*) describing the principles of the Toyota Production System at the automotive tooling company Hashida Giken, whose president, Hiroshi Hashida, is seated at the right

Born in Osaka in 1926, Tanaka worked in manufacturing at Daihatsu for more than four decades. He joined the company in 1949 and worked initially in equipment

how reducing the amounts of parts alongside the assembly line or reducing the amounts of work-in-process between the processes would promote kaizen. So I had viewed the parts and the work-in-process as something of a disinterested observer.

Ohno-san began appearing frequently at our Kyoto Plant in the early 1970s. Daihatsu was preparing to handle some of the production of the Toyota Publica there, and he was overseeing the introduction of the kanban system. I had no interest in kanban and had not paid any attention to what Ohno-san was doing at the Kyoto Plant.

Shortly after the production of the Publica got under way in Kyoto, a fatal accident occurred at the plant. That threw the plant into chaos. People were upset and didn't know what to do. My boss at the Ikeda Plant called me over to his desk and told me that he wanted me to move to the Kyoto Plant and get things back on an even keel.

I arrived in Kyoto a couple days after receiving the assignment. What I found there was appalling. All along the assembly line were mountains

planning for plants and in plant management and production control. Tanaka rose to the rank of production manager at Daihatsu's Ikeda (headquarters) Plant, in Osaka Prefecture, and in 1973 moved to the Kyoto Plant, which then specialized in producing passenger cars. He served as deputy plant manager and then plant manager in Kyoto before returning to headquarters in 1983 as a managing director responsible for production. Named a senior managing director in June 1992, he retired from full-time work later that year.

Tanaka thus occupied center stage in the development of production technology at Daihatsu throughout his career. And he has remained active in retirement as an adviser to Daihatsu and as the chairman of a study group that promotes advances in surface processing at plants in Osaka Prefecture.

Daihatsu was and is the only automaker based in the Kansai region, centered on Osaka, Kyoto, and Kobe, and it boasts a history older than Toyota's.

of parts. "Do you people think you're working in a warehouse?!" was my initial greeting to my new colleagues.

We were working hard on quality control activities at Daihatsu at that time, and I had thrown myself into those activities head over heels. But what I found at the Kyoto Plant gave me pause for thought. Posted all over the workplace were materials for administering the quality control effort. Producing and displaying the materials had become an end in itself. We needed to get to work on more-substantive kaizen based on the actual circumstances in the workplace. So I told everyone to get rid of any and all materials that didn't provide concrete guidelines for how to go about our work. We would retain only the materials that were obviously useful.

Thanks but no thanks

The production managers and group leaders at the Kyoto Plant were working feverishly on installing the kanban system when I arrived. But I

But in the late 1960s, it was distinctly inferior to Toyota in product quality and in cost competitiveness. Joining the Toyota Group in 1967 presented Daihatsu with the pressing challenge of swiftly attaining Toyota-like standards in its diesel technology, in its vehicle technology, and in its production technology. That challenge became especially pressing in 1973, the year that Tanaka moved to the Kyoto Plant.

Toyota was growing rapidly in the early 1970s, and its plants were unable to keep up with the surging demand in Japan, North America, and elsewhere for the company's small, dependable models. In 1973, the automaker entrusted some of the production of its smallest model, the Publica, to Daihatsu's Kyoto Plant. That was the fateful year of the first oil crisis, and demand for Toyota's fuel-efficient cars was soon to burgeon more dramatically than anyone could have guessed.

had yet to develop any interest in kanban. I simply observed their efforts from a distance and took part as little as possible in the endeavor.

Toyota had developed a somewhat upscale version of the Publica, the Publica Starlet, also to be produced at our Kyoto

The Daihatsu Consorte of around 1970, a sister model to the Toyota Publica

Plant. The Starlet remained an ultracompact mass-market model. It carried an extremely low sticker price and would therefore be a low-margin undertaking, at best. Earning any kind of profit on the Starlet would demand drastic cost cutting.

We were producing a Daihatsu model closely related to the Publica, the Consorte, and we produced both models on the same line, using bodies supplied by Toyota. Our Consorte would remain in production, but the

Despite Daihatsu's shortcomings, the company was posting annual growth in sales and earnings amid the booming growth in Japanese vehicle ownership. Toyota had therefore turned a blind eye to issues at its new affiliate. But the production team at Toyota took a closer look when it entrusted a Toyota-badged vehicle to Daihatsu. No less than Taiichi Ohno, then the executive vice president for production at Toyota, took a personal interest in the project.

Toyota had largely completed the task of adopting Ohno's principles in all its plants and processes, and it had accompanied those principles with the regimen of total quality control (TQC). In 1973, Toyota was in the midst of propagating the Toyota Production System and TQC at its principal suppliers. Toyota suppliers in the Nagoya vicinity worked directly with Toyota plants and had already begun to absorb the basic concepts. Daihatsu, however, had little daily interchange with Toyota, and introducing the Toyota Production System

Toyota's Publica Starlet of 1973

Starlet would entail a lot more parts than its predecessor. That would mean producing two very different models.

These days, automakers commonly produce two, three, or even more models on the same assembly line. But in those days, each assembly line produced only a single model. Our production team reviewed the proposal and determined that we would need a 10,000-square-meter building to handle the new Toyota model.

Ohno-san rejected our proposal out of hand. The Starlet, he insisted, was an economy model. Building a new plant would raise the fixed costs and render the project untenable from the outset. So much for Toyota, scoffed our production engineering people. What's impossible is

there would be a unilateral undertaking. Ohno required an on-site evangelist, and Tanaka was his man.

What emerges from Tanaka's talk is Ohno's rigorous emphasis on (1) the *gemba gembutsu* (also *genchi gembutsu*) principle of focusing management on the workplace and (2) eliciting wisdom and innovation from people in the workplace. Ohno, we learn anew, was more interested in getting people to think for themselves than in telling them what to do.

People have understandably tended to focus on the technical aspects of the Toyota Production System. Tanaka reminds us of the crucial importance of the human aspect of motivating people in the workplace through inspirational leadership. As famous as the Toyota Production System has become, questions remain about the applicability of the system in divergent corporate cultures and cultural milieu. Toyota's experience in transferring the system

impossible, they contended, and we could not possibly assemble the Starlet without a new plant building. Sentiment mounted in the company that we should refuse to accept the Toyota model.

Junichi Ono, Daihatsu's executive vice president for technology, came by my desk one day around that time and asked me for an opinion. "Ohno-san says that we should make the new car without putting up a new building. Our production engineering people say that's out of the question. What do you think?"

I replied in my typically irresponsible manner: "We might as well have a go at it. We don't know what's possible until we try. And if things don't work out, we can always take it from there." That was not to suggest that I was especially confident that we could produce the new model without a new plant. And my boss was no more confident than I was. But we decided to tell Ohno-san that we would have a go. My boss and I went to Toyota to deliver our response, but Ohno-san was out, so we simply left a message: "We'll do it without building a new plant."

to Daihatsu is thus a hugely instructive episode. That episode is, indeed, the original blueprint for transplanting the system to new and unfamiliar environments.

When I got back to the Kyoto Plant, the plant manager was away. I took the liberty of assembling the production managers and told them that we had decided to produce the Starlet. They exploded and pummeled me for about two hours with reasons that it was impossible. After listening to the litany of impossibilities, I explained that I understood perfectly well why it was impossible but that we had decided to produce the Starlet nonetheless. I told the managers that, henceforth, I was interested in hearing about ways to produce the new model and that I had no more patience for listening to why it was impossible. I called on them to join me in figuring out how to make the new project work.

The years have mellowed me, but back then I was as pigheaded as they come. People knew that once I had made my mind up they would never persuade me otherwise. The production managers were soon coming forward with ideas for achieving the necessary cost reductions. In one example, we were producing batches with a stamping machine that extended over 12 shifts, and we reduced the batch sizes to 6-shift lots. That halved the space required to store in-process stampings, and we would be able to use the freed-up space to store parts for the second model. Everyone got into the act.

People in every process found ways to save space over the next six months. We carefully maintained the newly available space to have it available when the time came to add a second production model. While

Daihatsu's Kyoto Plant around 1970

we were working successfully to free up space, I heard through the grapevine that Ohno-san had softened his stance. He had apparently told a subordinate to go have a look at our Kyoto Plant and to let us know that, if absolutely necessary, Toyota might acquiesce to a second plant building. I dispatched a defiant message to Toyota: "Thanks but no thanks. We'll get the job done with the facilities we have."

Ready, set, go!

Ohno-san came around about once a month during the preparations for mass production. He always brought along a Toyota general manager from production engineering by the name of Takemoto. I overheard him telling Takemoto, "If this project doesn't go right, you're out of a job. And so am I." Although Ohno-san was an executive vice president, I could tell from the tone of his voice that he meant what he said. That inspired me to work even harder to succeed.

At a meeting one day, Ohno-san asked our president, Sakae Ohara, who his contact person should be for the Starlet project, and Ohara-san named me. I was sitting about three rows back, but they called me up to the front of the room. That was exactly the fate that we all tried to avoid in dealing with Ohno-san. Everyone was interested in hearing what he had to say, but no one wanted to face questions directly from the man while standing at the front of a crowded room. That was because of Ohno-san's method. If he had 10 things that he wanted to tell you, he'd tell you 2 and expect you to think for yourself until you came up with the other 8.

You can imagine anyone's terror at having Ohno-san look them in the eye and ask, "What do you think?" I had yet to develop any interest in the kanban system, and I couldn't help thinking that Ohara-san had deliberately named the manager least passionate about Ohno-san's signature tool.

The day of the start of mass production finally arrived. I summoned all the production managers for a meeting a little before 8 a.m. "Ohno-san is bound to show up before the week is out," I cautioned them, "so let's make sure that we get things shipshape over the next few days." No sooner had I spoken than a woman entered the room to report that she'd just received a call from the guardhouse at the plant gate. Ohno-san had just entered the plant. I rushed to meet him, and we talked for about 30 minutes. Predictably, he grew impatient and insisted that we go have a look at the workplace.

We started at the body line. After Ohno-san had observed things for a while, he pointed at a man in a main process on the line and asked me, "Is he behind or ahead in his work?" I had no idea and could only answer honestly, "I don't know." Ohno-san, visibly unhappy, turned to the supervisor responsible for the shop and asked him the same question. I don't remember how the supervisor answered, but he gave a clear answer, either that the work was running ahead or behind. That exasperated Ohno-san all the more, and he barked at me angrily, "This guy is lying through his teeth. I'm standing here watching, and I can't see if the work is running ahead or behind. There's no way that he could know any better."

Ohno-san then demanded a blackboard, and I escorted him into a meeting room. He headed straight for the blackboard and, chalk in hand, drew a line. "When you ran races in school, you had a starting line, right? Everyone started at the same line, and ready, set, go! they all started running. You could see who was the fastest, who was the second fastest, who was the slowest. But if everyone starts at a different place, you can't tell who's fastest. That's what's happening in the work that we just saw. You can't tell who's running ahead and who's running behind. You can't see where problems lie, and you've got no basis for doing kaizen. You've got to work as if you were putting things on a conveyor, even where you're not actually using a conveyor. And to do that, you need a pacemaker."

Getting into the spirit

Our task, therefore, was to come up with an effective pacemaker. Toyota's Takemoto and I considered different possibilities and finally settled on a buzzer as the easiest for everyone to understand. We installed the buzzer at the middle of the main line so that it would be audible to everyone, even at the front end and back end of the line.

Ohno-san came around again about a week later and promptly denounced our pacemaker. "That's no good at all. Your workers will feel like they're under pressure all the time." This is a side of Ohno-san that you don't hear much about, and I want you to listen carefully. Contrary to the image that most people have, Ohno-san cared a great deal about employees in the workplace. You read that he was some kind of ogre who was always trying to squeeze one more drop out of a dry towel. But the real man was not like that at all.

"The last thing you want to do," he explained, "is make your people feel like they're always under the gun. If you want to use sound for your pacemaker, use a pleasant melody, not a shrill buzzer. And let the employees choose the melody. Also, you need to install the speakers at three places, not just one."

Ohno-san and I discussed several things for a couple of hours. Then he suddenly asked, "Have you worked out the new positioning for your pacemaker speakers? Are they already in place? When will they be ready?" I found a plant administration manager and asked him when we would have the speakers installed in three places. "We'll do it this Saturday," was the prompt reply. I conveyed that answer to Ohno-san without any sense of contradiction, whereupon he told me the following story.

"I was at the Takaoka Plant the other day. They had a lot of body shells hanging from the overhead conveyor in the paint shop. I told the general manager that he had too much work-in-process and instructed him to reduce the volume. He replied, 'We'll get right on it. Give us a little time.' I assumed that he meant an hour or two, and I went back after a couple of hours and asked, 'Have you taken care of the excess work-in-process?' His answer was, 'We'll get it done this Saturday.' 'Fine,' I said, 'and in the meantime, I'm going to trash all these body shells hanging here. Get me a ladder and a hammer. Now!' The general manager gained a new sense of urgency, and he got the job done right away."

On hearing that story, I began to feel extremely uncomfortable seated in the office. I excused myself and went out into the workplace to get the speakers installed.

Ohno-san needed to attend a meeting that evening in Nagoya and therefore needed to leave our Kyoto Plant by 4 p.m., at the latest. A little before three o'clock, I went to check on the speaker-installation work. When I told the people to hurry up, they protested that they were working as fast as possible but that they could not get the job done by four o'clock. I told them they could use temporary wiring or anything necessary to speed things up.

When we finally got the speakers installed, it was nearly five o'clock. Ohno-san was still in the meeting room when I went to report that the job was done. He hadn't spoken a word since one o'clock, and the atmosphere in the room was sort of eerie.

On receiving my report, Ohno-san simply got up and said, "I'm leaving now."

"Please come and have a look at the speakers," I begged.

"No, I'm leaving."

"Everyone worked really hard to get the speakers installed. The least you could do is stop by and have a look."

"You've finally got in the spirit of things, haven't you? As long as you've got in the mood to get things done, then I'm satisfied."

A friend of labor

Ohno-san came by the Kyoto Plant about once a week for the next six months. He reminded us frequently and severely what we needed to do:

"Make do with the equipment you've got."

"Don't automate anything."

"Don't spend any money."

"Limit your production output to the numbers in the sales plan."

"Your costs will eat up all your profit if you don't watch out, so don't hire more people."

As soon as we had complied with Ohno-san's insistence on monitoring the pace of work cycles, he raised the stakes. "Simply determining whether a cycle is too fast or too slow isn't good enough. You need to monitor the pace of work inside each cycle." So we divided the cycles into five parts and set up a sound system to play music at the completion of each part, including music to indicate the completion of the whole cycle. Everyone working on different processes in the same cycle knew when they should be one-fifth done, when they should be two-fifths done, and so on.

We rigged the processes so that a yellow *andon* lamp shined when the work was four-fifths done and a blue *andon* shined when the work for the cycle was completely done. A red *andon* light would shine at a process that was running behind. When the lamps at all the processes were shining blue, the music would stop and the next cycle would begin.

Our system prevented any process from moving on to the next work cycle before all the processes had completed the work in a cycle. That linked the pace of work to the pace in the slowest process, and it was difficult to get used to. People found themselves waiting all the time for someone in some process to catch up. Capacity utilization stagnated. We could only produce four or five vehicles per hour at first.

Ohno-san, however, was patient. "Improve things little by little. Make sure that the process that caused problems this morning doesn't cause problems this afternoon. The way to increase your hourly production volume is to recognize problems when they occur and to make the necessary improvements to prevent them from recurring."

We had formerly regarded our workflow as a conveyor that we started and stopped. Ohno-san's "ready, set, go!" concept changed our basic perspective. In our new approach, everything came to a stop if a process fell behind, and everything started up anew when all the work in a cycle was done. It was still a conveyor concept, but the conveyor started and stopped on its own. People in our plant formerly had pressed a button to indicate the end of a cycle. Pushing buttons is not the object of our work, however, and the act of pushing wasted a second or more of time. So we devised sensors that detected when operators had placed tools in positions that indicated the end of a cycle. The sensors triggered the *andon* lamps and the music.

One day, Ohno-san demanded—without offering any reason—that we get rid of the automated equipment for conveying side panels between processes. Side panels are big and heavy, and they are difficult for even two men to carry. Conveying them manually would mean considerably more work. Why Ohno-san wanted us to remove the automated conveyance was a mystery, even to Toyota's Takemoto.

The people in the workplace appealed to me to ask Ohno-san to reconsider his order. I was just a deputy plant manager at a Daihatsu plant. Ohno-san was an executive vice president at Toyota. I was in no position to challenge his judgment. So I reminded our people that Ohno-san was a production genius and that he surely had a good reason for wanting us to get rid of the automated conveyance. I understood perfectly well, however, that conveying the side panels manually would impose a huge burden on our employees, and I set about thinking of new ways to handle the task. One way would be to assign more people to the work, but that, of course, was not an option. Instead, we devised some jigs for hanging the panels from a rail and pulling them from one process to the next.

Our automated equipment had raised the side panels straight up and them moved them horizontally to the next process. But our manual pulley system pulled the side panels directly toward the next process along a diagonal path. So the manual system conveyed the side panels faster than the automatic system had. Sure enough, Ohno-san had noted the time loss that our automated system entailed. Only when we actually tried an alternative method in the workplace did we see how much time we were wasting.

Ohno-san cut right to the chase on his next visit: "Has the removal of the automatic equipment been causing headaches for people in the workplace?"

"It was a problem at first," I acknowledged. "And we experimented with a number of possible solutions. We finally settled on a pulley system, which has actually reduced the conveyance time."

"That's good to hear. I wasn't entirely confident about how things would work out. And I was thinking in the car about the trouble that I might have caused for your people. But I know that the workplace can be a source of incredible wisdom when the need arises. That really is good to hear."

Ohno-san repeated two or three times during our conversation that he had been worried about causing trouble for people in the workplace. He was the first senior executive who I ever heard express that kind of concern. I knew then that he really approached kaizen from the standpoint of the workers. I knew how wrong people had been to suggest that he was an enemy of labor.

Gemba gembutsu

Kaizen raised our productivity from four or five vehicles per hour to six and then to eight. Ohno-san turned his attention to time loss that he perceived in the conveyance equipment on our main assembly line. We were using a shuttle system, which he denounced as wasteful. Ohno-san noted the time that work-in-process sat waiting for the shuttle, and he instructed us to devise a way to send bodies on to the next process as soon as they were ready and needed.

Our shuttle system launched a body toward the next process as soon as the previous body was safely out of the way. But that could impose delays. I was beginning to get a feel for Ohno-san's way of thinking, or at least I thought I was. And what I thought was that he was interested in pushing things to the limit. I issued instructions to our people based on that understanding: come up with a system that will put the next body in motion as soon as the previous body starts moving.

Soon after we modified the system in accordance with my instructions, an accident occurred. An employee who had gone behind a body to work on the back panel got sandwiched between that body and the next body. Fortunately, he didn't get hurt. But I got a scolding from Ohno-san on his next visit. He asked what we had done about the time loss that he had noted on his previous visit. And I explained that we had squeezed things to the limit but that an employee had got pinned between two bodies.

"You're going about things completely wrong," he declared. "You're moving things in anticipation of needs in the next process. If you're going to do that, you need to make sure the coast is clear before you put things in motion."

I never heard anything again from Ohno-san about time loss in conveyance on our main assembly line. He was more interested, I had discovered, in our basic stance than in what we actually did.

Under Ohno-san, our basic stance came to include synchronizing activity in the production sequence with kanban, and what we did included using kanban as instructions to start work in each process. We didn't have any welding robots back then, so all sorts of cables for the hand welding tools where hanging down around the line. Those cables obstructed the operators' view of the work instructions, and we received a request from the workplace to install a television monitor to display the instructions.

I approved the installation of the monitors, and the operators reported happily that the displays made their work a lot easier. Our plant manager told me to get rid of them, however, on the grounds that Ohno-san hated television monitors. I argued that Ohno-san might hate monitors in principle but that he was a man who welcomed anything that made work easier for employees. I assured the plant manager that Ohno-san would acknowledge the value of the monitors, and I left them in place. We raised the subject with Ohno-san on his next visit. Declining to render judgment sight unseen, he said, "Let's go have a look." Ohno-san stood in the position of the welding operators and acknowledged forthrightly that the work instructions were difficult to see and that the television monitors were a good idea.

Gemba gembutsu [also *genchi gembutsu*: a commitment to seeing things (*gembutsu*) firsthand as they really are in the workplace (*gemba* or *genchi*)] was absolutely fundamental to Ohno-san's approach. He never rendered judgment simply on the basis of hearing about something. He always insisted on going to the place in question and having a look. On occasions when we might press him for an opinion, he'd say, "You're the one who has seen the thing. You know better than I do. How could I talk about something that I haven't seen?"

A key to kaizen

Ohno-san was extremely demanding in regard to kaizen results, but he had an uncanny sense for what was possible in the circumstances. Asked about our progress in raising productivity, I reported proudly that we were up to 8 vehicles per hour, and he said, "I see. So next week, let's get it up to 10." When I reported that we had reached that target, he said, "So now get it up to 12." That continued week after week. Takemoto reflected on the effort that everyone was putting into achieving the targets and wondered aloud if Ohno-san would ever be satisfied.

Something interesting happened when our output reached 16 vehicles per hour. Ordinarily, I had reported our latest rise in productivity with words like, "Ohno-san, we did it!" But when I announced our attainment of 16 vehicles per hour, I said something like, "We finally got it up to 16." I don't know if my words betrayed fatigue or not, but for whatever reason, Ohno-san never again broached the subject of hourly output. He still had a higher target in mind, however, and he steered us next to some modest automation. Sixteen vehicles per hour took us above the break-even point in our initial production planning. But Ohno-san was now aiming for 20 per hour.

To oversee the automation kaizen, Ohno-san brought along a man from Toyota by the name of Imai. "We've got a lot of people at Toyota," grumbled Ohno-san, "but hardly any of them have any real wisdom. Imai is an exception." I wondered what Imai would do for us in the way of kaizen, and for a week he did nothing at all. He simply watched what was happening in the workplace. On the Monday of his second week at our plant, he came by my desk and described his impressions and his plans as follows.

"I watched the activity in your workplace carefully for a week, and I saw that people are working extremely well. I struggled to think of something that I could do for you, and my conclusion was that I have no role to play here.

"I stopped by Ohno-san's house on the way home Friday evening and told him what I have just told you. He said, 'Your problem is that you're trying to think of something to teach the people at Daihatsu. You don't need to teach them anything. What you need to do there is help make the work easier for the operators. That's your job. Do some simple kaizen. Do some small-scale automation.'

"I finally know what I'm supposed to do here. And that's what I'm going to do."

My habit was to take a walk through the plant on my way home each evening. One evening, I noticed a light on in the body shop around eight o'clock. We didn't have much overtime at that time, so I was curious and went to have a look. A few men were holding a discussion. One was Imai. Another was a team leader. He explained that they were testing the ejection mechanism on a benchtop spot welder and that it wasn't working very well.

I suggested that they go ahead and try using the mechanism, as long as they had gone to the trouble of making it. At that point, Imai asked someone to bring him an acetylene torch, and he proceeded to cut off the ejection mechanism. I asked what in the world he was doing, and he replied that they would keep modifying the welder until the operators were completely satisfied.

"Good kaizen," said Imai, "depends on the active cooperation of your employees. You might think you're on the right track. But unless your employees are taking part actively, you'll never get the full potential of the improvements. That's why we're going to keep working on this until the people in the workplace think we've got it right."

About a week later, I again saw a light on late one night. This time, two operators were working on a new version of the ejection mechanism.

"We've just about got it right," said one of the operators. "But we want to make sure that we don't cause problems for people, so we're making some extra parts tonight."

The two operators working late had the same spirit as Ohno-san. And they had gotten that spirit by seeing his example. The people on the plant floor never talked directly with Ohno-san during his visits. They received his instructions through me. But they saw him there. They saw how he took an interest in their work. And they saw the results of his guidance. Plant managers always made a special effort to prepare for a visit by a VIP. But people in the workplace rarely paid any heed. Visits by Ohno-san, however, were different.

"When's Ohno-san coming next?" someone would call out and ask me when I was walking through the plant. "He'll be here again next week." "We'd better get things right by then," the operator would shout back.

The company union's officials called me in one day and complained that what we were doing at the Kyoto Plant was labor abuse. They had the same misconception about Ohno-san that I had before I met and worked with him: that he was an enemy of labor. I described how my own impressions had changed as I saw Ohno-san in action—as I saw how he genuinely cared about people in the workplace and how he went out of his way to make work easier and more fulfilling for the employees. And I added in the spirit of *gemba gembutsu*, "But don't take my word for it. Go have a look. Ask the people in the workplace what they think." I heard later that someone from the union office had gone to the Kyoto Plant and that none of the employees expressed any dissatisfaction.

The real purpose of kanban

What became clear during my work with Ohno-san is that his chief interest was something other than reducing work-in-process, raising productivity, or lowering costs. His ultimate aim, I gradually learned, was to help employees assert their full potential. And when that happens, all those other things will occur naturally. I put the question directly to Ohno-san at the end of our six months of intensive work under his guidance.

"Ohno-san, I'm grateful for everything you've done for us over the past half year. And I want you to know that I was completely wrong about the kanban. I thought of it entirely in terms of reducing work-in-process, raising productivity, and illuminating problems. Of course, it is good for all those things. But your basic aim is something else, isn't it? You use the kanban to create a positive tension in the workplace by reducing work-in-process, and that motivates people to do better than they ever thought they could do. Isn't that what you're really aiming for?"

Whenever someone said something wrong, Ohno-san was unhesitating with an unambiguous "No." But he never said "Yes." The way you knew he agreed with something was that he said nothing. And my question elicited an affirmative silence.

A professor from a German university came to our plant one time to learn about the kanban system. He started off by asking me about the purpose of kanban. I replied that the kanban was a tool for tapping people's potential by fostering a creative tension in the workplace. "I had always heard that kanban were for reducing inventories," he replied, "but your answer makes more sense."

In my talk, I have covered only some of the most trying incidents and most gratifying incidents in our work with Ohno-san. I hope that my remarks have conveyed the most important message: that motivation is everything. Tools and methods are secondary. Any tool or method will work if people are motivated. And no tool or method will work if people are not motivated. That's what I learned from Ohno-san.

To us, Ohno-san was like a god. But he was ever aware of his fallibility, and he was determined not to let his mistakes become a burden on people in the workplace. That's why he was always impatient to try out new ideas immediately. "I don't always get things right," he'd say. "And if I've got something wrong, I want to fix it right away." And that's why we scheduled our kaizen in minutes and hours, not in days and weeks.

Ohno Anecdotes and Aphorisms

1. Kaizen

Ohno-san would scold us, saying, "Simply staring at things is no way to find out how to make them better. Your eyes are wide open, but you're blind as bats!" "But Ohno-san," someone would protest, "blind is a derogatory term." "Is that right? Well then, you've got tinfoil over your eyes [to make them shine as if they were open]."

"If you're going to do kaizen continuously," he'd go on, "you've got to assume that things are a mess. Too many people just assume that things are all right the way they are. Aren't you guys convinced that the way you're doing things is the right way? That's no way to get anything done. Kaizen is about changing the way things are. If you assume that things are all right the way they are, you can't do kaizen. So change something!

"When you go out into the workplace, you should be looking for things that you can do for your people there. You've got no business in the workplace if you're just there to be there. You've got to be looking for changes you can make for the benefit of the people who are working there."

Here's an example of Ohno-san's approach. He was observing the work on an engine assembly line one time when he was a plant manager, and he noticed that one of the workers needed to lift a heavy engine block once during each work cycle. Ohno-san wondered why that was necessary. He called the production chief over and ordered him to go find out what was going on. The production chief came back and reported that the roller conveyor was broken.

"What in the world do you think you're doing here?" shouted Ohno-san. "We don't hire people to lift engine blocks. You go check and see right now if you're not sitting on other problems just like this one." The production supervisor soon reported three similar problems, and he received the predictable scolding from Ohno-san. "You're out here on the floor every day, but you're not really seeing anything: whether your people are having problems with something, whether waste is happening, whether you have overburden somewhere."

Ohno-san insisted that only about half of the activity in a typical workplace was value-added work. The rest was just spinning wheels, not making any money for the company. He taught us to see. I took a fresh look at the workplace, and I could see that he was right, that waste was happening everywhere.

Another thing Ohno-san said about kaizen was that we should never listen to the shop veterans. "They just get in the way of kaizen," he'd say. "As much as possible, get the opinions of the people who are actually doing the work. Wisdom is born from the ideas of novices. The veterans will spout off about what's possible and what's not possible on the basis of their experience and a tiny bit of knowledge. And when the veterans speak, everyone else keeps quiet. So kaizen can't even get started."

Here's a funny story in that connection. My uncle is 93 years old, and he's hard of hearing. The ear, nose, and throat specialist told him that he needed hearing aids, that it was only natural for someone in their 90s to wear them. So my uncle bought an expensive pair of hearing aids. One day soon after that, he happened to go to the barber.

"My hearing has failed recently, so I got these hearing aids."

"Have you had your ears cleaned lately?"

"Can't say that I have."

"Let's have a look," said the barber. And he promptly dug out a couple of huge clumps of wax from my uncle's ears. All of a sudden, my uncle could hear perfectly well—without the hearing aids.

I heard this story straight from my uncle. It's a pretty good example of how specialists, like his doctor, get hung up with their experience and expertise. The barber is a pure amateur from a medical perspective, so he doesn't get caught up with all the technical possibilities. Veterans [in the production workplace tend to] look at the world from the perspective of their experience and expertise, so you can't rely on what they say. You've got to listen to the novices.

Conditions in the workplace are the basis for all kaizen. You can't come up with useful kaizen sitting at your desk. You can think in terms of hours while you're sitting at your desk, but you can't think in terms of seconds. Ohno-san always reminded us that the processes move in seconds when we're making things, so we need to monitor the movement of things and people in seconds to find opportunities for kaizen. And he kept telling us to focus on what's actually happening in the workplace.

2. The Workplace as Fact

Ohno-san hated written materials. If you took him some papers to see, he might go through the motions of looking at them, but he wouldn't really pay any attention at all. You'd be trying to explain something in the documents, and you could tell from his eye movements that he couldn't care less. When you got done, he'd hand the papers right back to you. He'd give really detailed instructions in the workplace, but he almost never had anything to say in response to written reports.

I never saw any papers on Ohno-san's desk. That's no exaggeration. Literally, no papers at all. The only documents I ever saw him pay any attention to were the factual records of production and sales results: things like how many vehicles we sold yesterday, how many vehicles our plants produced yesterday, what the operating rates were, and so on. Those numbers were records of actual results, so they were indisputable facts. Ohno-san had no interest in any other written materials. He only trusted things that he could confirm with his own eyes.

I visited Ohno-san one time at Toyoda Boshoku (Toyoda Spinning and Weaving) when he was the chairman there. He was in a foul mood and promptly let me know why.

"Some guys in charge of kaizen at Toyota were just here. They said they were going to hold a jamboree to introduce case studies and that they wanted me to come. I got angry and told them that kaizen is about eliminating waste. I asked why they would hold a kaizen event that entailed the waste of preparing a lot of useless materials. People can see the kaizen in the workplace. I told them that they didn't have a clue. Their job is to eliminate waste, and they're the ones creating waste."

The group responsible for kaizen at our company came to me sometime after that encounter with Ohno-san and asked for some materials. I refused and told them how angry Ohno-san would be at such a request. They insisted that they needed to make a report about the kaizen activities. I asked why they needed to make a report when people could see the actual kaizen in the workplace. I told them to show people the kaizen in practice.

We have too many people these days who don't understand the workplace. They've got that tinfoil over their eyes. They think a lot, but they don't see. I urge you to make a special effort to see what's happening in the workplace. That's where the facts are. And the truth is hidden in the facts. Our job is to get a handle on the truth.

3. Problems

When Ohno-san sensed a problem, he'd spend an hour or even two hours at one spot. He'd peer at things while chain-smoking. Sometimes, he'd forget about his cigarette, and it would burn all the way to his lips.

One time, Ohno-san called me over as he was watching over a workplace while smoking. "Something's not right in the motion of that worker," he pointed out. I was one of those guys with tinfoil over their eyes, so I didn't see what he meant, and I said so. "Look at his hands and feet. He keeps changing the way they move. Either he's doing the work wrong or something is creating an overburden in the process. You need to find out what the problem is. If you stand here and watch for a day, you'll figure it out."

Ohno-san would keep looking at things for as long as it took to figure out what the problem was. He warned us that "waiting until you've seen the data is too late for kaizen. You can evaluate the day's data and figure out that 'hey, that machine stopped a lot' or 'that process was improving,' but the horse is already out of the barn. A whole day has passed while you were processing the data. You've got to act on the spot."

"Acting on the spot" is wonderful in principle, but you've got to know where to look. You need to look where the biggest problems are. That's where the *andon* lamps come in. The *andon* lamps [which light up when employees pull the line-stop cord to indicate trouble] tell you where the problems are happening. You need to go to those places and examine things carefully. If you watch carefully, you'll see what's causing the problems. Then, you can do your kaizen improvements. Doing that again and again is how you raise productivity. Of course, new issues keep arising, as when the *takt* time gets quicker [*takt* being the German word for (musical) "meter," and *takt* time being the time increments at which the following process requires parts] or when you reduce your staffing on the line.

4. The Line-Stop System

Everything was moving smoothly on our assembly line one day when Ohno-san arrived and I showed him around. No red *andon* lamps went on to indicate problems, and the line didn't stop at all. That had me worried. And sure enough, Ohno-san was irritable by the time we'd walked through about half of the line.

"You've got," he finally blurted out, "too many people on the line. You need to staff your line at a level where the line stops about 10% of the time. That's the only way to make sure of getting problems out into the open. People think that everything's great if the line keeps moving. But that's wrong. Even if your operating rate is 98%, you've got too many people. You can't afford to take pride in a line that keeps moving. You've got to make sure that your people on the line can stop the line and that your supervisors can't.

"Most of all, you've got to avoid making your operators think that they shouldn't stop the line. You need to have your operators abide by the standardized work and to turn out high-quality products. You can't put pressure on them to do any more than what is naturally possible. If the line stops, it's your job to figure out the problem and to do kaizen improvements to solve the problem. If the line stops, that means you've got a problem that needs solving."

So a high operating rate might simply mean that you have too many people on the line. You need to work continuously to get problems out into the open. That's the way to raise productivity.

5. Work-in-Process

Maintaining a lot of work-in-process lets you keep the line moving, even if work runs behind somewhere. As a result, you don't notice the problem [that caused the delay]. We might have three pieces of work-in-process between two processes on the assembly line. Ohno-san would come along and bark at us to get that down to just one piece. As soon as we did that, our operating rate would plunge. Our buffer of three pieces [of work-in-process] had been absorbing delays in work along the line. When we got rid of the buffer, the delays affected work everywhere on the line immediately.

Ohno-san would say, "If you've got three pieces of work-in-process, reduce that to two. If you've got two, reduce it to one. The ideal is to get it down to zero. But reducing work-in-process is not the object. The object is to expose problems. If problems stop showing up, reduce your work-in-process. None at all is best."

The line stops as soon as you eliminate your work-in-process. You don't know when or where the next delay will occur. That keeps your supervisors on their toes. It's like being out on the street. If you're walking along a broad street that has no traffic, you can waltz along without a care in the world. On the other hand, if you're walking on a narrow lane—and if one side of the lane is a cliff—you need to watch your step. Getting rid of work-in-process enforces that kind of alertness. You reduce the work-in-process to get everyone to feel that tension.

That's why Ohno-san said, "If your line never stops on account of some process keeping the next process waiting, you've got too much work-in-process. You want to have occasional stoppages caused by parts shortages. Of course, you don't want your line to be stopping all the time. But the occasional delay caused by a process keeping the next process waiting for an item is good. If that stops happening, reduce your work-in-process until it starts happening again. You've got to maintain that kind of intensity to make sure that problems become apparent. You shouldn't think that no shortage of parts is a good thing."

6. The Quality of Work

No one ever got a scolding from Ohno-san for getting something wrong as long as they were doing their best. But he'd turn red in the face and deliver a severe tongue-lashing to someone who was slacking and made excuses for messing something up. He was absolutely livid one time when he found us ordering parts with a fixed schedule. We were doing that because kanban were hard to use at first, and Ohno-san exploded.

"Are you trying to destroy your suppliers? Don't you understand the trouble that you cause the suppliers by issuing production instructions on the basis of a schedule? Can't you see that you'll stick them with unnecessary inventory if your production volume dips?"

Ohno-san was extremely attentive to the fundamentals of work and to the work process. He believed strongly that things would work out right in the end as long as everyone was doing their best and using their head. Anyone can work hard. But it was doubly important to work hard in a way that demonstrated some thinking. He was less interested in seeing people work up a sweat than in seeing them improve work in ways that let things get done smoothly.

7. Solid Work

Our assembly line stopped one time while Ohno-san was watching. A production manager ran to see what the problem was and came back with the following explanation: Someone had checked a part after attaching it and had discovered that the part was faulty. So the workers were removing the part and attaching another one.

On hearing the explanation, Ohno-san laughed angrily. "You guys are stupider than chickens. If you thought some food might be poisonous, would you gulp it down without checking it first?" Checking a part before attaching it takes no more time than checking it afterwards, and it can save a lot of trouble.

I taught myself a valuable lesson once when I needed to pick up some important visitors at Kyoto Station. I had gotten a call from our headquarters' secretarial division. Some transport officials from the government were going to visit our Kyoto Plant in a couple of days, and the secretarial division wanted me to pick them up at 3 p.m. I wanted to make sure I didn't miss them, so I asked for the number of the train on which the visitors would be arriving.

On the day of the visit, I double-checked the train number, and I learned to my surprise that the scheduled arrival time was one o'clock, not three. Fortunately, I had just enough time to get to the station before the train arrived, and everything went smoothly in the end. I had just happened to think to ask for the train number, and that had enabled me to avert a humiliating misconnection. The experience reminded me of the importance of making sure that you have information to check things against and of making sure that you do the checking.

Contingency planning is also essential in ensuring that work gets done right. Simply assuming that things will go according to your original plan is irresponsible. You've got to prepare for unexpected events.

8. Mutual Assistance

"You can't gauge people's capabilities with perfect accuracy, so you inevitably end up with some imbalances in allocating work. To keep work moving smoothly, the people in each process need to be prepared to help out in other processes. You need to provide multiprocess training so your people can help out wherever help is needed.

"Japanese these days seem to have lost the spirit of mutual assistance. An inscription at the site of the historic Antaka no Seki checkpoint [in

Ishikawa Prefecture] cites wisdom, courage, and benevolence as the conditions for overcoming adversity. [That checkpoint was the scene of an oft-cited but apocryphal incident in Japanese lore of the 12th century. Minamoto no Yoshitsune had jointly led the overthrow of Japan's ruling clan, the Tairas, with his older brother, Minamoto no Yoritomo. But he had angered Yoritomo with his subsequent conduct and was fleeing for his life, a flight that was to prove unsuccessful. Yoshitsune, disguised as a monk, was traveling in the company of the wise monk Musashibo Benkei. They famously secured safe passage past the checkpoint, thanks to the benevolent assistance of its overseer, Togashi Yasuie.]

"The wisdom of Benkei and the courage of Yoshitsune would not have been enough in themselves to secure safe passage past the checkpoint. The benevolence displayed by Togashi was indispensable. Assistance from third parties can be essential in coping with challenges."

9. Automation and Intelligent Automation

[The Japanese word for automation is *jidoka*. It comprises three kanji: 自 (ji), for self or auto; 動 (do), for motion; and 化 (ka), which corresponds to the "-ation" suffix. The *jidoka* familiar to students of the Toyota Production System shares the first and third kanji with its homonym, but the middle kanji is slightly different: 働. Toyota has replaced the kanji for mere motion with the kanji for work. The additional element on the left side of the kanji (亻) is, by itself (as 人), the kanji for person.]

"Toyota's *jidoka* means investing conventional automated equipment with capabilities ordinarily associated with human wisdom: the ability to check quality and the ability to stop when problems occur and to call attention to the problems. When we install automated equipment, we need to add the element of human wisdom and make it *jidoka* equipment [in the Toyota sense]. And we need to provide equally wise linkage between the machines. That means devising [pull] linkage that synchronizes the operation of the preceding machine with the operation of the following machine rather than [push] linkage that arbitrarily feeds items from one machine to the next [regardless of the pace of work in the following process].

"*Jidoka* linkage prevents absolute timing loss. Push linkage with a conveyor causes problems. Volkswagen and other automakers would station a person at conveyor connections [to deal with those problems]. Those problems and the timing loss that they entail are the result of using push linkage. To prevent that loss, you need to use synchronized [pull] linkage.

"You've got to remember that the purpose of automation is to raise profitability for the company, not to make things look pretty. The guys in production engineering sometime automate stuff for the sake of appearances. Sometimes, they automate stuff just for the sake of automation. The right way to automate is to start by doing thorough kaizen in the processes as they are. Then you automate just enough to achieve what you need above and beyond what the processes are capable of delivering otherwise."

10. Rationalization

Ohno-san would get angry when he saw workers running around and working up a sweat. He'd say, "What's the big hurry? Mistakes happen when people are rushing back and forth like that. You're making a huge mistake if you think that a lot of running around means that people are doing a good job. You've got to arrange things so that people can get their work done more easily."

Rationalization is a matter of arranging things so that your equipment and your people can generate value-added continuously and efficiently.

A workplace where rationalization has been done right doesn't look that way to the untrained eye. Amateurs assume that a rationalized workplace is one where you see lots of automated equipment and where everyone looks really busy. That's not true rationalization.

[Ohno-san also warned us not to let automation detract from rationalization.] "When you install automated equipment, you need to position it so that fluctuations in production volumes don't result in awkward increments of work. Automated machines tend to become bottlenecks when production volumes fluctuate. Let's say that a one-minute cycle becomes a two-minute cycle. If you've got one person working between two machines, you could end up with just a half-person's worth of work for that person to do. You've got to position your equipment and your people to avoid that kind of problem.

"An increase in production volume shouldn't necessarily mean a decline in unit costs any more than a decline in volume should mean an increase in unit costs. Those sorts of things happen as the result of arranging things poorly."

11. Other Ohnoisms

"Machines are there for people to use, not the other way around."

"Some people love to make things complicated. The key is to make things simple."

"A lot of people think that rationalization means turning out more stuff. In fact, the essence of rationalization is turning out better stuff."

"Attaining a target doesn't mean that you've finished anything. Targets are just tools for tapping people's potential. When you've attained a target, raise the bar."

"Learning from mistakes is common sense. You also need to learn from what you've done when you're successful and put it to work in tackling new challenges. When you've just attained a target, that's no time to pat yourself on the back and relax."

"Do things that no one else is doing. Your efforts might not come to anything, but if they do, you need to learn from the process, too."

"The way you evaluate people shapes their behavior. Production at the Takaoka Plant slumped one time [on account of weak demand], and the plant was operating only half days. At times like that, the people should simply take the rest of the day off. But when I went to the workplace, I found the lights on and people sweeping up and getting ready for the next shift. I noted that they were wasting electricity and asked what they were doing. They answered that their evaluations would suffer if they weren't doing something that looked like work all the time. When you've got idiots for managers, people in the workplace end up wasting money."

"The right approach to maintenance is to keep your machines and equipment in perfect condition and make repairmen unnecessary." [*Tanaka:* The maintenance guys at Toyota would hang out in a room during the day and play mahjong. Someone mentioned that to Ohno-san, and he responded] "It's a good sign if your maintenance guys can sit around and play mahjong. You're in trouble if they're busy running around. [If your maintenance guys can sit around playing mahjong] that means you're doing a good job [of keeping your machines and equipment in the right condition]."

"The ultimate criterion is cost. In deciding how to proceed, you make your decision on the basis of cost."

"If you think there's no alternative, you're just failing to see the other possibilities. If no one [disagrees with you and] comes forward with a different idea, then come up with an alternative on your own. You need to understand the alternatives before going ahead with anything."

"You need to stop the line if a defect turns up." [*Tanaka:* We established a reworking process one time to deal with defects. Ohno-san scolded us, saying] "You get defects because you set up a process like that. If a defect occurs, stop the line. That way, everyone will do their best [to prevent defects from occurring and, when they do occur, to determine the causes and take countermeasures]. You don't want to be setting up a separate process to rework stuff." [*Tanaka:* People working hard on the line don't necessarily notice defects naturally. So you need to stop the line when a defect occurs and show people what has happened and why. That teaches them how to avoid creating defects. It's a lot better (than resigning yourself to the occurrence of defects and letting a reworking process deal with the problems).]

"Set things up so that production cannot continue when a defect has occurred." [The president of a company in Kyushu that made a certain product came to consult with Ohno-san. His company recovered unsold products and recycled them into new products. (The main reason for the unsold products was defects, and) the president was interested in reducing the volume of returned products. He sought advice from Ohno-san about how to proceed.] "You can't reduce the volume of returned products as long as you keep recycling them. Do you have a place at your factory where you could dig a hole to bury the returned products? If you really throw away the stuff that comes back, your people will see what a terrible waste it is. That sense of waste is crucial."

"Telling lies is bad, but being fooled by lies is worse." [*Tanaka:* Making decisions on the basis of written materials can produce bad decisions. If you've got doubts about something, you need to go to the workplace and see for yourself. The president at a company came from an administrative background, and he couldn't determine what was what when a technical issue arose at a board meeting. So he went to the workplace to see what the problem was. He discovered that half of what a director responsible for production had said at a board meeting was untrue. The president started visiting the workplace occasionally. Word got around that he was keeping an eye on things, and the directors stopped making false reports.] "Managers and general managers are good liars. But directors are even better."

Conclusion

I urge all of you to maintain a sense of urgency. Ohno-san had a sense of urgency, and that's why he came up with the idea for kanban after seeing a U.S. supermarket. Anyone can gain knowledge through study. But wisdom is something else again. And what we need in the workplace is wisdom. We need to foster people who possess wisdom. The only way to do that is to set our goals high and force people to accomplish more than they might have thought possible.

Once people really resolve to do something, the necessary wisdom arises. The people grow, and they assert new capabilities. The kanban didn't arise from textbook learning. It arose from practical experience in the workplace, and the best way to learn about kanban is to use them. Ohno-san told us, "Books are appearing about kanban, but only someone who actually uses kanban can really understand how they work. You guys have learned about kanban by using them, so you don't need to read my book." So I never did read his book.

Ohno-san was a man who defied the conventional wisdom. He devoted his life to kaizen. He kept finding new things to improve and new ways to do kaizen. You need to avoid thinking that the present way of doing things is the best way. You need to be eager to change things. Everything begins with trying something. Without that determination to try something, all the knowledge in the world is useless.

If you got anything at all today from my comments about Ohno-san, then please try putting it to work. Different companies have different ways of doing things, and no single system is the best for everyone. Different factories will naturally have different approaches. But what we need to do everywhere is create a sense of tension and to motivate people to get things done.

Questions and Answers

Q: You say that you were dubious about the kanban at first? Why were you doubtful?

Tanaka: I just didn't understand it well enough. I couldn't see the connection between reducing in-process stock and doing kaizen. Only after we tried it did I see how reducing in-process stock highlights problems. I had figured that we could simply change the processes to make the necessary improvements. And Ohno-san never explained his reasons, so the only way to learn was by doing. Nothing was clear to me at first, so I doubted that the kanban would really work.

When I joined Daihatsu, I went straight to work in production engineering without ever having worked on the plant floor. That was unfortunate. I should have gained some hands-on experience in production first. Then I could have been more useful to our production people when I worked in production engineering.

Anyway, my first job was in production engineering, where I participated in planning a new plant. I went to work in production when the new plant opened. Only then did I realize that I had been a "catalog engineer." I had simply collected catalogs and other materials and looked at the pictures and decided that I wanted to make this or that. Of course, some of what I did was useful, but it wasn't in tune with the expectations of our production people. What they wanted was a working environment that made work easier to do. If I had been more aware of circumstances in the workplace, I could have come up with better layouts.

Eiji Toyoda was a person who truly enjoyed spending time in the workplace. When he arrived at a plant, he'd head straight for the shop floor. I showed him the automated line at our new Shiga Plant when he visited one time. He said, "You guys are just dragging me around to show off your automation." He saw right through us.

Most corporate types who came to the plant would compliment us on our impressive new facility and on all the fancy equipment. But Eiji was looking carefully at the relationship between the equipment and the people. He told us that the matching was lousy between our automated machines and our people. He meant that we wouldn't be able to respond flexibly when production volumes fluctuated and that work loss would occur as a result. You can't afford to focus exclusively on your automated equipment. A line of impressive-looking machines is not necessarily a good thing.

Q: I'm responsible for a production line. I have been careful in deploying people, and I have eliminated inventory buffers so that the line stops immediately if a problem occurs. But we keep having problems with dumb mistakes. I'm not making any progress in tackling this problem, and I'm getting really frustrated.

Tanaka: Humans are imperfect animals, so mistakes happen. Work is a combination of processing and checking. In crucial processes, you need to incorporate and enforce checks to avoid mistakes that would place the employees at fault. Workers naturally tend to forget things and to become careless. I assume that you are already doing this, but you can help prevent mistakes by detailing important processing steps in the standardized work manual and by having your people check themselves against that sheet.

Q: I prepared a collection of Soichiro Honda sayings in connection with the evolution of production engineering at Honda [Motor]. What he said resonates perfectly with what we have heard from you, and everything makes perfect sense. A love for making things seems to be the common thread.

Soichiro Honda was originally infatuated with making tools for making cars that would evoke [the beauty of] production engineering, and he would make a beeline for the shop floor whenever he came to a plant. His passing has underlined the importance of conveying that spirit to the next generation, but imparting that spirit to new employees is hard. What suggestions do you have for passing on the spirit that you have been discussing?

Tanaka: The example set by management is important. If management sets a bad example, the people down below will let things slide. If you're going to tackle the challenge of rationalization, someone's got to take charge. People who achieve great things, including Honda-san, have some important things in common. They tend to display a *genchi gembutsu* commitment to the workplace, and they tend to believe only what they can confirm with their own eyes.

I remember watching the great film director Akira Kurosawa on a television show. He was describing what he had learned while working as an assistant director under Kajiro Yamamoto. Kurosawa recalled walking out of the studio with Yamamoto and passing an actress dressed in a kimono and carrying a pouch. Yamamoto asked him what she was carrying. He wasn't sure and said something like, "Isn't it a medicine pouch?" That earned a scolding from Yamamoto. "Don't try to BS people. If you don't know the answer, don't say anything until you can find out for sure."

Kurosawa then became a *genchi gembutsu* person [a person committed to seeing things firsthand as they really are]. His *genchi gembutsu* commitment is the same thing that we require in manufacturing. The most important thing for people in manufacturing is to keep one foot in the production workplace and take a good look at things there before making decisions. People who excel at anything tend to be people who insist on seeing things for themselves. That's because the facts are in the things that we can actually see, and we can only get at the truth through the facts. Just thinking about things in your own head won't [lead you to the truth].

The way to pass this spirit on to the next generation is to go out into the workplace and scold people. If someone screws up, take them into the workplace, show them exactly what's gone wrong, and give them a good scolding. When someone gets a scolding in the workplace while looking at what's actually happened, they can't make any excuses. The scolding presents the person with a higher standard to meet.

On the other hand, you can't be strict all the time. Ohno-san cautioned me one time after I'd been scolding people in the workplace. "You need to be careful not to discourage people who already have the right motivation." I asked him what he meant, and he replied, "Motivated people want to do things, even when they think they can't. And some things really are impossible for some people. At times like that, motivated people can get discouraged. So even if you say something strict, you also want to find an opportunity to extend a helping hand."

Extending a helping hand lets people know that you value their effort, even if they were unsuccessful. [Managers] who never extend a helping hand can never earn the trust of their subordinates. We need to accompany strictness with a readiness to help. And to do that, we need to know what's going on in the workplace. If you don't know what's happening in the workplace, you can't do anything for the people there.

Managers who are happy when problems stop showing up and operating rates rise are no good. Managers need to let their people know that they're happy to see problems show up. Ordinary people tend to want to hide problems. We shouldn't ever think badly of people who reveal one problem after another. We should welcome situations where problems become clear.

When Ohno-san gave guidance to companies, he always started with the president. "All the training in the world will come to nothing unless senior management displays a strong commitment. If you demonstrate the right commitment, I'll provide your people with the training they need."

Q: At [what is now the Toyota subsidiary] Kanto Auto Works, a lot of the engineers were from Nakajima Aircraft [which was Japan's premier manufacturer of aircraft and which was disbanded after the war]. That engineering tradition entailed a lot of conflict between the product engineers and the production engineers. I'm interested to know whether or not the situation there was different from what you've discussed in your talk today.

So I have two questions. One, are the people you describe who love to rationalize systems different from the people who simply love to make things? I see that as a difference between Soichiro Honda and Taiichi Ohno. My second question is about those people who just love to work, regardless of what's happening in regard to targets. When people like that clashed with Ohno-san, how did he set them right?

Tanaka: I never received any guidance directly from Honda-san, so I can't comment with confidence on the difference between him and Ohno-san. My gut feeling is that Honda-san and Ohno-san had similarities but that they were basically different. Honda-san participated directly in creating products. Ohno-san was more interested in fostering human resources and in creating systems, but he devoted himself to the practical side of those challenges, not to the theoretical side. As a result, a lot of people grew and developed through receiving guidance from Ohno-san. Their way of thinking came to resemble his way of thinking.

Q: I am studying that subject carefully, and I have obtained some pertinent materials from Honda [Motor]. I've learned that [Soichiro] Honda also devoted a great deal of attention to fostering human resources. If you want to get any work done right, you need to spend a lot of time on that task. Honda-san could never have achieved such impressive success if he had ignored the task of fostering human resources.

What emerges most clearly in the materials I've obtained is [Soichiro Honda's] emphasis on motivating people and on encouraging people to tackle self-improvement. If those materials all became public, they would highlight an important similarity between Honda-san and Ohno-san. I think that we need to take another look at the two men's approach to manufacturing.

The message in your talk that resonated with my experience was that nothing happens unless management demonstrates a strong commitment. I was at Kobe Steel, and I spent a year supervising [what should have been] a thorough rationalization of operations at the Saijo Plant, near Hiroshima. The plant manager was dead set against our efforts.

I secured a strong show of support from the company president. He declared that he would fire anyone who stood in the way of our efforts, even the plant manager. That changed everything. I went into that assignment without any relevant experience, and I learned a lot about the deep-rooted resistance you encounter on-site when you try to reform factory operations. You've got to listen to people in the workplace, but you've also got to push ahead with new ideas [and new ways of doing things].

Tanaka: You're absolutely right. You walk into an old plant and tell someone that they've got to change the way they do things. They'll tell you,

"I've been doing things this way for 20 years, and it works just fine." I answered like this: "If you've been doing things that way for 20 years, don't you think it's time for a change? Can't you see that doing things the same way for 20 years means that you're not making any progress?" People's own wisdom and experience don't necessarily highlight the need for change.

Another issue is differences in how people perceive the appropriate goals. I was anti-kanban at first, and that was because I didn't understand the aims of the kanban system. Circumstances later provided me with the opportunity to understand those aims, and I went to work [on putting the kanban system in place and making it work]. Different perceptions of suitable goals can happen like that when people haven't had the chance to come to terms with what you're trying to do.

Q: You describe putting in place [what some people called] the New Production System. I understand that you and others set up the system at 37 or 38 companies. The guiding principle appears to have been to rationalize plant operations without spending any money and to defer any large-scale automation as much as possible. You determined what resulted in the smoothest flow. And after you had simplified the flow as much as possible, you automated what you had at that point.

I've been listening without really understanding fully what you were saying. I'd be interested to hear what you went through before arriving at that approach. Once you arrived at that approach and everyone understood how things would proceed, I assume that you didn't have arguments about whether or not to automate things. Were you still operating in a kind of flux?

Tanaka: We definitely felt like we were proceeding in a state of flux when we were first putting the system in place. An operating procedure ultimately took shape, but that was maybe five years down the line. Clear criteria for automation came even later. The mood of the times presented a lot of pressure to automate and to computerize, and our younger employees were impatient. We lost some people then that I felt bad about losing.

Q: Tell us more about the initial resistance to the kanban system.

Tanaka: That was only natural. You can't understand the kanban system until you give it a try. When you just walk in and tell people to start using kanban, they're bound to resist. It's something that you learn by doing. I could easily have ended up on the outside looking in. I only stuck with it because I happened to get the chance to see how [kanban] could work.

I didn't think at the time that any particular method was the be-all and end-all, and I still don't think so. What matters is motivation. You need to start by motivating people, by getting them excited about accomplishing something. Once you do that, they'll be happy to learn and use whatever method you propose. The kanban system is simple. But unmotivated people will not learn the system. The motivation has got to come first.

Q: At Toshiba's Omi Plant, they were making desktop computers on two 20-meter-long assembly lines until two years ago. They got rid of the conveyor lines and started having individuals assemble whole computers. I was amazed. Productivity doubled. That's because a conveyor line ends up flowing at the pace of the person who has the lowest productivity. A veteran assembler can put together about 50 computers a day. And putting individuals in charge of assembling complete computers reduced the in-process stock dramatically.

I know of lots of similar examples. And that trend is narrowing the difference in productivity between low-wage small companies and high-wage big companies. The only thing left to differentiate a company is motivation. I think we've entered an era when [the people at] big companies can't take anything for granted.

Tanaka: Small companies that assert unique strengths have high profitability. They do things that big companies aren't doing. Their people operate outside the organization-man mentality. Niche strategies can work.

Q: I have a question about your story of Eiji Toyoda pointing out a mismatch between people and automated equipment. We are in an era of violent fluctuations in demand. What kind of operating rate is reasonable to aim for in matching people and automated equipment?

Some mismatching is inevitable, but the degree of the imbalance depends on your priorities. Has kaizen produced an ideal allocation of human and mechanical resources at Daihatsu? And what is the logic behind the allocation that has resulted there?

Tanaka: If you were operating a line entirely with human labor [and with no automated equipment], fluctuations in production volume wouldn't affect your productivity a bit. If you install automated equipment and position individual workers between machines, you can't reduce the staffing [when the production volume declines]. You've got to arrange things so that one operator can [operate a broader or narrower range of equipment, depending on the production volume].

In general, installing highly automated equipment means higher unit costs when the production volume declines. A strong and inverse relationship between unit costs and production volume indicates a bad approach to manufacturing. Fancy equipment will raise unit costs sooner or later.

Toyoda Boshoku [now Toyota Boshoku (Toyota Spinning and Weaving)] once assembled vacuum bottles for [a consumer products company], and it wasn't making any money at all from that business. It was assembling the vacuum bottles on a conveyor line when Ohno-san became the chairman there [after retiring from Toyota]. So you'd have spells of waiting between people on the line, and you'd end up working at the pace of the slowest person. Ohno-san got rid of the conveyor belt and had the people do their work standing [alongside a workbench]. Productivity went up 30% or 40%, and Toyoda Boshoku finally started to turn a profit on the vacuum bottle business.

Yes, the era of the conveyor as the be-all and end-all is over. We can discard the assumption that mass production is synonymous with conveyor lines.

Q: My question is about how the production engineering sector should support the kaizen efforts by people in the manufacturing workplace. You've mentioned progress in computer technology, and the production engineering people are presumably supervising the creation of advanced systems. Meanwhile, the people on the shop floor are pushing ahead with the [practical] ideas promoted by Ohno-san. How do those different efforts interact?

Tanaka: Creating systems needs to be a matter of going out into the workplace, seeing the problems that are occurring there, and developing systems [to address those real-world circumstances]. You won't get far in the workplace with systems based on ideas that you've simply dreamed up in your head.

All [good] systems originate in the workplace. Ohno-san wasn't consciously working on any system at first. He was simply [solving problems] and ended up creating a system. A system that someone just dreams up [in an office or somewhere] won't work in the production workplace. If anything, it'll trigger a backlash.

Q: Product development engineers are showing up increasingly on the plant floor these days, along with the production engineering people. That seems to be a trend, doesn't it?

Tanaka: The development people also need to abide by the *genchi gembutsu* principle of seeing for themselves in the workplace. They need to see for themselves if the things they've designed are truly easy to assemble and whether the quality [of the assembled products] is what they envisioned. That kind of attention results in higher quality and lower costs.

We say that providing management with information feedback is the job of the production workplace. Conversely, management is responsible for absorbing information from [the plant floor]. Amazing things result when both ends of the flow fulfill their responsibility. Things get out of whack in the workplace when a know-it-all comes along [and starts spouting off].

Q: Kanto Auto Works adopted the Toyota Production System in bits and pieces. At Toyota, the system extends all the way from sales to product development, manufacturing, and purchasing. But at Kanto Auto Works, a new idea that took hold in the plants didn't have any effect on product development. Instead, product development would absorb some idea from Toyota. So even if the Toyota Production System was transforming operations in the plants, the basic approach to product development didn't change. You must have had a similar experience at Daihatsu. How did things play out at your company?

Tanaka: Here is an example of something Ohno-san did to prevent that sort of problem. He instructed us to report the number of parts shortages that occurred [when the flow-based production line stopped because of a work delay in any process on the line]. Ohno-san told us to leave everything else up to the people on the shop floor. The people in the production workplace got in trouble when parts shortages occurred, so they worked hard on kaizen improvements to prevent shortages.

Ohno-san also told us to have the quality assurance people play a more-active role in managing flows of information [among the processes and among the different sectors of operations]. And he laid down a general rule for everyone to follow: "If you come out to the workplace with nothing better to do than complain, then stay away. If you have a positive suggestion about ways to maybe improve things, then come."

In the relationship between sales and production, Ohno-san told the production people to make more stuff because things were selling well. And he told the salespeople to sell more. But he knew what our production capacity was, and he never insisted on pushing production to an unsound level just to keep up with strong sales. He knew that putting unreasonable pressure on the workplace would simply cause problems, and he cautioned us, "You've got to maintain quality. Making unreasonable demands causes quality to deteriorate."

Ohno-san carefully managed any discrepancies between the number of vehicles that the salespeople were demanding and the number of vehicles that we could reasonably produce. That earned him the absolute confidence of the people in manufacturing. They accepted anything he said as the truth.

Q: At our previous gathering, we heard from [Masao] Nemoto [a former senior managing director at Toyota (see chapter 5)]. He led the introduction of TQC at Toyota, and he told us that the Toyota Production System and TQC complemented each other [and had both been essential to Toyota's progress in raising productivity, ensuring quality, and lowering costs].

Nemoto-san observed that the Toyota Production System gets a lot of credit [for Toyota's success]. And he noted that people have forgotten that TQC was indispensable, for example, in putting the kanban system in place. What was the positioning of TQC in the guidance that you received from Ohno-san?

Tanaka: Ohno-san always said, "Kanban won't work right anywhere that TQC isn't working right. Quality control is fundamental. The kanban system only works when you're making quality products."

The main difference [between Ohno-san and some of the proponents of TQC] was his dislike of written materials. He warned us not to waste time producing useless documentation. He insisted that we could convey information better by showing people the workplace than by turning out documents.

Ohno-san said, "Supervisors and managers should go 'read' the situation in the workplace when the line stops. They shouldn't waste their time gathering data. When a defect occurs, stop the line and go see what's happened. That's the way to discover the causes of problems. What good is preparing a bunch of data?"

He also said, "If you deal with problems on the spot when they occur, the person responsible for the problem will understand what he or she has done wrong. If you simply gather data and pass it upstairs, no one will feel any sense of personal responsibility when the report comes out. You've got to make people feel responsible for their mistakes. You need to maintain a healthy sense of tension [in regard to preventing defects]."

Chapter III

Putting a Pull System in Place at Toyota

Two Talks by **Kikuo Suzumura**

As recorded and edited by **Hiroaki Satake** *and*
Takashi Matsuo

Background

Issues that Toyota encountered in implementing the kanban system figure prominently in Suzumura's talks. Kanban are a crucial tool for operating the Toyota Production System as a "pull system." Indicating what, how, when, and in what quantities to make and move things can take place in accordance with either (1) a production plan or (2) actual demand. Kanban correspond to the latter. They link production activity to demand.

About the Text

This chapter reprises talks given on July 25 and August 8, 1998, by Kikuo Suzumura, a legendary figure in Toyota Production System lore. Suzumura was formerly a manager in the office responsible for propagating the Toyota Production System, now the Operations Management Consulting Division, and his retelling of his experiences is extremely specific. The descriptions can be difficult to understand, however, for people who have not participated directly in the Toyota Production System. They are especially challenging for anyone who lacks a detailed knowledge of automobile manufacturing.

To make the material more understandable for nonspecialist readers, the editors have reorganized the content thematically. They have obtained and

Production instructions based on a plan break down the plan into agendas for each process. People can account for deviations in performance from the plan, but the ultimate basis for the production instructions is an abstract formulation. In contrast, kanban—production instructions based on performance—link production to the consumption of processes' output in the following processes.

Every item that moves through the Toyota Production System carries a kanban. Toyota uses two main kinds of kanban: production instruction kanban and withdrawal kanban. Production instruction kanban circulate inside processes. Withdrawal kanban circulate between processes. The interlocking cycles of withdrawal kanban and production instruction kanban pull work through the Toyota Production System (fig. 1).

Withdrawal kanban cycles

When a process begins work on an item, it removes the kanban from that item and returns it to the previous process to withdraw another item. A process needs to use a withdrawal kanban to obtain an item from the

incorporated clarifications from Suzumura about several subjects, and they have supplemented his descriptions with explanatory material as necessary, including a preliminary background section.

The audiences for the talks related here consisted of individuals with whom Suzumura shared an intimate working relationship, and he was utterly unrestrained in his characteristically brusque tone. The editors have sought to retain that tone even as they have reorganized the material to simplify understanding.

Table 1 presents a chronological summary of Suzumura's activities in the context of Toyota history. The editors have prepared the table on the basis of Suzumura's talks and Toyota's official histories. Note that Suzumura's

Fig. 1: Basic Kanban Formats

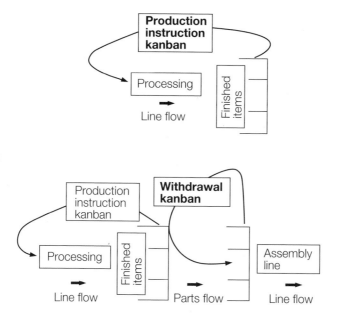

descriptions rely heavily on memory and that the editors have been only partly successful in cross-checking those descriptions with third parties.

About the Speaker

An understanding of Suzumura's activities at Toyota is indispensable in grasping how and in what kind of circumstances the Toyota Production System took shape. Taiichi Ohno justly receives credit for initiating, or "inventing," the system. But Suzumura, along with Itsuo Mamiya and Shozo Yoshii, was instrumental in translating Ohno's ideas into practical methods. Suzumura also was directly responsible for conceiving important elements of the Toyota Production System.

Table 1: Suzumura Chronology

	Toyota	Suzumura	Important new models	Annual production (vehicles)
1950	Labor dispute			11,706
1951	Starts five-year equipment modernization plan	Begins developing flow-based production and related work procedures		14,228
1952	Completes ¥1 billion investment in rationalizing machine tools			14,106
1953	Shifts production of Type S engine to Toyoda Automatic Loom Works			16,496
1954			Toyoace	22,713
1955	Completes wave of improvements on vehicle assembly lines, including installation of trolley conveyor and intercom system		Crown, Land Cruiser	22,786
1956	Builds No. 4 machining shop; Taiichi Ohno visits United States	Installs "Tokaido Line" (page 79); hears about U.S. supermarkets from Ohno		46,417
1957	Builds heat-treatment shop	Develops "bucket system" for transmission production (page 87)	Corona	79,527
1958	Completes wave of improvements in Nos. 1–3 machining shops	Installs parts conveyor in engine assembly shop (page 92)		78,856
1959	Upgrades machining shops in support of expanded vehicle production. Opens Motomachi (vehicle assembly) Plant			101,194
1960				154,770
1961	Builds second vehicle assembly line at Motomachi Plant		Publica	210,937
1962		Develops "iron computer" for transmission production (page 106)		230,350
1963				318,495
1964	Builds second machining shop at Motomachi Plant	Experiences failure of automation in production of Type 2R engine (page 109)		425,764
1965	Opens Kamigo (engine) Plant	Witnesses excessive investment in Type M engine production (page 111)		477,643
1966	Opens Takaoka (vehicle assembly) Plant	Develops production line for Type K engine to accommodate rapid growth in Corolla production (page 113). Devises information "lifting" for vehicle assembly line at Motomachi Plant (page 119)	Corolla	587,539

Sources: Suzumura's comments and official Toyota histories

previous process, so it can only withdraw as many items as it actually consumes. Withdrawal kanban thus link the flow of items between processes to the pace of production in the following processes.

Production instruction kanban cycles

When process A withdraws an item from the previous process (process B), it replaces the kanban on the item with a withdrawal kanban. The kanban that comes off of the item goes back into process B as an instruction to produce another item to replace the one that has been withdrawn. A process needs a production instruction kanban to begin work on a new item, so it can produce only as many items as the following process uses. Production instruction kanban thus link production in each process to the pace of production in the following process.

Kanban function in accordance with principles that are basically simple. Applying kanban to different items in different processes gives rise, however, to countless issues, as Suzumura describes.

Suzumura is thus well known inside Toyota and at Toyota suppliers as a leading figure in implementing the Toyota Production System. Although he retired more than a quarter century ago, people at Toyota and at Toyota suppliers continue to relate anecdotes about his exploits. This chapter redresses the paucity of attention that Suzumura has received in research and business texts about Toyota and about the Toyota Production System.

A native of Toyota City, Suzumura was born there in 1927, when the city's name was Koromo. He joined Toyota in 1948 on graduating from what is now the Nagoya Institute of Technology. His first assignment was to a machining shop at the Honsha (Headquarters) Plant, then known as the Koromo Plant. The fallout from a serious labor dispute in 1950 thinned the ranks of workplace

The Talks

1. Adopting Flow Production in a Machining Shop in the Early 1950s

Suzumura:

Those were hungry days for Japan when I joined Toyota [in 1948]. And no sooner had I joined the company than it spun off the marketing operations as a separate company and started laying off people left and right. Toyota had around 8,000 people altogether, and it dumped some 2,000. The guys who lost their jobs were to be pitied. But those of us who survived the layoffs weren't much better off. Sort of like out of the frying pan and into the fire.

People lost faith in each other. The company was one big heap of distrust. I could see that we couldn't afford to let something like that happen ever again. Meanwhile, the production system we were using amid all that was something to behold. It was an end-of-the-month scramble [because the parts required to assemble vehicles were rarely available in total until the end of the month (see Ohno's description on page 10)]. That's

supervisory personnel, and Suzumura soon became a group leader. He gained hands-on experience in production management in that capacity and subsequently as a production engineer. Suzumura moved to the forerunner of the Operations Management Consulting Division in the 1960s and participated in developing, refining, and propagating the Toyota Production System until his retirement in 1982. He passed away in 1999.

how guys learned to make stuff at Toyota. Pretty unbelievable.

Then came a surge in demand sparked by the Korean War, and we had to crank up production. We had been turning out something like 700 vehicles a month when the company let go of 2,000 people. Our output went up to 1,000 a month to meet the

A gathering of employees during the labor dispute that rocked Toyota in 1950

Korean War demand. We needed more people. We needed hundreds more. But management refused to take on any new employees. So we had to figure out ways to increase our output without hiring any more people. The company was grievously short of group leaders. So it promoted five of us who had been to school. We each took charge of a manufacturing workplace.

The group I led was in a machining shop [run by Taiichi Ohno]. In that shop, machines of the same kind were all clustered together in groups: drills over here, lathes over there, and so on. So the first thing I did was have our people rearrange them by processing sequence. Getting that done took five or six years. Our shop was just a backwater at the Honsha Plant. No one would do what I said the first time around. We were always hollering back and forth. I'd ask someone to take a new position, and I'd get an angry refusal, like "I'm a turret press operator. That's what I do!" Or maybe, "I grind gears! I don't do drilling. And I don't do milling."

We needed to arrange our machines to let work flow naturally from one process to the next. That meant having the right kinds of machines for each line. People tended to think that machines ought to be as fast and powerful as possible, that more-expensive equipment was better. But we didn't need high-output machines. We just needed enough of each

Prewar forging work at Toyota—with the kind of equipment that Ohno and Suzumura inherited and used

kind for all our lines. So we went out and bought equipment from plants that had been bombed in the war, like old naval armaments plants. We fixed it ourselves and installed it in our machining lines. We finally came up with enough equipment to get the lines laid out in the flow of work by around 1955.

We'd accommodate fluctuations in demand by changing the speed of the machines. But changing the speed unevenly among the machines would increase our manpower needs unnecessarily. So we made sure that we changed the speed of all the machines on the same line the same amount. That way, people could only produce the amount needed, even if they wanted to produce more. We established cycle times for each machine. That is, we'd let the operators know how many seconds they had for each work cycle, and we made sure that they observed those times.

We established standardized work guidelines when we built the lines. And we drew up charts that detailed the work sequence for each job. I prepared all the materials by myself at first. But within a couple of years, the other group leaders were taking responsibility for producing the materials.

Our colleagues began to imitate us when they saw how our improvements made life easier. Copies of our work began showing up in other workplaces. The group leaders would egg each other on. "Hey, if I can do this, you ought to be able to do it, too." To this day, the group leaders are the ones who determine the standardized work. And that's only natural. People who can do the work themselves are the right ones to teach others how to do that work.

A word from the editors:
Building production lines by arranging processes in the natural workflow
was a precondition for linking the processes and lines as a pull system.
And training and assigning operators to handle multiple jobs was essential to the flexibility required on flow-based production lines.

Taiichi Ohno famously began experimenting with multiprocess handling and with flow-based production lines in a Toyota machining shop
for engine components around 1949. Suzumura later became the group
leader responsible for crankshaft production in Ohno's machining shop.
The work in that shop spawned the principles of standardized work and
cycle time, which became fundamental to the Toyota Production System.
Readers should note, too, how the traumatizing experience of labor unrest
and mass layoffs motivated Suzumura and others to seek a better production workplace.

2. The Tokaido Line

Suzumura:
We finally got the processes [in our engine parts machining shop] arranged in the workflow sequence around 1955. Our attention then turned
to a machining shop that made parts and assembled units for steering and
suspension systems [units, in the parlance of Japanese automakers, being
components, such as engines and transmissions, that comprise multiple
parts and perform core functions]. That shop still operated in accordance
with a production plan, and it was a perfect example of Toyota's traditional end-of-the-month scramble to meet the plan's target. People would
kick back and relax at the beginning of each month, and they'd work like
crazy toward the end of the month.

We couldn't bear to watch the machining shop operating like that, but
we knew that we couldn't wean the shop from plan-based production

overnight. So we kept the plan-based production for the time being, but we insisted on distributing production evenly by breaking the monthly targets down into daily targets.

Steering and suspension units began piling up at the end of the line, especially in the first half of the month. One piled up on top of another. The pace of vehicle assembly picked up toward the end of the month, and that would finally eat up the stocks.

We made kaizen improvements in the way we conveyed things to resist surges. We were using a trolley on rails to move parts from the fabrication lines to the unit assembly line. We brought in a modified Toyota Toyoace truck and used it like a tractor to pull the trolley. We used the Toyoace to pull parts frequently to the assembly line (fig. 2).

We'd array the parts along the rail. The trolley would pick up parts along the right side of the rail on the way to the unit assembly line and along the opposite side of the rail on the way back. It would pick up the different parts needed for steering and suspension units for five vehicles on each round-trip, and it would unload the parts each time it arrived at the front end of the assembly line. I told the people in the shop that since we were running on rails they should think of the system as a train line. Soon, everyone was calling it the Tokaido Line [after the main train line that connects Tokyo, Nagoya, Kyoto, and Osaka].

We distributed empty containers to keep the parts fabrication moving at the pace of five vehicles' worth at a time. The containers were for operators to go get parts from the previous process to replace ones they'd finished working on. That took some getting used to. But that was how people still bought stuff like tofu back then. These days, tofu comes in a package. But in those days, the tofu peddlers would come around with their carts, and people would take their pots to go buy the tofu.

So I pointed that out to the operators. "When you go buy tofu, you take along a pot to carry it home, don't you?" They nodded in agreement.

"And if you didn't take along a pot, you wouldn't be able to buy any tofu, would you?" I needed to explain things like that to get people to understand. I needed to show that you can only get something when you have something to put it in.

We later replaced the trolley on rails with a trailer on tires. As for the timing for picking up parts, here's how it worked. We'd place one set of parts at the front end of the unit assembly line. We let the operators go get more parts from the "train" when they started using parts from that set. The idea was that the next set of parts should arrive before the assembly line had used up the previous set of parts.

We wanted the operators who made parts to make more when—and only when—the unit assembly line had used what they had already made. So we needed production instruction kanban. When we made our first kanban, we were starting from scratch, so we were free to make whatever suited our purposes in the workplace. No one would make too much of anything as long as the supervisor was keeping his eyes peeled. But the supervisor couldn't be watching everyone continuously. So we figured out a way to let people know when it was okay to make what.

In short, we started issuing production permits. Kanban were basically permits for making specified items. When the following process withdrew something from a process, the permit came off [and went back into the process as a production instruction]. Only when that permit arrived did anyone have the right to make something.

I gave orders to halt the train and wait if parts were not ready for pickup at any stop along the way. So the train would stop for the first guy who had failed to have his parts ready on time. And while it was stopped, the next guy down the line who was running behind would have the chance to get caught up. Our production instruction kanban ensured that we would keep making parts until we had everything needed for a full load.

Stopping the train wherever parts weren't ready meant stopping the unit assembly line until the parts arrived. It also meant stopping the fabrication lines—all of them. On the other hand, it meant that we could all see immediately who had stopped the train. We'd all head straight for the line where the train had stopped and help get the problem solved. We were like a community fire brigade rushing to the site of a fire. And you can be sure that everyone at the problem line, from the group leader on down, would be looking pretty embarrassed.

No one wanted to be the first one to stop the train, and everyone started working hard to avoid that humiliation. Our system gave rise to that kind of spirit. And we really did need the system. Without it, parts would always be piled up in heaps at the front end of the unit assembly line,

Fig. 2: The Tokaido Line

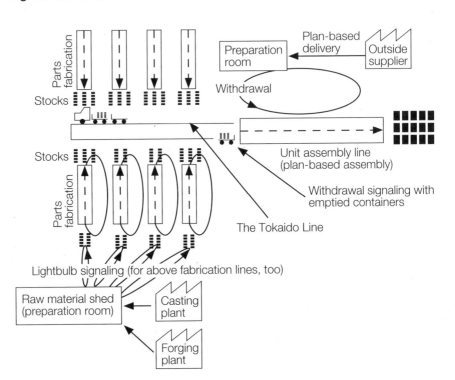

and no one would feel any special urgency about getting their parts ready. People would have the attitude like, "Hey, it doesn't make any difference up there if I finish my parts now or if I finish 'em five or six minutes from now." By keeping the whole shop waiting when anyone was behind, we made everyone aware of their responsibility for keeping things moving.

What's more, the group leaders started making suggestions for improvements. They'd come forward, for example, with ideas for better tools. But they couldn't draw up their ideas properly in diagrams. I was the only one around who could do that for them. And that made them beholden to me. They knew that they had to listen to Suzumura.

When you're making different kinds of assemblies, the temptation is strong to concentrate on one kind at a time: one in the morning, for example, and another in the afternoon. That simplifies life for the guys on the unit assembly line. But it wreaks havoc for the upstream guys who make the parts.

For example, the guys who make the parts for the unit you assemble in the morning will go crazy trying to keep up, but they might end up sitting on their hands in the afternoon. You'll have all sorts of shortages of parts, and your unit assembly line will stop again and again.

So if you're going to make different kinds of assemblies, you need to distribute the production of the different kinds evenly through the day. You've got to produce each kind of assembly in small volumes at a time. Otherwise, your parts-fabricating people will face hell on wheels when they show up in the morning, and you'll run into problems with insufficient capacity. That's the way things are, and that's what led to our discovery of leveled production. Or perhaps I should say that it's what caused us to stumble into leveling production.

If you don't level production, you'll keep running out of parts. You level production by changing the order in which you make things. You tell your people, "This is the order in which you've got to assemble things."

You keep writing out the order for people to see. But even if you think you've leveled the monthly production, you've still got a month's worth of work ahead of you. And dumping the information for a whole month's production on everyone will lead to all sorts of mistakes down the line. Someone is bound to get the model specs wrong or something wrong.

What's worse, everyone loves to make stuff in batches. And if you give them all the information up front, the first thing they'll do is start batching their production. The way we prevented that was by being stingy with information. We would just tell the guy who drove the train to pick up parts for what we were going to assemble next.

That's integrated command. It's integrated information. It's what finally put us in a position to really manage the pace of work throughout our shop. Until then, we had to assign a supervisor to monitor the pace of work on every line—what they now call production control. He'd go around and tell guys what to make and when to make it. Simply changing the way we doled out information eliminated the need for that supervision.

So the assembly line people would use the train to gather parts from the fabrication lines. They'd know it was time to go get some more parts when a withdrawal permit arrived. As for timing, the parts needed to arrive at the assembly line before it had used up all its parts. You could only get the timing right if you conveyed the parts by having the following process pick them up. You'd screw up the timing if you simply pushed the parts onto the following process according to a production plan.

This story I'm telling you is how things sound after we've figured out the logic. But we sure didn't start with the logic. We simply tried something. Later, we figured out that we were using a pull system. And the first place where we tried the pull system was in the machining shop at the Honsha Plant. We used it to connect parts fabrication to unit assembly. And it was a hard time coming.

Around that time, I heard the story of American supermarkets from Ohno-san. Everyone takes supermarkets for granted these days. But they were a revolutionary idea for us [in Japan, where shopkeepers still fetched the merchandise for customers]. I was amazed at the idea of retailers letting you choose freely from a bunch of merchandise on display, put your stuff in a basket, and pay on the way out. I couldn't get used to the idea of shopping without shopkeepers.

What would happen, I asked, if someone went in and ate a bunch of food without paying? That stumped Ohno-san. He finally said that he supposed that Americans were a people of integrity and that they just wouldn't do something like that. And he repeated that our production system was like going shopping at a supermarket. In fact, people really did call our system the supermarket system at one time.

We used to have a place called the preparation room, where we stored finished parts from our own lines and from suppliers. Our train line prevented the parts from our lines from making the detour into that room. Before that, inspectors would handle the stocking forms for the parts, and they would insist that group leaders bring withdrawal forms when they came to get more parts.

Even after we stopped routing our own parts through the preparation room, we still brought suppliers' parts through there. The inspectors in the preparation room were completely in charge. The guys from the assembly line had to beg for parts.

The preparation room was a storage place for castings and forgings, as well as for other parts. A guy in the preparation room would shout for parts, and someone would bring a cartload of parts and leave 'em there. Then the prep room guy had nothing more to do for a while, so he'd just kick back and have a cigarette. That's how things worked. It was like we were moving the carts once in a while just to keep them from sprouting weeds.

Everyone thought it was great when we got some forklifts. But we still faced the problem of when to move what. So we installed sets of black toggle switches in the machining shops for steering and suspension systems, transmissions, and engines ... in four places, maybe six. We connected them to rows of lightbulbs in the casting shop and the forging shop, and we created a kind of code for communication. We assigned a combination of lights to each kind of part. One bulb shining meant this part. This bulb and that bulb were for that part. And so on.

You can do a lot without computers. We had an electrical signaling system, not an electronic one. Lightbulbs would go on in the casting shop or in the forging shop, and a forklift operator would then turn off the lights and take a load of the requested parts to the place where the order came from.

Of course, people needed to keep an eye on the lightbulbs. If they didn't, they'd keep the people in the machining shops waiting for parts. That caused some rowdy exchanges.

Our lightbulb signaling system was basically a matter of sending electricity to pick up parts instead of taking a kanban. And we made sure that a forklift that brought a load of parts would always take back a load of empty pallets. Ohno-san would read us the riot act if he ever saw forklifts driving around not carrying anything.

A word from the editors:
Toyota still managed production in accordance with monthly plans when Suzumura went to work in a machining shop at the Honsha Plant. The necessary parts rarely became fully available until the latter half of each month, and that resulted in the "end-of-the-month scramble" cited by Suzumura. It also resulted in large production batches on the assembly

line and on the parts-fabrication lines. Suzumura addressed those problems in the following ways.

The linkage Suzumura established between his parts-fabrication lines and his unit assembly line eliminated the need for supervisors to tell people when to make what. It transferred the authority and responsibility for deciding when to start work on a new set of parts to the lines. Toyota's official 20-year history records that the company pulled the supervisors formerly responsible for that function off of the assembly lines and machining lines in February 1957.

Toyota's vehicle assembly lines remained an "end-of-the-month scramble" for some time after Suzumura converted his machining shop to pull production. So the units produced by his assembly line piled up at the end of the line during the first half of each month. That problem would continue until Toyota adopted pull production on its vehicle assembly lines.

3. A Bucket System for Machining and Assembly

Suzumura:

Once we got things going in the right direction with units like axles and steering columns, we went to work on transmissions. We tackled the transmission assembly line with the same approach we'd used on the other lines. But transmissions have gears. And gears require heat treatment. After the cold processing, you need to carry them off to the furnace. So we needed to deal with more than just machining and assembly.

The heat processing took place in the same plant [as the machining and assembly]. But it was under another division. So this was the first time that we had to work across divisional lines in building a pull system. And you can be sure that it was a knock-down, drag-out fight.

We had a hell of a time persuading the group leaders in the other divisions to go along with our ideas. It all sounds so easy and natural today, but you can't imagine how much browbeating and cajoling went into the effort. But we somehow managed to build a working relationship between the divisions, one step at a time.

The next question is how we proceeded. Well, we considered lots of possibilities. In those days, we used a tunnel kiln from the United States for the heat treatment. Batch kilns were also available. But we had a tunnel kiln. And that was the state of the art at the time.

A tunnel kiln lets you run a huge volume of parts through the kiln while maintaining a constant temperature inside. But you don't necessarily want the same temperature for every kind of part. You want different temperatures for different kinds of parts. With a tunnel kiln, you want to process as many parts as possible once you're at the target temperature, say 1,100 degrees centigrade. You want to keep things going for three or four days. A tunnel kiln has just one entrance and one exit. So you end up with really long lead times.

We were in a fix. We needed to come up with something, so I had a talk with the shop supervisor in charge of heat treatment. I proposed that we divide the parts by treatment temperature. For example, we'd have a group for 1,100 degrees, group A; one for 1,000 degrees, group B; and another for 900 degrees, group C. And I asked him to let us get the batch sizes down to where we could cycle through the temperature range at least once a day.

The idea was to run the parts of group A through at 1,100 degrees, then lower the temperature to 1,000 degrees and run group B through at that temperature, and then lower the temperature to 900 degrees and run group C through at that temperature. It was just a matter of turning down the gas. When the temperature got down to 1,000 degrees, we'd start feeding in the next lot. And we'd feed in another lot when the temperature dropped down to 900 degrees. Then, we could turn up the gas and raise the temperature back up to 1,100 degrees and start the cycle over again.

Turning a kiln on and off would waste a lot of energy, so heat treatment goes on around the clock and uses three shifts. I was asking to run three lots a day at three temperatures. And a cycle a day was a tough sell. The guys in heat treatment naturally wanted to run the kiln at 1,100 degrees for a couple of days or so once they'd got it to that temperature. "No one does that in the United States," they'd say. Or, "We can't run any parts through the kiln until the temperature stabilizes, so changing the temperature means a lot of waste."

I argued back that running more stuff than you need through the kiln was more wasteful. Finally, I simply put my foot down and shouted, "Just shut up and do it!" I figured that the results would prove my point.

Toyota, by the way, had paid a small fortune for the tunnel kiln. The exchange rate back then was ¥360 to the dollar.

We had storage places at the back end of the grinding line for gears. When the transmission assembly line withdrew finished gears from there, a production instruction kanban would come off the gears. It would go back to the front end of the grinding line as an order for more material.

The raw material for the grinding process consisted of items that had come through the sintering process. A withdrawal kanban would come off when grinding work began on a new lot of sintered material, and the grinding process would use that kanban to withdraw a new lot. But even though the grinding process might be hungry for another lot of sintered material, the heat-treatment shop was determined to handle stuff in huge batches.

I tackled the problem at the front end of the heat-treatment process. I had the people there set up roller conveyors, and I had them put the material for processing at different temperatures on different conveyors: A, B, and C. When the grinding process started work on a new lot of sintered material, the withdrawal kanban came off, as usual. But it [didn't then go to the back end of the sintering line. It] went all the way back to the front end of the heat-treatment process.

Someone from the grinding process would take the withdrawal kanban to where machined material was lined up waiting for heat treatment. He would withdraw a lot of machined material for the same kind of material that the kanban came off of, and he would place that lot on the conveyor for the appropriate heat-treatment temperature. Then, he would go to the back end of the heat-treatment process and pick up a lot of sintered parts. He would pick up the same amount as he had placed on the conveyor at the front end of the process. And he would bring that lot to the grinding process and place it at the front end of the process. In other words, we exchanged machined material at the front end of the heat-treatment process for sintered material at the back end.

A lot of people in Japan still got their water by digging wells and hoisting water out in buckets (*tsurube*). So I told the guys in the transmission shop to think of our system as fetching water from a well with a bucket. The heat-treatment process was the well. We'd take machined material for one kind of gear to the front end of the process and fetch sintered material for the same kind of gear from the back end.

We leveled production on the transmission assembly line, too. We withdrew material alternately from groups A, B, and C in an even mix and used the different kinds of material in an even mix on the assembly line. Production on the vehicle assembly lines was still an end-of-the-month scramble, so our transmissions piled up during the first part of the month. But we did what we could do.

So we started assembling transmissions in leveled production, and that made us want the different kinds of gear blanks to come out of the kiln in an even mix. Having a big amount of one kind come out all at once was useless. We figured out that we should stop feeding material into the kiln in big amounts of each kind and that we should break it up into small amounts of different kinds. The heat-treatment kiln was a long tunnel, and we'd get behind if we didn't use an even mix in loading the machined material and in withdrawing the sintered material. We gradually figured that out after getting things wrong again and again.

All of this was happening in the late 1950s. We needed two or three years to get things right. We didn't have any models to look to for guidance. Trial and error was the only way to proceed. We finally got the bucket system to work, but the errors along the way were monsters. Fail to load the right material at the right time, for example, and the kiln would have moved on to the next temperature setting. Go to the kiln and ask for a 1,100-degree material after the kiln has moved to 1,000 degrees, and you'll learn to your dismay that there's no more 1,100-degree material to be had. Miss your timing, and you'll have to wait until the next day for the material you need. Things spent four or five hours in the kiln.

I once put the wrong number of kanban into circulation and caused a vehicle assembly line to shut down for half a day. Try shutting down a vehicle assembly line for half a day and see what happens. It's like getting attacked by a swarm of bees. You can peek through the window on the kiln at the material you wish you had, but you can't yank it out. I stood at the back end of the kiln stomping my feet in frustration. You could hear people murmuring, "Ah, Suzumura screwed up." I really thought that it might get me fired. After all, I'd shut down the main assembly line.

I went to the office of the director responsible for our plant to apologize. The director, Shoichi Saito [later chairman of the company], came walking out of his office just as I arrived. I explained what had happened, and he simply said, "So you got things wrong, did you? Well, that happens." Saito-san was my savior.

A word from the editors:

Using large batches in heat treatment pressured the machining and grinding processes to use similarly large batches. That would result in mountains of inventory at the front end of the transmission assembly line. It would also result in frequent shortages of the kinds of parts required at different times. Simply adopting the kanban system, meanwhile, was an inadequate solution. Someone who brought a withdrawal kanban from the gear-grinding line to the previous process, heat treatment, would encounter large-batch processing. The parts that he had come to withdraw might not be available when he got there. Suzumura addressed those problems with his "bucket" (*tsurube*) system.

4. Supplying Parts for Toyoace Engines on a Conveyor

Suzumura:

So we made our system work with steering and suspension units, and we made it work with transmissions. Our next target was engines.

Toyota was outsourcing the manufacturing of large engines to an affiliated company at that time. That was part of a policy for increasing the output of trucks in the Toyoace family. But it left things flopping around in our factory, which we needed to do something about.

I assumed that we ought to do the same thing we had done with the steering and suspension stuff and with the transmissions. And I figured that we might as well make things easy for ourselves by doing the same sort of stuff we'd done before. It would be pretty much just a matter of going and picking stuff up. So the thought occurred to me that we could make things even easier by using a conveyor (fig. 3).

Using trailers to carry material from the processing lines to the assembly line was common sense in those days. So using a trailer would have been the easy thing to do. But I decided to try something different. I took advantage of a realignment of the production lines to put in a conveyor. And that was the beginning of all sorts of headaches.

Each of the processing lines maintained its own stocks of raw material. That was proof that they weren't using something. And that something was the production instruction kanban. The only difference in what I was doing was that guys would withdraw material with the conveyor rather than bringing a trailer to pick stuff up. We mounted hangers on the conveyor, and we put cards on the hangers to tell people what to put where. A guy at the front end of the assembly line would choose the cards. Three hangers would carry enough parts for one engine.

When you're using a conveyor to gather material, you can't have some guy loading the material on at each process. So we built automated loading mechanisms. When a hanger came along on the conveyor, the device at the process would stop the conveyor and load the appropriate parts onto the hanger. At least that's what was supposed to happen.

Fig. 3: The Conveyor Linkage between the Engine Assembly Line and the Processing Lines

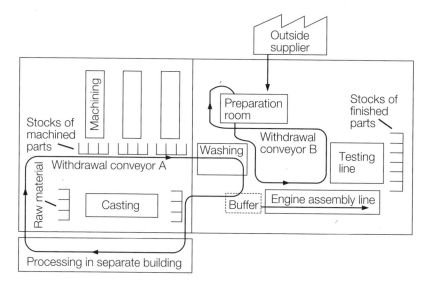

So the conveyor would pick up parts from the machining lines and bring them on hangers. It would carry them directly into a washer. The washer consisted of four or five zones. The first zones used caustic steam, and the later zones rinsed everything off with hot water. Our conveyor would stop to let the parts on the hangers get washed off in the steam. Of course, things got pretty hot.

We discovered that the temperature fluctuations were causing changes in the length of our conveyor: a full hanger's length between morning and noon. That was a problem, since it meant that we couldn't position the conveyor accurately. The conveyor was about 200 meters long, and it snaked around the machining lines. It would shrink and stretch about 2%—four meters—on account of the temperature fluctuations.

We needed to do something. We thought about the problem from every angle, and we realized that the conveyor was bound to shrink and stretch. So our only choice was to find a way to accommodate that shrinking and stretching. We decided that the answer was to allow the loading mechanisms to move in parallel with the hangers. Then things ought to load properly. We'd run a cycle like that and get everything loaded, and then the mechanisms would move back to their original positions. Our solution was a last-ditch effort. No one else was using anything like it. But we'd installed the conveyor, so we had to make it work.

We made only the main parts for our engines in-house. Most of the parts—about 70%—came from outside suppliers. We made the big stuff that required a lot of precision, like the cylinder heads and the housings, in-house. We got the starters, the piston rings, and lots of other things from suppliers.

All of the stuff from suppliers came into a preparation room. And that was an issue. We needed to figure out how to incorporate the preparation room into our system. What we decided was to treat the room as just another processing line.

We ran a conveyor through the preparation room to carry parts to the engine assembly line. And we told the guys in the preparation room to sort the stuff that arrived from suppliers into two groups: material for using on the machining lines and stuff for routing through the preparation room [to the engine assembly line]. We installed hangers on that conveyor, too, and devised them to stop at the same place each time and to arrive at a pace that allowed for using the parts immediately in engine assembly.

We put color-coded boxes along the assembly line to hold bolts and nuts. When a box was empty, the assembly guy would put it back on the conveyor. The guys in the preparation room would replace the empty box with a full one. So we had a pull system for bolts and nuts, a pull system that worked in box units.

The guys in the preparation room were in control. The guys in each process on the assembly line had to take whatever came along on the conveyor and use it. The assembly guys had no choice in what to take off of the conveyor, and they had no occasion to exercise any judgment.

We did lots of things to make sure that the right parts and enough parts went onto the hangers. We used gauges to check hole diameters. That let us monitor quality at the same time that we were making sure we got the right stuff onto the conveyor. The jigs on the assembly line conveyor were in multiples of five, and each set of five jigs was painted a different color from the sets before and after. So we arranged the hangers on the parts conveyor in the same combinations and in the same colors. That helped make sure that people withdrew the right parts at the right place.

The preparation room became like a machining line. We made it like that. We took the guys in the preparation room, who had thought of themselves as special, and we locked them into the production line. That made things interesting. The preparation room was under the plant administration division, not under the machining division. And you've got a shop supervisor out on the floor. That raises the issue of who the guys in the preparation room take their orders from. Their administrative colleagues are off in an office. I'm standing next to them in the preparation room from morning to night.

Naturally, the guy standing there carries more clout. This is the workplace. And I'm right there, day after day. You can be sure that they listened to me. This time, it wasn't a matter of working out arguments between divisions. Considerations of job descriptions and lines of authority went out the window. We took things into our own hands. And we got away with it. You can get away with stuff when you produce results.

So Toyota was still assembling vehicles in accordance with a production plan. But we went in and converted the production lines for steering units and suspension units to a pull system, and we did the same thing with transmissions and then with engines. Ohno-san could never have done all that by himself. We managers got together to put his ideas to work, and we got the cooperation of group leaders and team leaders and of the shop foremen. None of this was anything that just one or two people could have done.

A word from the editors:
Engine production at Toyota relied more on outsourced parts than the production of steering units, suspension units, and transmissions did. But the parts made in-house, such as cylinder blocks, cylinder heads, camshafts, and pistons, were heavy, so Suzumura decided to install a chain conveyor for withdrawing parts. The conveyor supplied parts to the assembly line in the sequence required for assembling the engines.

Meanwhile, Suzumura needed to accommodate the large number of engine parts that arrived from outside suppliers. So he also installed a conveyor line between the preparation room, where the parts arrived, and the engine assembly line. That conveyor line moved at the same pace as the conveyor line from the machining processes and delivered parts in sets. It integrated the preparation room, which was under the jurisdiction of the plant administration division, into the production workplace.

The production of steering units, suspension units, transmissions, and engines still took place in the context of monthly production plans. But Suzumura managed to convert all of that production to a pull system inside the larger context of production planning. Plan-based production persisted on the vehicle assembly lines, however, and large inventories accumulated at the ends of the pull-system shops in the first half of each month. The "end-of-the-month scramble" on the vehicle assembly lines ultimately consumed those inventories, but the need for converting vehicle assembly to a pull system was becoming painfully apparent.

5. Faxing Production Instructions on the Vehicle Assembly Lines at the Honsha Plant

Suzumura:

The engines that emerged from our newly improved assembly line just piled up at the end of the line. We didn't have any linkage yet between the engine line and the vehicle assembly lines. So we went to work on setting up linkages to the vehicle assembly lines for steering units, suspension units, transmissions, and engines.

Vehicle assembly at Toyota then was still an end-of-the-month scramble. Things piled up during the first part of the month: steering units, suspension units, transmissions, engines, everything. Heaps of stuff. Then toward the end of the month, the vehicle assembly lines started withdrawing stuff like crazy, and things disappeared.

When the vehicle line started assembling Land Cruisers, for example, they'd want to go three or four days straight without changing a thing.

That was before we built the Motomachi Plant, so we were also making the Crown [passenger car at the Honsha Plant]. When the time came to assemble passenger cars, they'd take down all the truck stuff and gear up to run just Crowns on the line. That was a pain for the guys on the assembly line, the way things were always switching back and forth. People could see that something needed to change. So Toyota built the Motomachi Plant, and the assembly of the Crown gradually shifted over to that plant.

Ohno-san became a manufacturing general manager, and that gave him authority over everything from vehicle assembly to body parts and painting. The timing was perfect, and we went to work.

We started by supplying the vehicle assembly lines with steering units, suspension units, transmissions, and engines in five-vehicle lots. A vehicle assembly line would send an empty trailer over to the end of the steering unit and suspension unit lines. It would leave the empty trailer there and bring back a trailer loaded with parts. It did the same thing with transmissions and engines. The right to withdraw parts resided in the trailer.

We let everyone know that we were going to proceed pretty much in that manner. Frames were big, so we [used the bucket system that we had developed for transmissions. In other words, we] used withdrawal orders from the vehicle assembly lines to manage the flow of frames from the frame lines to the painting line.

When a vehicle assembly line had used five frames, it would send an empty trailer to the end of a frame line. It would then pick up a trailer loaded with five frames to take to the front end of the painting line, and it would pick up a trailer loaded with five painted frames at the back end of the painting line.

The Honsha Plant had two vehicle assembly lines. It also had two frame lines, and people would've liked to make each frame line correspond to one vehicle line. But that didn't always work very well. Depending on the model or model variation, the frames for the vehicles being assembled on the No. 1 assembly line might be coming from the No. 1 frame line or from the No. 2 line. And likewise for the No. 2 assembly line.

You might be better off producing a frame on one line or the other, depending on the size of the frame and on the amount of work involved. The guys on the frame lines used Arabic numerals to number the frames being produced for the No. 1 assembly line and Roman numerals to number the frames for the No. 2 assembly line.

We established the order of vehicle assembly in single-vehicle units. So we gave instructions to produce frames in corresponding orders on the frame lines. But for some reason, the order was a mess when the frames came out of the painting shop. Part of the problem was the way the frames from the No. 1 and No. 2 lines merged on the way into painting. The problem was also partly due to the retouching work that occasionally became necessary. We could hardly maintain big buffer stocks of bulky stuff, like frames, so things naturally got out of sequence as we hoisted the frames that passed muster onto the vehicle assembly lines.

As I mentioned, we parceled out information to make sure our lines produced steering units, suspension units, and engines in exactly the order we intended. But when the frames got out of sequence, that screwed up the linkage. So we needed to set up a central command post to integrate the information about what was happening in every process.

A new tool called the Interwriter [an early version of the facsimile machine] appeared around that time. The Interwriter had a tape on which you'd write something with a pencil and then push a button. Then a terminal on the other side of the plant would print out what you wrote, like magic. We used the Interwriter to issue production instructions. The central command post issued instructions to the front ends of the assembly lines for engines, for transmissions, for steering and suspension units, and for frames.

Frames didn't come out in the order of the first instructions, so when activity on the vehicle assembly lines reached a certain point the central command post dispatched a revised set of instructions to the withdrawal guys on each line. The order didn't change dramatically, but when it had changed for any reason this was our chance to make adjustments. We'd let people know that this was the final order. The guys at the back ends of the machining lines would arrange things in that order, and the guys at the front ends of the assembly lines would take empty trailers to exchange for trailers loaded with parts.

We had the central command post issue the scheduled order with the Interwriter. The guys at the back ends of all the machining lines arranged the parts for withdrawal—for example, suspension units—in that order. They cut off the Interwriter tape and put it on the parts. The tape for the engines went on the engines. The tape for the transmissions went on the transmissions. But the final confirmation would come later, and the guys had to wait for it.

So we issued the scheduled order well in advance of withdrawing the parts, but we issued a revised order right before the withdrawals happened. That was a final confirmation. When we were lucky, the final version was the same as the first version. But we didn't issue it until the last minute. If we issued a revised order and then made changes again, the guys in the workplace would go crazy with the changes upon changes. We kept things to ourselves until the last minute. That way, the final confirmation didn't seem like a change so much as a fresh set of instructions, and people accepted it without resistance. That's how we integrated the instructions for ordering parts for withdrawal.

Frames had the longest lead time, so the central command post issued the final withdrawal order for them first. That was well before it issued the final confirmation for the engines and the other components. For them, the guys in the central command post waited. Only when the vehicle assembly line reached a certain point did they hit the switch and send the confirmation for the engines or whatever. Only then did the assembly line withdraw engines, transmissions, or whatever and begin installing them in vehicles. Installation took place in the specified order. All that the guys on the assembly line needed to do was install things in the order they arrived.

We were dealing with lots of part specifications: about 80 sets of specifications for transmissions alone. Trying to keep stocks of 80 kinds of transmissions would be insane. So we managed the tail ends of the branching variations at the vehicle assembly line. When the time came to assemble the transmissions, we only made ones that we'd actually install in vehicles. We worked out the required transmission specifications when we worked out the vehicle variations. That greatly reduced the number of transmission variations that we needed to think about.

Some transmissions required some really complex combinations of gears, so we used the Interwriter to let the transmission guys know as soon as we had a tentative schedule. When we sent the confirmation later, they simply tore off the Interwriter output and put it on the corresponding transmissions for withdrawal by the vehicle assembly line.

The unit plant that was furthest from the Honsha Plant was a Toyota Auto Body plant that made truck cabs. It was about 20 kilometers away, in Kariya. We had that plant make cabs in the same order we'd install them on the vehicle assembly lines. A truck would go pick up the cabs and load them on in the order we'd specified. When the truck got back to our plant, we'd take 'em right off the transport truck and put 'em right onto the trucks that we were assembling. It took us awhile, but we finally got to where we could do that. That was around 1959. At least we got things to work as far as the Honsha Plant was concerned.

This provided the basis for the lifting system that I'll talk about later. The trailers [and transport trucks] were the equivalent of withdrawal permits. Take an empty trailer and come back with a full one. And do that again and again. We finally got the shop supervisors, the group leaders, the team leaders, and the operators to go along with our methods. The leaders who didn't get their people to do it right got a scolding when we got back. They decided it was better to get their people to do things right than to get a scolding.

We never would've been able to get things to work if we hadn't gotten the cooperation of the shop supervisors, the group leaders, and the team leaders. And I did all that without ever having been formally assigned to the vehicle assembly lines. I was just an engineer in a machining shop.

We had a bunch of trailers, but we didn't have many tractors to pull them. So we devised a linkage that let us detach the trailers from the tractors. We then needed to think of ways to route the tractors efficiently in taking empty trailers and in picking up full ones. I studied freight-handling diagrams from Japan National Railways. I drove the tractors myself to time how long it took to get from one point to another; for example, how long it took from the painting line exit to the entrance to the vehicle assembly line. And I drew up diagrams on my own.

We finally got intercoms in the plant. I liked trying new things. So I used intercoms to connect the central command office to sites in the workplace. That way, we got immediate reports about what was busted where. The guys in the central command office worked out responses in advance for various kinds of problems. They were like the guys in flight-control towers. And right next door was the plant manager's office. So the plant manager could also see what was going on in the plant, see where problems where happening.

We told people to report problems immediately and to shut up when things were going all right. Management is not a matter of having all

sorts of information about everything. It's just a matter of know-
ing what's wrong. You decide a
permissible range for things, and
when something slips outside
that range you jump on it. That's
the essence of management. I figured that out around that time.

Toyota's Motomachi Plant soon after it opened
in 1959

Ohno-san moved to the
Motomachi Plant between late
1959 and early 1960. I wanted to go with Ohno-san to the Motomachi
Plant, but he refused to let me come. I asked why he was abandoning me
like that, and he said, "Motomachi is too far. You don't have a car." Of
course, no one else had a car either. I got to go overseas for the first time
in 1961. And when I got back, I bought an old run-down Crown. I still
remember the price: ¥180,000.

So Ohno-san left the Honsha Plant for Motomachi, and I lost my main
supporter. I was all alone. I wasn't even an assistant manager yet, and I
took a job in the central command office. That office was under plant administration. But I'd set up the system, and I wasn't about to take any guff
from the administration general manager. I knew I could handle things.
At least I knew that I wanted to try.

We got all the necessary information integrated at the central command
office. That eliminated the need for the supervisors who used to monitor
the flow of production. We finally had an autonomic nervous system in
place for the vehicle assembly lines at the Honsha Plant and for the production lines that supplied them with parts.

To get things running on their own momentum, you've got to keep
your defect rate below 10%. We'd gotten to where we took a defect rate

of 2% or 3% for granted. The stuff I'd been involved in had taken about 10 years to get done.

A word from the editors:
Suzumura's next task was to link the production lines for frames, steering and suspension units, transmissions, and engines to the vehicle assembly lines. That included working out ways to manage the order in which the production lines upstream supplied parts to the vehicle assembly lines downstream. In 1959, Taiichi Ohno became a manufacturing general manager responsible for vehicle assembly, body fabrication, stamping, painting, and other core processes. That became the occasion for linking the unit production lines to the vehicle assembly lines.

6. Handling Outsourced Parts

Suzumura:
What caused the biggest problem for us around the time I'm talking about was parts. We didn't have computers back then, so what we did was take the monthly plans and break them down. "If we need this much stuff in January, then this is what we need each day." We'd divide the total by 25 and write down how many we'd need per day. We'd get the supervisors who monitor the production flow to write out production orders. Writing by hand takes forever, so we'd stick in some carbon paper to get 50 orders out of 25. One of the sheets eventually reached a parts maker.

Some of our suppliers back then would deliver parts in cardboard boxes for shipping tangerines. So we decided on packaging guidelines. We decided that some parts should arrive, for example, 20 to a box. That way, we knew how many parts we were getting when boxes arrived. And we were able to take inventory in just an hour or two. Taking inventory used to take all night. No one knew how many parts were in each box, so they had to count everything. That's why we decided to specify the number of parts per box.

Our new way of doing things got the inventorying done in two hours or less. Everyone expected inventorying to take all night, so guys would sign in for hours up to midnight or whatever, and they would sit around and play shogi [a Japanese game similar to chess] after the inventorying was done. Some of our suppliers were still delivering parts in cardboard boxes in 1968 and 1969. So you can see that changing things completely took several years.

We devised a system of red cards and blue cards for the boxes of parts on our shelves. A red card would pop up when we were running short of something even though it had come in on time. The red card meant to stock 10% more next time. Our cards went up and down like the pantographs on an electric streetcar that was switching lines. A blue card would pop up if we had too much of something—so much that the box would overflow if the next delivery was in the same amount as the last delivery. The blue card meant to stock 10% less next time and to put everything in that box.

A red card called attention to a potential shortage before the shortage occurred. A blue card called attention to an excess and warned us to stock less next time. The cards later gave way to delivery kanban (also known as supplier kanban). I began experimenting with [withdrawal] kanban in purchasing [at the Honsha Plant], but Ohno-san was dead set against using delivery kanban at the Motomachi Plant for some reason. They didn't get around to using delivery kanban there until a lot later.

A word from the editors:
Toyota continued purchasing parts from outside suppliers in accordance with monthly plans after it had synchronized its internal unit production and vehicle assembly. And it purchased those parts in generally large

batches. Suzumura improved the purchasing process by breaking down the monthly purchasing into daily production orders and by distributing the purchasing of different items evenly through the month. In an era before the appearance of computers, he had his people write out the purchasing orders by hand. His system of red and blue cards, meanwhile, helped cope with deviations from the planned production volume.

7. A New Transmission Shop and an "Iron Computer"

Suzumura:

Toyota later shifted the production of large transmissions to its affiliate Aisin. At that point, the big shots at Toyota were making the decisions. All that guys like me could do was say "aye, aye, sir." As a result of the shift, we ended up with more space than anyone knew what to do with. The biggest hole was the one left by the plating shop for transmission parts. We moved a shop for small transmissions into that space. That was around 1962 or '63.

As long as we were shifting things around, I figured that we might as well move everything. So we rearranged our processes and set up the shortest-possible hanger-conveyor line to gather parts. The information about what to withdraw went out over the Interwriter. That left the guys in assembly with no choice but to put together things in the order they arrived. It established the order for assembling things.

Our new layout made it more important than ever to make sure that things arrived properly at the assembly lines. Spacing the hangers on the parts conveyor to match the spacing on the assembly line conveyor was hard. We'd have a series of hangers, A, B, C, and so on. They'd carry the parts for one transmission. The first guy on the assembly line and the guy five places down on the line would use different parts. So we needed to load stuff on the hangers to arrive at the right place on the line at the right time. That meant getting things phased right, taking into account the pace of work, as well as the spacing.

We tried everything to get things in the right places at the right time for everyone on the assembly line. Even after we got it right, I couldn't get anyone, not even Ohno-san, to understand why we did things the way we did.

Matching the spacing on the conveyor to the spacing on the assembly line is easy for one transmission. The parts from outside suppliers were generally small, and we handled them on a separate conveyor. They moved along at the same intervals as the spacing on the transmission assembly conveyor. In other words, the conveyor for the parts from outside suppliers moved in synchrony with the transmission assembly line. But problems occurred when we tried the same spacing on the conveyor for the parts from our own machining shops. It simply didn't work.

We had things, like splined shafts and gears, that we needed to pre-assemble on subassembly lines [which stick out like branches from the trunk of the main line]. Some parts needed to get to the subassembly lines early. I finally worked stuff out by calculating back from where we needed the parts and by telling people to think of the path of each part as a separate conveyor. But no one was inclined to think that way.

We needed each part to arrive at a certain place. So I told people to think of one part at a time and to envision it as being on its own conveyor. Then I told them to think of the parts as all being mixed up together on the same conveyor. Let's see how that would work. We needed to stagger the parts' positioning—their phases—to keep things from getting in each other's way. For example, think of five parts, each positioned five positions apart: 1, 6, 11, 16, and 21. That's one conveyor. The other conveyors have nothing to do with those five parts. That's all.

We ran lots of experiments. I finally decided that we pretty much had something that would work. Problem was, no one understood what I was trying to do. I used a thread and set up a model. "When it's here, we turn things like this." Explaining my idea like that finally persuaded Ohno-san. He still had lots of complaints, though. I'd get confused myself trying to deal with him. It was the kind of stuff that computers remember for us these days.

We needed to send signals to indicate where to get which parts ready. Figuring out how to send the signals was a challenge. Today, you just type stuff into a computer. But we didn't have computers back then. We had to do something, so I put up flagpoles on the hangers. We made them in three lengths. That gave us three kinds of indications. We'd stick a flagpole on the hanger for the first box in a set.

We installed limit switches at the place where the conveyor was headed. Actuating a combination of switches at process No. 2, for example, might signal process No. 6 to send a part. We put wooden rings on the flagpoles and used ring combinations to provide more-complex switching and signaling. At least that's how I promised Ohno-san it would work.

In fact, the system did work. And it gave us all sorts of possible combinations. This was a new kind of withdrawal kanban. We created even more possibilities by attaching three colors of flags to the flagpoles.

I like doing what I like to do. I liked thinking up stuff like that. I was thinking of stuff like that all the time I was in the central command office. I spent about a month on the signaling system to get it set up and running right. I'd be up on a grating looking down on the line. "It just went," I'd shout into a transceiver. "Did the part arrive?" We were doing with people what everyone expects computers to do now.

I heard this story directly from Ohno-san. A vice president from Ford visited our plant after the system had been up and running for quite a while, maybe 1965 or '66. Ohno-san was showing him [and our president] around. The Ford guy froze at one place and wouldn't budge for about 30 minutes. He was staring at our signaling system. When he finally spoke, he said, "That's an iron computer!"

"It was awful," Ohno-san said. "Here is our president. And the guy asks, 'Who was responsible for this? You've got to come to Ford.' Just like that. The guy was trying to hire me away, right in front of our president."

That was about the only computerization we had back then. We had it in parts management.

A word from the editors:

The number and variety of transmissions produced at the Honsha Plant continued to grow, despite the shift of some production to Aisin. So Suzumura installed a hanger conveyor between the fabrication lines for transmission parts and the transmission assembly line. The idea was to supply transmissions to the frame assembly line in the order that the frames were assembled. Suzumura made several innovations to deliver parts to points along the transmission assembly line when they were needed, as he describes.

8. The Type 2R Engine and Automation's Limitations

Suzumura:

We were making an engine for the Corona [passenger car] called the 2R, and that production also moved to the Motomachi Plant [from the Honsha Plant]. We were increasing production head over heels. That included putting up new plant buildings. We shifted a parts shop to Motomachi [from the Honsha Plant] around 1963. And we started making a clearer distinction between work for people to do and work for machines to do.

Also around that time, we were getting concerned with issues of how closely parts fit together, how well they fit together. We'd assemble an engine and then start it up to see how things worked, and we'd need

The Type 2R engine

to adjust it to get it just right. We began using a turntable for engine testing when we started making the 2R. We'd stick each engine on the turntable and start it up. If it ran okay, it went to the store place for engines. We worked out an automated sorting system for sending each engine to the right place in storage. We set up conveyors to take the engines to the right places.

We committed a monumental error around that time in engine assembly. We had wanted to automate something, and we had found that automation was difficult when the jigs were fixed to the conveyor and went by continuously. So we decided to use stand-alone jigs that we could remove from the conveyor, and we started running the assembly line on the basis of *takt* time [the pace of demand].

We found that we didn't have enough time for the automated assembly work after stopping the jigs. We needed to shorten the time required to move stuff between processes. We were trying to handle one engine every 60 seconds, and conveyance between processes was eating up 10 seconds of that time. I told the guys to get that down to 5 seconds.

The more we speeded up the conveyance, the more inconsistent the positioning became. We could've dealt with the problem more easily if we were handling everything with automation. But we were still handling stuff manually in some processes. And grabbing an engine that was covering about two meters in five seconds was too scary to try.

In hindsight, we didn't really need to automate so much. We shouldn't have tried so hard to eliminate the manual work. If doing something by hand required three seconds or so, then so be it. We should've taken it from there instead of fretting about the three seconds that the manual work required. We had no business trying to automate everything.

We decided to let the assembly line conveyor run continuously and to get rid of the stand-alone jigs. We detached the machine tools from their mounts and suspended them from the ceiling. No problem. The machine didn't need to position things automatically. The operator could nudge everything into more or less the right position, and the machine would then lock on. All we needed to do was get stuff done in 60 seconds, which wasn't really so difficult. That taught me the limits of automation.

A word from the editors:

Suzumura describes an unsuccessful experiment with stand-alone jigs. Recognizing his mistake, he got rid of those jigs and entrusted the initial assembly work to human hands. He left the subsequent processing to the machines. Suzumura also abandoned the intermittent, *takt*-based conveyor operation and reverted to continuous operation. Toyota went through a similar wave of disaffection with excessive automation in the 1990s.

9. The Type M Engine and Excessive Investment

Suzumura:

Next up was the Type M engine, an in-line six-cylinder engine. We made it at the Kamigo Plant [which Toyota built in 1965 to produce engines]. This is another classic story. We needed some serious horsepower for high-end passenger cars, so we made the in-line six-cylinder Type M engine. Everyone was sure it would be a big success, so we geared up to make 10,000 a month. When a big shot announces something like that, it takes on a life of its own. People spring into action everywhere.

Japanese were starting to make some money at that time, and Toyota was making good money, too. We got a fancy surface broach from

The Type M engine

Cincinnati Milling Machine. It let us cut holes at the drop of a hat. It was expensive. But, hey, we were going to make 10,000 engines a month.

We were off and running, but we were only [selling enough cars equipped with the new engine to call for] making 1,600 or 1,700 a month, not 10,000. The project was in the red. It wasn't even making enough to cover the depreciation. We were getting an earful about the red ink from the accounting division.

Later, we made the Type K engine, too. It was for the little Corolla, and Toyota was making money hand over fist with that model. But the Type M remained in the red. People got disgusted with the project and considered mothballing the broach. Of course, putting the machine away in a warehouse wasn't going to do anything about the depreciation. But the limited way we were using it wasn't ever going to cover the depreciation either. I sat down and did the calculations one day, and I figured out that the fancy machine would operate in the red even if we left the labor costs out of the equation. That was a wake-up call about the danger of overinvestment.

At that time, I was still just an engineering supervisor in a machining shop at the Honsha Plant. But Ohno-san had said, "I'm in charge of that [the Kamigo] plant, too. And you engineers in the machining shops at the Honsha Plant are also supposed to be helping out." So we built the fancy machine into the layout for the Type M engine at the Kamigo Plant. Simple. Clear-cut. And when we got running, we were deep in the red. But we learned a lot from the experience.

A word from the editors:
Toyota built the Kamigo Plant in 1965 to make the Type M in-line six-cylinder engine for a full-blown passenger car. The episode proved a painful reminder of the importance of planning investment prudently.

10. The Corolla's Surging Production Volume and the Type K Engine

Suzumura:
A year or so after the Type M engine fiasco, we received orders to go to work on the Type K engine, for the Corolla. People had learned their lesson with the Type M engine, and the production target for the Type K was a more-modest 8,000 engines a month. The plant would operate in two shifts. That would mean about 160 people with our usual way of doing things. We looked at the production processes for the Type M engine and for the Type 2R engine and calculated all the work that people would need to handle with the Type K. At two shifts and 8,000 engines a month, that worked out to about 160 people, including assembly. And I'd received orders to find ways to reduce that number.

The equipment technology was advancing, and the assembly work was getting pretty automated. If we could automate the conveyance between machines, we wouldn't need people there. I divided the processes into work that we ought to be able to automate and work that would continue to require some manual positioning before feeding stuff into a machine. Mounting an engine block, for instance, required handling by two people. I grouped work like that, which required the human touch,

The Kamigo Plant in 1966

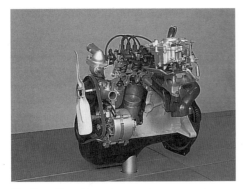

The Type K engine

together with all the necessary parts. We'd continue to do that work with people.

We'd learned better than to use automation where it wasn't called for. If we were to reduce our staffing, we needed to make the reductions in places where automation already made sense.

I took a good look at the specification sheets and identified places where we ought to be able to eliminate manual handling. I also took a good look at the ways we were conveying stuff from process to process. I worked out a plan at my desk.

I explained the plan to Ohno-san. He listened carefully and then asked, "How many people will you use to produce 8,000 engines a month with two shifts?"

"I'll run it with 100 people. I think it'll work with 100 people."

"I don't recall saying that we could use 100 people," he shot back. That was pretty galling. But he was a managing director. I was just an assistant manager.

Ohno-san went on talking. I could tell that he didn't have any concrete idea about how to proceed. But he emphasized repeatedly that he had never condoned using as many as 100 people. I finally blurted out, "Well, what do you want us to do?" For my temerity, I received a harsh rebuke: "You idiot! Deciding what to do is your job." I could see that I would gain nothing by persisting. I could also see that I would need to make the Type K engine with fewer than 100 people. And I could see that offering to try it with 99 people would simply draw more harsh words from Ohno-san. I finally made the engine with 86 people. Reducing the staffing caused one problem after another, and all we could do was deal with the problems as they popped up. I put together a group of accomplices, and I came across like the leader of a gang of young toughs. But in my own mind, I was fighting for truth and justice.

The Type K was originally supposed to be a 1,000 cc engine. But just before launching the Corolla, they increased the engine displacement 100 cc, to 1,100 cc. And the car sold really well. In less than six months, our production mandate nearly doubled, to 15,000 engines a month. This was no longer an end-of-the-month scramble. It was now a daily scramble.

Customers couldn't get enough of the new Corolla. The thing sold like crazy. Our dealers were screaming for deliveries. They even came to the plant. Dealers actually brought cash to the vehicle assembly line [at the Takaoka Plant] and pleaded for more cars. The guys there said, "Hey, we can make as many cars as you need, but a car's gotta have an engine. You need to talk to the guys making engines at the Kamigo Plant. They made fun of us, saying that we were the brakes in the system, not the engine.

The dealers were serious. They offered to send mechanics to help out on the line if we were undermanned. But our problem was not a lack of people. It was a lack of capacity in the equipment. The last thing we needed was a bunch of inexperienced mechanics wrecking our machinery and making the problem worse. I explained that we weren't making the engines by hand. But that just made the dealers angrier. I was still 42 or 43, and they thought that I was being a smart aleck.

I needed to do something, so I ordered the guys in our shop to increase the cutting speed. Theoretically, that ought to have given us more parts faster. But at the end of the day, we didn't have any more parts than we did

The Takaoka Plant soon after it opened in 1966

before. The only thing that had increased was our cost for cutting tools. Raising the cutting speed had simply worn out our cutting tools faster. We had to spend a lot of time replacing those tools. We were always shutting down the machines to replace the cutting tools, so we were using the machines less than before to actually make stuff. We went back to the slower cutting speed.

I turned my attention to the transfer machines, which were becoming common. We might have transfer machines at 10 stations, and the last one to get its work done would determine the pace of production. The transfer machines might be done with their work at 9 stations, but if one was still waiting on its process, no one could move on. I naturally focused on the place where things were moving the slowest. A good example was the station where we drilled eight-millimeter holes. That work took the most time of all. Everybody else on the line would be done and ready to trot, but we could only move at the pace of the slowest process.

My solution was to change the division of labor between processes. I decided to let one process pass the work on when the hole was half done. We pulled out a machine that was a relic but could finish drilling the hole. That would ordinarily require human participation. What I did instead was fill a burlap bag with sand and put it on top of the drill handle. That lowered the bit onto the work piece. And since the hole was already half drilled, the hole served as a guide for the bit. Pushing the handle down was all we needed to do to finish drilling the hole all the way through.

Our method worked pretty well. But we still came up 200 or 300 engines short of the 15,000 a month that we needed.

A word from the editors:

Automation was streamlining fabrication work, and the last hurdle in automating things almost completely was the conveyance between processes. Suzumura identified the work that would continue to require the human element and work that would allow for further automation. And he focused on the latter in pursuing dramatic reductions in staffing needs.

A last-minute change in engine size necessitated a frantic but successful response. Then Suzumura and his team faced a nearly twofold surge in demand soon after the new Corolla went on sale. Buying new equipment to cope with that surge would have entailed a breaking-in period. So Suzumura opted for the quicker option of pulling a vintage machine out of mothballs. He used that machine in connection with a brilliant idea for eliminating bottlenecks by dividing work into multiple processes.

11. The Production Survey Office and Production Control Division

Suzumura:
Right when I was in the middle of this and that I underwent an operation on a kidney. They had the wrong idea that I had cancer. No one had told me [as was common Japanese practice at the time in regard to cancer diagnoses], but a series of checkups had indicated cancer, and that's what the doctors had reported to the company.

I thought something strange was going on. Ohno-san came to visit me in the hospital, which was pretty unusual. His boss, Shoichi Saito, also came by. Saito-san said, "I just happened to be in the hospital, so I stopped by to see how you were doing. You ought to think of this as a message from the gods to take things easy for a while."

The doctor who had done the operation said, "You're lucky that it was just kidney stones." Back in those days, cancer was a death sentence. And the guys in the central control office had figured that I was a goner.

People at the hospital were wondering why in the world someone like Saito-san would come visit a mere assistant manager. After all, Saito-san was the No. 2 man at Toyota, after Eiji Toyoda. And here he was, offering some rarely heard gentle words of encouragement.

I jumped right back into my work as soon as I got out of the hospital, but a fever sent me back. I'm certain that what happened next was the result of Saito-san saying something like this to Ohno-san: "You can't leave him in the workplace. You ought to put him in the production control division." In production control, I sat right next to Ohno-san. I received stern orders to stay off the golf course, to stay out of mahjong parlors, and to stay off the plant floor.

I was in the [production control division's] Production Survey Office [now the Operations Management Consulting Division]. We had about 10 full-time people on the office staff, including [now Toyota chairman Fujio] Cho-san and [now Kanto Auto Works adviser and former chairman Susumu] Uchikawa-san.

Our office concentrated on calculating needs for parts from our internal operations and from outside suppliers. I knew that we could arrange things so that no one needed to calculate that stuff, and I immediately went to work on teaching [what we'd learned in the workplace] to the guys in the office. The Crown was selling pretty well, so I picked it as an example. The biggest issue was how to manage the stocks of parts in each process. We had lots of fights about how to do that.

A word from the editors:

After a stay in the hospital, Suzumura moved from the production engineering team on the plant floor to the production control division. Ohno and Saito apparently ordered that move out of concern for his health. Toyota set up the Production Survey Office (now the Operations Management Consulting Division) in the production control division around 1970, and Suzumura became a member of that office. The Operations Management Consulting Division is familiar to researchers as the propagator and guardian of the Toyota Production System, but no one has systematically analyzed how it has fulfilled that role. This is what Toyota's official 50-

year history has to say about the establishment of the Production Survey
Office:

> The Toyota Production System had become a more or less complete
> system. It was the cumulative result of decades of effort, and it was a
> framework for integrating work throughout the company. Toyota adopted
> the name Toyota Production System in 1970 to recognize the system-
> atic workings of the constituent concepts and methods. It accompanied
> that move with the establishment of the Production Survey Office in the
> Production Control Division. The members of the newly established of-
> fice were responsible for implementing the Toyota Production System at
> Toyota plants and at the plants of Toyota suppliers.

The Production Survey Office started out with a secretariat of about 10
full-time people. Supplementing the secretariat were employees seconded
from pertinent divisions for terms of two or three years. The staff totaled
no more than 30 people, including support personnel. At the writing of
the Japanese version of this book, the Operations Management Consulting
Division had more than 50 members, including about 25 core members
and more than 25 employees seconded from other divisions.

12. Vehicle Assembly at the Motomachi Plant and "Lifting" Information

Suzumura:
Toyota's production technology for full-fledged passenger cars originated
at the Motomachi Plant. But we had a tough time there making the Crown
right. We distributed the production instructions for different body specifications evenly and issued them continually to the body line in finely
tuned increments. The bodies that came off of that line headed into the
painting line.

At the back end of the painting line was a storage area. How many bodies to store there was a matter of style. As it was, the storage area was long and narrow. We didn't like that. We insisted on making it broad to accommodate different models and model variations.

Two-door and four-door models entail different amounts of work on the assembly line. Think about that from the perspective of a guy on the assembly line. The last thing in the world that he wants is a series of vehicles that require all kinds of work. And each vehicle that comes along requires something different in the way of seats, trim, engine, and whatnot. A superdeluxe model entails extra work. A standard-grade model entails less work.

You've got to put together a mixed salad of variations. Otherwise, people will choke on the surges in work requirements that are bound to occur. A line that encounters a surge is like a snake that has swallowed an egg. Everyone ends up waiting for the stuff to work its way through the previous processes. That's no good at all. Meanwhile, the proportions of different specifications in the composition of demand vary a lot at different times through the year.

So the guys in the central command office paid attention to the amount of assembly work entailed by each model. They took that into consideration in determining the order of body types before issuing production instructions. But when the bodies reached the painting line, the guys there couldn't keep them in the order they arrived.

We had two-tone color schemes. We had paint specs that required coating twice and baking twice. We had specs that called for coating three times and baking three times. Those specs all required different amounts of time to handle.

Meanwhile, the painted bodies lined up in storage in the order that they came off of the painting line. Obviously, bodies that went through painting processes four times came out at different times from those that went through twice. That's why we wanted to have a broad storage area that would allow for lining up bodies with different paint specifications, keeping them all accessible for easy withdrawal. When lining bodies up more than one deep was unavoidable, the overlapping bodies were of the same painting specs.

The width of the storage area was for lining up bodies of different painting specs. The depth was for paint specs that we handled a lot. The specs that were most common came off of the painting line the most often, but they also got withdrawn the most often. We needed plenty of width to handle that coming and going. If we were going to have 50 bodies in the storage area, we'd be a lot better off with 10 bodies across and only 5 deep than with just 3 bodies across and 17 deep.

At the beginning of each month, we determined the proportions of different painting specifications for that month. And we rearranged the storage pattern to simplify the work of fishing bodies out in those proportions. That was a key to keeping things moving smoothly.

Bodies of small-volume specifications would get in the way, so we moved them out of the storage area. That made those bodies a little inconvenient to handle, but their small volume meant we didn't have to handle them very often. We could afford to handle them separately. But we distributed different specifications as evenly as possible through the day.

When we fished bodies out of storage, we'd send information about the order of the bodies to the engine line, to the transmission line, to the seat line, and to the other lines. They'd then arrange their output in the same order. The vehicle assembly line would send an empty truck to the Kamigo [engine] Plant, and the driver would bring back a truck loaded in advance with engines arranged in the right order. It would pick up seats in the same way from [the supplier] Takashimaya Nippatsu Kogyou.

All activity originated at the vehicle assembly line. And information about the order in which we fished bodies out of the painting-line storage area determined the production sequence. So we needed to make sure that we kept everything moving in that order. Keeping the defect rate below 5% was absolutely essential. Otherwise, we'd run into all kinds of problems.

A word from the editors:
The defect rate came down to a manageable level, and Toyota achieved a workable balance in the workflows from the unit assembly lines to the vehicle assembly line. Suzumura then began experimenting with ordered withdrawal.

13. Supplier Kanban

Suzumura:
The Honsha Plant was still using kanban for only some of the parts from outside suppliers. A supplier kanban is a variation on the withdrawal kanban. Trying to withdraw things directly from each line at a supplier's plant can be inefficient, so people didn't like that approach. We transported stuff in fixed quantities [as specified by the kanban] and at variable timing [as determined by the pace at which the following process was actually consuming parts]. Otherwise, things would get out of synch.

Let's say that the following process comes to withdraw something from the parts arrayed by the previous process. That'll work as long as you're just withdrawing one piece at a time. We might have the No. 1 and No. 2 assembly lines coming to the same place to get parts. And as long as they're working one on one like that, withdrawing stuff in fixed quantities will work. It'll work, but withdrawing a single box of parts might not make sense if fetching it means driving a truck 30 minutes or an hour or longer. You might want to bring the kanban from the No. 1 and No. 2 assembly lines and pick up the parts for both lines with the same truck.

We would've preferred to have everyone withdraw in fixed quantities at variable timing. But logistics forced us to do the next-best thing: pick up stuff at fixed timing and in variable amounts. Still, we really would rather have had the processes go pick up stuff when they needed it. And we could have stuck with fixed-quantity, variable-timing withdrawal, even if the pickup points were a little distant, if we were dealing with simple one-on-one relationships.

Unfortunately, things were more complicated than that, and people complained about the loss that occurred with fixed-quantity, variable-timing withdrawal. So I gave in and went with the fixed-timing, variable-quantity pickups. But I warned everyone not to bring any more than the amounts specified by the kanban.

Kanban can be useful even if you're using a push system. Say you've got boxes that hold 10 parts each and you order 100 parts. You've only got 10 kanban. That simplifies the management of quantities.

We're putting a kanban on each box. So if a supplier sticks in an 11th box when we've only ordered 10, we'll end up with a box that doesn't have a kanban. And that really happened sometimes. But we decided to pay for stuff on the basis of the number of kanban—paying for a number of parts defined as the number per box times the number of kanban. As a result, people gradually became careful about the delivery quantities.

The next thing we did was to put carts out on the delivery docks. This "train" was bound for the No. 1 line, this one for the No. 2 line. We decided which handcart was for which line, and we lined them up like that. When someone brought a lot of parts, he'd load it on the right cart and deliver it to the right place. We put a box beside each handcart to hold kanban. When the guy brought the cart back, he'd grab the kanban that was sticking out of the box and take it back with him.

A word from the editors:

Toyota had sophisticated reasons for adopting kanban for outsourced parts in the late 1960s and early 1970s. Supplier kanban were more than just a means of improving the flow of orders and deliveries. They were also a way of promoting production-control reform at suppliers that were using large-batch production based on anticipated orders.

Introducing kanban in business with outside suppliers required a commitment to reform on the part of the suppliers. The suppliers needed to abandon large-batch, make-to-sell production and, instead, produce items only in amounts that corresponded to the kanban that had been withdrawn. And that required guidance from Toyota. Replacing make-to-sell production with a pull system was counterintuitive for the suppliers, and it encountered a great deal of resistance.

Summary of the Chapter

The Toyota Production System Methodologies in a Historical Context

An important purpose for the editors in preparing the present volume was to reconstruct the Toyota Production System in theory. For that purpose, the editors set out to identify the constituent methodologies of the system and to elucidate how Toyota put those methodologies into practice.

The kanban system is well known as a tool employed in the Toyota Production System. But the two are not identical. Exactly which methodologies constitute the Toyota Production System is a question that has received insufficient analytical attention in studies of the system.

Two chronological tables prepared by Toyota illuminate the range of methodologies employed in the Toyota Production System. One table appears in a July 1975 revised edition of an unpublished textbook produced for employee training. The other, based on the table in the textbook, appears in Toyota's official 50-year history, published in November 1987. Fukui Prefectural University's Hiroaki Satake presents a notably convincing comparison of the two tables in a 1998 paper.

We can recreate the origins and the development of the Toyota Production System by analyzing the methodologies introduced in the two tables and by studying the circumstances of the creation of those methodologies. In table 2, the editors present an overview—based largely on the two tables prepared by Toyota—of the methodologies employed in the Toyota Production System. Distinct stages are evident in the development of the pull-system methodology, as summarized below.

First stage: to 1955

Toyota begins deploying production equipment in the sequence of successive processes rather than in groups of similar machines. That is a prerequisite for the development of a pull-system methodology. Toyota begins using multiprocess handling. Each employee handles a broader or narrower range of work, depending on the workload, and the company provides the employees with training to handle multiple processes.

Second stage: 1956 to 1965

Toyota develops pull-system methods for integrating production lines. That effort focuses initially on linking lines that produce units, such as engines and suspensions, with the lines that fabricate parts for those units.

Third stage: 1966 to 1975

Toyota develops pull-system linkages between the vehicle assembly lines and the processes, including outside parts manufacturers, that supply

Table 2: The Evolution of Toyota Production System Methodology

	Compensation	Training	Pull system (just in time)			
			Process flow	Conveyance	Tool and die changeovers	Kanban
1947						
1948	Compensation by job category					Pull system
1949						
1950	Four categories of piece-rate work		Flow-based production in machining Synchronization of machining and assembly			
1951						
1953				On-call conveyance in machining shops		Kanban in machining shop Leveled production
1955	Piece-rate conferences		Synchronization of body parts production and vehicle assembly			
1957						
1959				Synchronized transport among Toyota plants		
1960			Synchronization of work at all plants			
1961						
1962					Shortened changeover times for stamping dies	Kanban throughout Toyota plants
1963						
1965						
1966						
1969	New system of job ranks					
1970	Indicators for productivity and standard mass production rate	TPS training for supervisors Establishment of Production Survey Office to propagate TPS		On-call conveyance at all plants		
1971					Simplified die changeovers at Toyota plants	
1973				Synchronized deliveries from suppliers		
1974						
1975			Introduction of equipment suited to flow production		Simplified die changeovers at suppliers' plants	
1976		Autonomous study activities				
1977				"Milk run" and relay transport		
1978		Course for standardized work trainers				
1980		Course for managers Course for technicians				
1986						
1988	Revision of job ranks and new system of skill qualifications					
1992	Revision of divisional breakdown					

Note: The above table is a simplified—for purposes of clarity—version of a table that appeared in the original, Japanese edition of this book.

| Purchasing control | Production instructions | Multiprocess handling (*jidoka*) | | Order-to-delivery linkage | Equipment | |
		Multiprocess handling and standardized work	Visual control and in-process quality assurance			
		One operator per two machines				1947
						1948
		One operator per three or four machines				1949
			Visual control *andon* signal lights			1950
					Capacity sheets by part and by process	1951
		Systematic standardized work				1953
Fixed-quantity purchasing						1955
	Sequence sheets					1957
						1959
						1960
Red and blue cards for purchased parts						1961
			Fully integrated process management			1962
	Interwriter technology (facsimile machines)	Multiprocess handling, U-shaped assembly line				1963
Kanban-based orders and deliveries						1965
			Automated production lines for engines	10-day order system		1966
						1969
			Automated production lines for body parts	Daily order system		1970
	New system for production instructions (inc. instruction stickers)					1971
						1973
				New order system		1974
		Mixed-model production			Flexible manufacturing equipment at vehicle plants	1975
						1976
Barcode labeling						1977
					Flexible manufacturing equipment at unit plants	1978
	Automated processing of production instructions		New automation on production lines			1980
	New production instruction system					1986
						1988
						1992

components to those lines. It synchronizes the fabrication of parts on in-house production lines and at outside suppliers with the production sequence on the vehicle assembly lines.

Fourth stage: since 1976

Toyota employs electronic communications equipment to link activity alongside the vehicle production lines with activity in the previous processes. That helps fine-tune the timing of production instructions and of sequential delivery.

Suzumura's talks center on the second stage in the development of pull-system methodology at Toyota. He describes in detail how he used pull-system principles to create linkages between unit assembly lines and parts-fabrication lines.

Suzumura also touches on events of the third stage. He discusses how Toyota built a system for monitoring the usage of parts along the vehicle assembly lines and for supplying parts and assemblies in direct correspondence to that usage. His discussion extends to related improvements in production control at Toyota suppliers.

A new round of innovation became necessary in the fourth stage. The increasing diversity in vehicle models and model variations necessitated innovations in replenishing line-side stocks of parts and assemblies. Toyota needed to create sophisticated in-house logistics systems, and it needed to tap the potential of newly emerging electronics and communications technologies. Advanced technology became part of the tale of the Toyota Production System.

The Toyota Production System as Shared
Experience and Responses

Suzumura describes the adoption and application of kanban in the production workplace at Toyota from around 1955 to around 1965. His talks
provide a compelling portrait of the spread of pull-system principles from
parts-fabrication lines to unit assembly lines to vehicle assembly lines.

   Toyota's production system has justly received immense attention as
the wellspring of the company's competitiveness. That can engender the
misimpression that Toyota started out with the system, fully intact, or that
the people at Toyota set out consciously to build the system. But as we
hear from Suzumura, the Toyota Production System evolved gradually,
step-by-step.

   Taiichi Ohno, Kikuo Suzumura, and others conceived elements of the
system and worked heroically to put their concepts into practice. But none
of those individuals ever possessed a comprehensive vision of the Toyota
Production System as an integrated framework. They were simply tackling
problems that arose in the workplace, one by one, and their solutions accumulated and gradually became—collectively—what we now know as
the Toyota Production System. Determining when and how each of the
system's principal methodologies took shape is therefore essential to an
in-depth understanding of the system.

   The first application of the pull-system principle took place in a small
part of a machining shop—a shop that had been operating in accordance
with monthly production plans. And it relied on the ever so un-Toyota
approach of maintaining large inventories of raw material at the front end
and of finished parts at the back end. The inventories were a necessary
buffer to cope with the uneven pace of output in the previous processes
and in the following process. That uneven pace resulted from the other
processes' adherence to the end-of-the-month scramble that went with

plan-based production. Every process was at the mercy of the vagaries of production in the previous and following processes. In retrospect, the people in that machining shop at Toyota had a natural interest in insulating their process from the vagaries of their operating environment.

New issues arose each time Suzumura and his cohorts applied their nascent insight in a different workplace, such as the transmission shop or engine shop. And their portfolio of methodologies grew as they dealt with those issues in turn. When they encountered the seemingly unavoidable large-batch processing in the heat-treatment shop, their response was more improvisational than systematic. Suzumura and his colleagues were equally improvisational in dealing with the part matching and processing automation that Toyota adopted in the name of improving product quality.

Some observers of the Toyota Production System perceive what they regard as a dogmatic resistance to robots and other high-technology automation. Any resistance to automation, far from dogmatic, is the painful lesson of the dangers of imprudent investment in automation. The Toyota Production System is entirely amenable to automation that is demonstrably useful.

We could characterize the Toyota Production System as the result of repeated problem solving in accordance with a conceptually consistent approach. That would be to attribute a more-systematic unity to the undertakings, however, than the historical record warrants. Historically, the Toyota Production System is anything but a framework of physical tools, such as kanban, and procedures based on a preexisting conceptual format. Rather, it is the shared experience and responses of the people who have participated in creating the system.

In the early 1970s, Suzumura participated in shaping the Toyota Production System from the standpoint of what is now the Operations Management Consulting Division. He threw himself into teaching young employees, including administrative employees, the principles of problem solving in the workplace. He also participated actively in propagating the principles of the Toyota Production System in vehicle assembly plants and at the plants of outside suppliers.

The Operations Management Consulting Division remains in the vanguard of the continuing quest to apply the principles of the Toyota Production System more widely and more thoroughly. The division's very existence in the Toyota organization underlines the role of personal transference in bequeathing and inheriting the spirit of the Toyota Production System. That personal transference remains central even as Toyota works to convey the essence of the system through training and education programs.

Chapter IV

The Evolution of Buffering at Toyota

Remarks by **Kaneyoshi Kusunoki**
As recorded and edited by **Takahiro Fujimoto**
with **Takashi Matsuo**

The Remarks

Practice trumps theory. That principle is fundamental to the Toyota Production System.

Ohno-san was a man of the plant floor who despised theory. You won't find anything new in the Toyota Production System in regard to production control theory. The system is basically just Taylorism. Toyota simply refined [the scientific management theory of Frederick Taylor] through the trial and error of kaizen improvements and built an integrated system.

About the Text

This chapter centers on a reconstruction of remarks by Kaneyoshi Kusunoki to Takahiro Fujimoto and Takashi Matsuo on April 17, 1996. The meeting took place at the Tokyo headquarters of Hino Motors, where Kusunoki, a former executive vice president at Toyota, was serving as chairman. As with the interview with Taiichi Ohno in chapter 1, the editors refrained from tape-recording the proceedings and reconstructed the gist of the speaker's remarks from their notes. The text reflects subsequent editing by Kusunoki.

The editors focused the discussion on the subject of buffers in the production flow; specifically, buffering between the body-welding line and the paint shop and between the paint shop and the assembly line. They opted for that

Toyota began using the supermarket system [in the mid-1950s. That was a matter of letting the following processes withdraw the parts they needed from the preceding processes when they needed the parts and in the quantities that they needed. It contrasted with the traditional practice of having the preceding processes "push" their output onto the following processes].

Production technology was beginning to take off in Japan. Around 1960, we began to get access to the PB reports [compiled by the U.S. Commerce Department's Publications Board from the findings of different research organizations in the United States and elsewhere. Those were initially confidential and became available in Japan first to companies that were producing equipment for the U.S. military and later to companies that were producing civilian goods]. That occasioned a lot of advances in production technology.

---

focus because (1) the time available with Kusunoki was brief and (2) buffers are a central issue in operating the Toyota Production System.

Buffers are a subject of endless and sometimes heated debate at Toyota. After all, minimizing inventories between and inside processes has been a relentless emphasis in the Toyota Production System from the beginning. Toyota's Masao Nemoto makes that point in chapter 5: "Workers tend to want to keep inventory on hand to allow for covering up problems that occur. Toyota took away the inventory buffers to expose problems immediately. Shining a light on problems in that way has been crucial to everything that we have done."

Daihatsu Motor's Michikazu Tanaka confirm's Taiichi Ohno's perspective on this subject with the man himself in chapter 2: "You use the kanban to

1. Adapting Production Technology to Japanese Circumstances

We did more than just import technology blindly. We adapted things to Japanese circumstances. For example, we got our first transfer machines in the mid-1950s. But our production volumes were still small, so we only needed fairly rudimentary transfer machines and only in small numbers. Our early automation consisted primarily of extremely simple equipment.

Launching the Crown in 1955 presented a huge challenge. We'd been outsourcing our body production to Mitsubishi Heavy Industries and to Kanto Auto Works. But we decided to make the bodies for the Crown in-house. We didn't know anything about stamping body panels or making bodies for passenger cars. So we began studying body technology, and that's how we learned about things like stamping dies.

I received orders to learn about bodies, and I taught myself how to make dies. I developed a new method of cutting dies with a tracing model. I also learned about cold forging, die casting, injection molding, and other things.

create a positive tension in the workplace by reducing work-in-process, and that motivates people to do better than they ever thought they could do."

Nemoto provides a further reason for minimizing inventory in chapter 5: "Having stocks of semifinished items on hand was convenient and reassuring, but it could result in waste if changes occurred in the production plan. We minimized inventory risk by processing raw material on a strictly just-in-time basis."

On the other hand, handling things in exactly the same order in every process of the production sequence was unrealistic. Bodies emerged from the painting shop, for example, in a different order from that in which they entered the shop. Some sort of buffer was necessary at the back end of the

We installed our first full-scale transfer-stamping line at the Motomachi Plant around 1960. The company took on some debt to help finance the investment, but we could still only afford two lines. They were from the U.S. companies Danly Machine and Clearing. We learned a lot from installing and working with those lines. Toyota was still a high-variety, low-volume producer, so we needed to find ways to do the die changeovers in as little time as possible. The changeover took two hours at first, but we managed to get that down to less than 10 minutes.

When I went to work at Toyota in 1946, [the company was still mainly a truck producer. And] we were pursuing a target of increasing our production volume to 1,000 trucks a month. That meant about 40 trucks a day, since we were operating about 25 days a month. We figured that monthly output of about 10,000 vehicles was the threshold production volume for lasting viability as an automaker. But we had a hard time even getting our output up to 1,000 a month. Not until 1960 did Toyota's monthly production volume reach 10,000 vehicles.

Production technology assumed growing importance in our operations as our manufacturing expanded. We used a growing range of transfer

---

paint shop to allow the assembly line to withdraw bodies in the sequence it required.

Kikuo Suzumura describes Toyota's response in chapter 3: "We had two-tone color schemes. We had paint specs that required coating twice and baking twice. We had specs that called for coating three times and baking three times ... . Bodies that went through painting processes four times came out at different times from those that went through twice. That's why we wanted to have a broad storage area that would allow for lining up bodies with different paint specifications, keeping them all accessible for easy withdrawal."

Re-sequencing bodies between the paint shop and the assembly line became increasingly important as Toyota's exports grew and the range of

machines, adopted chipless machining, introduced steel-panel transfer presses, and adopted aluminum die casting.

2. Working Under Ohno

I became responsible for production control at Toyota in 1973. That placed me under Ohno-san,

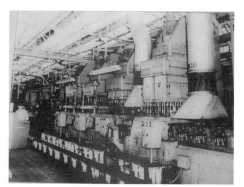

Toyota's first transfer machine

who was then the senior managing director responsible for manufacturing. I had come up through production engineering, whereas he had come up through production operations on the plant floor. Although we had worked under the same overall production umbrella, our paths and specialties had been utterly different.

Ohno-san was opposed to private offices. He believed that everyone should work together in a large office space. So I occupied a desk for three years beside Ohno-san's, which provided a rare learning opportunity.

---

vehicle specifications expanded. Distributing the workload evenly is a big consideration in determining the sequence of bodies on the assembly line. And different specifications can mean big differences in the amount of labor entailed in assembly. Cars equipped with air-conditioning, for instance, require a lot more time to assemble than those without. A continuous series of especially labor-intensive specifications could cause people on the assembly line to fall behind in their work, and a line stoppage could occur as a result.

The ideal sequence for the downstream work of vehicle assembly thus differs from the ideal sequence for the upstream work of painting. Buffering was a means of accommodating the different sequencing necessary to optimize work in the different processes.

Ohno-san's style was to blithely try out new ideas immediately on the production line. He never bothered to explain what he was doing, and he was not the least bit concerned about the possibility that he might bring production to a halt. He'd just try things and learn from what went wrong. When people didn't carry out his experiment in the manner he'd intended, he'd scold them severely. He'd insist that people keep at it until they'd done things in accordance with his plan.

Ohno-san, meanwhile, was building the Toyota Production System—not on a blackboard somewhere but out on the plant floor. And he encountered a lot of resistance. Some people were dead set against his ideas. In the face of that resistance, he carried on with a missionary zeal. He was so dogmatic and passionate that he sometimes seemed to be getting too carried away with things. But I guess he felt that any compromise, that any loosening of standards, would undermine his mission.

The anti-Ohno faction was especially aghast at his single-mindedness in carrying out his experiments to completion, even when that meant bringing the production line to a halt. He was able to get away with that because he had the backing of [the heads of the company] Eiji Toyoda

---

Toyota had another reason for using buffers. The company automated its stamping, welding, and painting work extensively in the 1960s, and production stoppages caused by mechanical breakdowns occurred frequently in those upstream processes. Toyota could ill afford to let those stoppages interrupt work on its labor-intensive assembly lines. Stoppages there would be extremely costly in terms of labor costs.

Kusunoki was the right person to ask about buffers. He had dealt closely with Ohno from the standpoint of production engineering, and he had a solid grasp of the theoretical and practical aspects of buffering. He explored the topic carefully with his interviewers. His comments were invaluable in bridging the perspectives expressed by the other individuals who appear in this volume.

and Shoichi Saito. I've heard that Eiji had to tell him a couple of times to back off. Sure enough, even Ohno-san would give in and try another tack when Eiji put his foot down.

3. Articulating a Conceptual Framework

The Toyota Production System was working, but it lacked a formal, conceptual framework. That became a serious concern for me around 1975. Toyota's production methods had begun to receive a lot of attention since the oil crisis [of 1973]. We began getting visits from "kanban tourists," including visitors from overseas. The only materials we had on hand to explain our production system were some case studies. They were woefully inadequate to provide a good understanding of our approach to Japanese academics or to the foreign visitors. I was especially worried that people overseas would jump to the conclusion that we at Toyota were just a bunch of kamikaze fanatics.

So we went to work on preparing a systematic description of our production methodology. The responsibility for developing that systematic

The editors have included in this chapter a reprint of the first English-language academic paper that describes the Toyota Production System. Kusunoki coauthored that paper in 1977 with three Toyota colleagues, including the company's present chairman, Fujio Cho. It remains an invaluable source of insight into the thinking that underlay Toyota's historic innovations in manufacturing.

About the Speaker

Kaneyoshi Kusunoki, born in 1924, joined Toyota in 1946. He spent most of his career in production engineering. That included work in developing new manufacturing technologies, and he headed a unit established in 1970 to develop

description fell to a group in the production control division's Production Survey Office [later known as the Operations Management Consulting Office, now the Operations Management Consulting Division]. That group was a mix of managers from engineering and nonengineering backgrounds: Fujio Cho [who is now the chairman of Toyota], who studied law at the University of Tokyo; Kosuke Ikebuchi [who later became a Toyota vice-chairman], who studied welding technology at Osaka University; Susumu Uchikawa [who later became a senior managing director at Toyota], who studied economics at Kyoto University; Yutaka Sugimori, who studied economics at Nagoya University; and Junichi Yoshikawa, who studied engineering at the University of Tokushima. The general managers above them were Kikuo Suzumura and Itsuo Mamiya. Furnishing assistance in preparing the description in the format of an academic paper were professors Rintaro Muramatsu, of Waseda University, and Eiji Ogawa, of Nagoya University.

Ohno, of course, hated that kind of deskwork. If he saw people poring over written work like that, he'd tell them to get out onto the plant floor. So the team couldn't do its work within his sight in the Production Survey

---

production technology for catalytic converters and related items necessitated by air-quality legislation in the United States and elsewhere.

Kusunoki became a member of Toyota's board of directors in 1972, and he took charge of the company's production control division in 1973. He subsequently headed Toyota's entire production engineering organization and served as the plant manager of several plants, including the Tsutsumi and Tahara vehicle assembly plants.

When Toyota built its first wholly owned vehicle plant in the United States, it dispatched Kusunoki to oversee the construction project and the plant startup. He served as the inaugural president of what is now Toyota Motor Manufacturing Kentucky, which Toyota established in 1986 and which

Office. Fortunately, I was responsible for production engineering, as well as for production control. And the company let us have private offices in production engineering, since we were handling sensitive information about equipment planning and investment planning.

The team took up residence in my office. Under the guidance of Muramatsu [and Ogawa], the members undertook a scientific analysis of our production system and wrote up their findings. We delivered our paper in August 1977 at the Japan Industrial Management Association's Fourth International Conference on Production Research in Tokyo (see page 151). That was the first time that Toyota presented a formal description of its production system to an external audience.

Our paper expresses the number of kanban in circulation in a process, y, with the formula $y = [D \ (T_w + T_p) \ (1 + \alpha)] \ / \ a$, where D is the demand per time unit presented by the following process, T_w is the waiting time per kanban, T_p is the processing time, a is the number of parts per container, and α is the policy variable [or discretion]. Of special note here is α. Ohno-san taught us not to settle for the number of kanban necessary to maintain production at some rate but to work continuously to achieve

begin producing Camrys in 1988. He headed Toyota Motor Manufacturing Canada, too, which was also established in 1986 and which also began operation in 1988. Returning to Japan in the late 1980s, Kusunoki served as an executive vice president at Toyota before taking on the chairmanship of Hino Motors. He retired in 1998.

Kaneyoshi Kusunoki (*center, left*) celebrating the production of the 10-millionth transmission at Toyota's Kinuura Plant in 1987

a leaner flow by reducing the number of kanban as much as possible. He always said that steering that effort is the responsibility of workplace leaders.

Without the policy discretion expressed by the α element, our formula would be a mere calculation that any clerk could perform. We knew that Ohno-san would never approve the paper if it did not contain that element. So we showed him that we had faithfully reflected the discretion of the workplace managers in the formula. He signed off on the paper, and we submitted it to the Japan Industrial Management Association. [The paper received a good reception and] two other Toyota managers later presented a similar paper under Muramatsu's guidance at another international conference in Amsterdam.

4. Buffering: Between the Paint Shop and the Assembly Line

Buffering was necessary between the paint shop and the assembly line for two reasons: (1) to accommodate the changes in body sequence that occurred in the painting process and (2) to insulate assembly work from the mechanical breakdowns that occurred frequently in the paint shop. We didn't have a formal system for managing the buffer between the paint shop and the assembly line when the Motomachi Plant opened in 1959. We just sort of kept on hand a number of painted bodies that seemed sufficient to keep things flowing smoothly. Ohno-san was not yet in charge of production overall. Reaching decisions was a matter of spirited discussion and debate among the production engineering people, the facilities construction people, and Ohno-san. I was working in the technological development unit of our production engineering organization at that time.

By the time the Takaoka Plant opened in 1966, we had a well-established system for buffering. We maintained three rows of 10 painted bodies each between the paint shop and the assembly line there. The plant was producing about a car per minute, so that gave us about 30 minutes' worth of buffer. Each row contained bodies for a mix of vehicle specifications in regard to the amount of labor required in assembly. Red, white, and yellow markers indicated the different labor requirements. We sometimes used space upstairs to increase the size of the buffer when production volumes surged. But for the most part, we worked with a 30-body buffer.

When I started working for Ohno-san in the early 1970s, he told us to use more rows and fewer bodies per row in the buffer. We were using up to seven rows in the buffers at some plants by the mid-1970s. But the only time we could easily adopt a new configuration for the buffer was when we built new plants. That was on account of the structural constraints imposed by the plant buildings.

A 30-minute buffer kept our downstream operations insulated from all but the most serious problems with upstream equipment and processes. Nonetheless, we encountered plenty of problems at our Kentucky Plant and at other overseas plants that were too serious to absorb with the buffer. Serious equipment breakdowns occurred mainly in body welding. Serious processing problems happened mainly in the paint shop. For example, we had a really hard time achieving consistently high quality with black paint at the Kentucky Plant. We had to resort for a while to importing black Camry bodies from the Tsutsumi Plant—the Kentucky Plant's mother plant in Japan.

The maintenance and repair capabilities were generally lower at our overseas plants than at our Japanese plants. A problem that would get fixed in 10 minutes in Japan might take 30 minutes or even an hour to resolve. We therefore used larger buffers overseas than in Japan. That was necessary to keep the plants operating smoothly and to keep our overall production costs down. As the operations stabilized, we gradually reduced the size of the buffers.

Kaneyoshi Kusunoki (*center*), Eiji Toyoda, and employees at Toyota Motor Manufacturing Canada celebrating the production of the company's first Corolla in 1988

We experimented in the late 1970s with eliminating the painted-body buffers and linking the paint shops directly to the assembly lines at our Japanese vehicle plants. That experiment continued for about a year, and it didn't work out very well. The people in body welding inevitably end up arranging bodies in the optimal order for welding work. [As described earlier] that resulted in surges of labor-intensive work on the assembly line and caused line stoppages.

The disparity in labor requirements among vehicles was especially big on the assembly line at our Canadian plant. That's because the plant produced cars for the U.S. market, where air-conditioning was basically standard, and for the Canadian market, where it was less common. The painting capabilities at the Canadian plant were pretty low initially, and that necessitated a lot of touch-up work. So the buffer between the paint shop and the assembly line was chronically small. We also had a lot of equipment problems initially on the body-welding line in Canada. The buffer at the end of that line also ran chronically small—only five or six bodies—so a serious breakdown in welding would also interrupt work in the paint shop.

The shortage of painted bodies sometimes forced the assembly line people to withdraw bodies directly from the paint shop, rather than from the buffer. That prevented them from sequencing the bodies in an order that would optimize the distribution of assembly work. And work stoppages caused by surges of labor-intensive work occurred as a result.

Stoppages will occur occasionally on any assembly line, even in Japan, that handles product specifications that present diverse labor requirements. We didn't have much of a problem with stoppages of that kind on the assembly line in Kentucky. That's because all the cars that we made there initially were air-conditioned four-door sedans. The vehicle specifications didn't present much variation in labor requirements.

5. Buffering: Between the Welding Line and the Paint Shop

Welding equipment, like painting equipment, is prone to mechanical breakdowns, and that necessitates some kind of buffering between the welding line and the painting shop. People at Toyota are instinctively wary, however, of anything that resembles inventory, and Toyota allocates no special storage area for welded bodies ready for painting. Instead, Toyota provides for a minimal buffer of welded bodies on the conveyor line that connects the welding line to the paint shop. That differs from the practice in conventional automobile manufacturing, whereby vehicle assemblers set aside large storage sites for welded bodies.

People at Toyota regard the buffer as a necessary evil, at best, and make every effort to keep it as small as possible. The appropriate size for the buffers between the welding lines and paint shops is a subject of continuing debate. People on the plant floor and in production engineering want to maintain buffers that correspond to the line downtime per shift. On the other hand, the people in the Operations Management Consulting Division want to keep the buffers smaller. They believe that comfortable buffers make people less vigilant in identifying and resolving the root causes of problems. They inherit Ohno-san's preoccupation with finding solutions rather than settling for fixes.

People mainly concerned with financial considerations, such as investment efficiency and equipment utilization rates, favor ample buffers to prevent production from stopping. The people in the Operations Management Consulting Division respond that the natural fear of a line stoppage motivates people to pursue kaizen. They argue that a 30-minute buffer between welding and painting is sufficient for an assembly plant that is producing a vehicle a minute, and they insist that people in the plant should work to reduce the size of even that minimal buffer.

I was the first person to head both production engineering and production control at Toyota, so I was the first person to have the chance to establish integrated policy [for buffering and other issues]. That included accepting increases in the size of our buffers when we were working hard to increase production output. But we didn't expand the sites of the buffers or add new buffer sites. Instead, we used available space inside and between the processes—including the overhead conveyor line—to hold more inventory. Even Ohno-san and his disciple Kikuo Suzumura approved of increasing our in-process stock like that as necessary.

Increasing the buffer stock without actually expanding the buffer sites was a typically Toyota innovation. It contrasted with the readiness of U.S. and European automakers to allocate more space to hold inventory. Even at Toyota, employees at our overseas plants worry about being held accountable for production shortfalls caused by line stoppages. They demand extra buffer space when we are building new plants. And since adding buffer space after building a plant is practically impossible, erring initially on the side of larger buffers makes sense. You can then work with your people in finding ways to gradually shrink the buffers.

We provided too little space for the buffer between welding and painting when we built our first vehicle plant in Canada. So we made sure to expand the buffer space appropriately when we expanded the plant's capacity to 80,000 vehicles a year, from 50,000. In contrast, the buffer line between welding and painting was too long at our California joint venture with General Motors, New United Motor Manufacturing, Inc. (NUMMI). That was because NUMMI inherited a GM plant. We shortened the buffer line when we renovated the plant.

As I have described, buffers make sense between the body welding line and the paint shop and between the paint shop and the assembly line. But the latter positioning is more useful than the former. That's because paintwork is especially sensitive to any number of variables, and the frequent need for retouching plays havoc with the order in which bodies emerge from the paint shop.

You'd be amazed at the things that can cause inconsistency in paint jobs. We once traced a paint problem in Kentucky to a new cosmetic compact that a female employee was using. Paint characteristics vary slightly among suppliers, such as Nippon Paint, Kansai Paint, DuPont, and PPG Industries. Fingerprints show up immediately. And special colors can be especially difficult, as with the problem we had with black paint in Kentucky.

6. Stamped Parts Inventory

We also lacked a system for managing inventories of stamped parts when we opened the Motomachi Plant in 1959. We had borrowed ¥10 billion from the Export-Import Bank of Japan to install stamping lines. But that bought us only two lines, so we had to produce a diversity of stampings on each line.

Ohno-san's approach of reducing the die changeover times dramatically and changing dies frequently hadn't taken hold completely at Toyota. And the people at the Motomachi Plant strove initially to minimize the frequency of die changeovers. They amassed big inventories of stamped parts and commissioned a nearby logistics company to build a warehouse to store those inventories.

When Ohno-san became the plant manager at Motomachi, he ordered people to make do without the warehouse, and he forbade them to hold more than four days' worth of inventory of stampings. We used the same four-day limit for stamped parts inventory when we opened the Takaoka Plant in 1966, and we gradually lowered the limit.

We started out with a simple triangle kanban in the stamping shop. That kanban—literally no more than a metal triangle that you could hang on things—worked fine as long as the variety of stampings was small and as long as the variation in lot sizes was minimal. But it became inadequate as our models and model variations multiplied and as we therefore began handling a greatly increased diversity of stampings.

[The triangle kanban was for large-volume lots. Using it as production instructions for all the stampings we needed would have pushed our inventory over Ohno-san's limit.] The production supervisors responded by running small-volume stamping lots based on mental calculations and without using kanban. They'd sneak those lots in midway during the kanban-based processing of large lots. That enabled them to secure the parts they needed without violating the four-day inventory limit, but it undermined the kanban system.

When we figured out what was happening, we reduced the lot size per kanban to, say, 50 stampings, from 200. That enabled us to handle a greater variety of parts within the kanban system without exceeding our overall inventory limit. Desktop computers were becoming common in our plants, and they helped us cope with the increasingly complex combinations of stamping work that we needed to handle each day.

7. Line-Side Parts Inventory

Team leaders at our vehicle assembly plants really took to the desktop computers. And that raised the energy level on the assembly lines impressively.

We designed the assembly lines at the Takaoka Plant for high-volume, low-variety production. They didn't easily accommodate the diversity of product specifications that we later produced there. We needed to array parts along both sides of the assembly lines, so the aisles between the lines became extremely narrow. And we needed to adopt one-way traffic rules for the trolleys that deliver the parts to points along the lines.

Mix-loading the trolleys in accordance with the kanban sequence meant stopping each trolley at the delivery points along the assembly lines. Unloading heavy items, such as batteries, took a lot of time, and that caused traffic jams, since we dispatched the trolleys at fixed time increments. We solved that problem by reducing the size of the different lots that the trolleys carried. Our desktop computers enabled us to calculate the optimal lot sizes for keeping the trolleys moving while keeping the lines supplied with the required parts.

The kanban remained invaluable in managing the interchange among processes, and the computers helped us keep that interchange working smoothly. That was a great example of using computers effectively. The guys using the computers were team leaders in their 30s. They brought a lot of energy to the work.

Our rule of thumb for inventories is a four-hour supply. We arrived at that figure through the painful experience of accidents, disasters, and highway congestion that disrupted deliveries of parts, along with careful consideration of inventory costs.

Meanwhile, we simply don't have enough space for even four hours' worth of inventory at Takaoka or at some of our other plants. At Takaoka, we are storing parts for special needs in a building next door that we'd been using to store old machine tools and inventories of parts imported from the United States. We also maintain extra winter stocks of parts that are subject to delivery delays caused by snow. Letting the weather interrupt the operation of expensive equipment on our lines would make no sense at all.

8. Closing Comments

A defining characteristic of the corporate culture at Toyota is that managers don't scold you for taking initiative, for taking a chance and screwing up. Rather, they'll scold you for not trying something new, for not taking a chance.

Leaders aren't there to judge. They're there to encourage people. That's what I've always tried to do. Trial and error is what it's all about!

We had no money after the war. We tried everything, like divvying up employees' wages in small chunks, but we finally got to the point [in 1950] where we couldn't meet the payroll and had to let people go. But even during those tough times, we maintained the spirit of trial and error.

When cash is short, your best shot is to speed the flow of material through your system. You don't need capital spending to move things faster and shorten lead times. You simply need to improve the way you do the work.

Eiji [Toyoda]'s support is what made the Toyota Production System possible. Eiji left production control to Ohno-san, production engineering to other executives, and finance to yet others. Those guys engaged in some knock-down, drag-out fights, and it was Eiji who held everything together.

The people at Toyota can be excruciatingly slow in deciding what to do, but once they reach a decision, their execution is something to behold.

Literal Reproduction of Original English-Language Document

4th International Conference on Production Research (Tokyo)

Toyota production system and Kanban system —materialization of just-in-time and respect-for-human system

Y. SUGIMORI, K. KUSUNOKI, F. CHO and S. UCHIKAWA
Production Control Department, Toyota Motor Co., Ltd., Japan.

The 'Toyota Production System' and 'Kanban System' introduced in this paper was developed by the Vice-president of Toyota Motor Company, Mr. Taiichi Ohno, and it was under his guidance that these unique production systems have become deeply rooted in Toyota Motor Company in the past 20 years. There are two major distinctive features in these systems. One of these is the 'just-in-time production', a specially important factor in an assembly industry such as automotive manufacturing. In this type of production, 'only the necessary products, at the necessary time, in necessary quantity' are manufactured, and in addition, the stock on hand is held down to a minimum. Secondly the System is the respect-for-human system where the workers are allowed to display in full their capabilities through active participation in running and improving their own workshops.

1. Starting point of concept—making the most of Japanese characteristics

The starting point of the concept of Toyota Production System was in the recognition of Japan's distinguishing features.

The most distinctive feature of Japan is the lack of natural resources, which makes it necessary to import vast amounts of materials, including food. Japan is placed under a disadvantageous condition in terms of a cost of raw material when compared to the European and American countries. To overcome this handicap, it is essential for the Japanese industries to put forth their best efforts in order to produce better quality goods having higher added value and at an even lower production cost than those of the other countries. This was the first thing that Toyota recognized.

The second distinctive feature is the Japanese concept toward work such as consciousness and attitude differed from that held by the European and American workers. The Japanese traits include: (1) group consciousness, sense of equality, desire to improve, and diligence born from a long history of a homogeneous race, (2) high degree of ability resulting from higher education brought by desire to improve, (3) centering their daily living around work.

Such Japanese traits have also been reflected in the enterprises. Customs such as (1) lifetime employment system, (2) labour unions by companies, (3) little discrimination between shop workers and white-collar staff, and (4) chances available to workers for promotion to managerial positions have been of great service in promoting the feeling of unity between the company and workers. Japan also does not have the problem of foreign workers, unlike European countries.

As related above, from the standpoint of labour environment, Japan is much better off than the European and American countries. In order to make full use of the Japanese advantages, it is of importance that the industries have their workers display their capabilities to the utmost. This was the second thing that Toyota recognized.

2. Toyota production system and its basic concept

Upon recognition of the matters related above, Toyota is planning and running its production system on the following two basic concepts.

First of all, the thing that corresponds to the first recognition of putting forth all efforts to attain low cost production is 'reduction of cost through elimination of waste'. This involves making up a system that will thoroughly eliminate waste by assuming that anything other than the minimum amount of equipment, materials, parts, and workers (working time) which are absolutely essential to production are merely surplus that only raises the cost.

The thing that corresponds to the second recognition of Japanese diligence, high degree of ability, and favoured labour environment is 'to make full use of the workers' capabilities'. In short, treat the workers as human beings and with consideration. Build up a system that will allow the workers to display their full capabilities by themselves.

2.1 *Cost cutting by thorough removal of waste*

For materialization of this system, Toyota has attached special importance to 'just-in-time production' and 'Jidoka'.

2.1.1 *Distinguishing features of automotive industry.* In order to have an efficient production system in the automotive industry, it is required that the following three distinguishing problems be solved.

(1) The automotive industry is a typical mass production assembly type where each vehicle is assembled from several thousand parts that have undergone numerous processes. Therefore, a trouble in any of the processes will have a large overall effect.

(2) There are very many different models with numerous variations and with large fluctuation in the demand of each variation.

(3) Every few years, the vehicles are completely remodeled, and there are also often changes at a part level.

The ordinary production control system in such an industry consists of fulfilling the production schedules by holding work-in-process inventory over all processes as a means of absorbing troubles in the processes and changes in demand. However, such a system in practice often creates excessive unbalance of stock between the processes, which often leads to dead stock. On the other hand, it can easily fall into the condition of having excessive equipment and surplus of workers, which is not conformable to Toyota's recognition.

2.1.2 *Just-in-time production.* In order to avoid such problems as inventory unbalance and surplus equipment and workers, we recognized necessity of schemes adjustable to conform with changes due to troubles and demand fluctuations. For this purpose, we put our efforts in development of a production system which is able to shorten the lead time from the entry of materials to the completion of vehicle.

The just-in-time production is a method whereby the production lead time is greatly shortened by maintaining the conformity to changes by having 'all processes produce the necessary parts at the necessary time and have on hand only the minimum stock necessary to hold the processes together'. In addition, by checking the degree of inventory quantity and production lead time as policy variables, this production method discloses existence of surplus equipment and workers. This is the starting point to the second characteristic of Toyota Production System, that is, to make full use of the workers' capability.

(1) *Withdrawal by subsequent processes*

The first requirement of just-in-time production is to enable all processes to quickly gain accurate knowledge of 'timing and quantity required'.

In the general production system, this requirement is met as follows. The production schedule of the product (automobiles in the case of automotive plant) is projected on the various parts schedules and instructions issued to the various processes. These processes produce the parts in accordance with their schedules, employing the method of 'the preceding process supplying the parts to its following process'. However, it can be seen that this kind of method will make it vastly difficult to attain production adaptable to changes.

In order to materialize the first requirement, Toyota adopted a reverse method of 'the following process withdrawing the parts from the preceding process' instead of 'the preceding process supplying the parts to the following process'.

· The reason for this is as follows: Just-in-time production is production of parts by the various processes in the necessary amounts at necessary timing for assembling a vehicle as a final product of the company. If such is the case, it can be said that only the final assembly line that performs the vehicle assembly is the process that can accurately know the necessary timing and quantity of the parts.

Therefore, the final assembly line goes to the preceding process to obtain the necessary parts at the necessary time for vehicle assembly. The preceding process then produces on the parts withdrawn by the following process. For the production of these parts, the preceding process obtains the necessary parts from the process further preceding it. By connecting up all of the processes in chain fashion in this way, it will be possible for the entire company to engage in just-in-time production without the necessity of issuing lengthy production orders to each process.

(2) *One piece production and conveyance*

The second requirement of just-in-time production is that all processes approach the condition where each process can produce only one piece, can convey it one at a time, and in addition have only one piece in stock both between the equipment and the processes.

This means that no process for any reason is allowed to produce extra amount and have surplus stock between the processes. Therefore, each process must approach the condition where it produces and conveys only one piece corresponding to the single unit that is coming off the final assembly line. In short, all the shops are withheld from lot production and lot conveyance.

Toyota has succeeded in reducing the lot size through greatly shortening the setup time, improving production methods, including the elimination of in-process inventory within the process resulting from ordering of multi-purpose machining equipment in accordance with the processing requirements for a product line, and improving conveyance resulting from repetitive mixed loading. All of these have been carried out, including at large numbers of subcontractors.

(3) *Levelling of production*

Provided that all processes perform small lot production and convey-ance, if the quantity to be withdrawn by the subsequent process varies considerably, the processes within the company as well as the subcon-tractors will maintain peak capacity or holding excessive inventory at all times.

Therefore, in order to make a just-in-time production possible, the prerequisite will be to level the production at the final assembly line (the most important line that gives out the production instructions to all pro-cesses). A degree of this levelling is determined by top managers.

(1) Final assembly lines of Toyota are mixed product lines. The produc-tion per day is averaged by taking the number of vehicles in the monthly production schedule classified by specifications and dividing by the num-ber of working days.

(2) In regard to the production sequence during each day, the cycle time of each different specification vehicle is calculated, and in order to have all specification vehicles appear at their own cycle time, different specification vehicles are ordered to follow each other.

If the final assembly line levels the production as related above, the production of all processes practising subsequent process withdrawal and one-piece production and conveyance are also levelled.

The second significant point in levelled production is to observe the basic rule of just-in-time; to produce only as much as possibly sold, on the one hand adjusting its production level according to the change in market, on the other hand producing as smoothly as possible within a certain range. Even after the monthly production schedule has been de-cided, Toyota will still make changes among the different specification vehicles on the basis of daily orders, and even when it comes to the total

Literal Reproduction of Original English-Language Document

number, if there is necessity to meet the changes in market conditions, Toyota will make revisions in the monthly schedule so as to reduce the shock of market fluctuation as much as possible.

When the production system related above is compared with the generally adopted scheduled production system, the former system can operate with smaller production changes than the latter system. Consequently, it will be possible to do with the less equipment capacity and more stable number of workers. (This is specially important to Japanese companies that have lifetime employment system).

A production control system which has been developed to practice the above three general rules; (1) withdrawal of parts by subsequent process, (2) small lot production and conveyance, (3) levelling of production, is the Kanban System.

(4) Elimination of waste from over-producing

The underlying concept in just-in-time production systems is that the value of existence of inventory is disavowed.

In the conventional production control system, existence of inventory is appreciated as a means to absorb troubles and fluctuations in demand and to smooth fluctuations in load of processes.

In contrast to this, Toyota sees the stock on hand as being only a collection of troubles and bad causes. We consider that virtually most of the stock on hand is the result of 'over-producing' more than the amount required, and is the worst waste that can raise the production cost.

The reason why we consider inventory resulting from over-producing is the worst waste is that it hides the causes of waste that should be remedied, such as unbalance between the workers and between the processes, troubles in various processes, workers' idle time, surplus workers, excessive equipment capacity and insufficient preventive maintenance.

Such latency of waste makes it difficult for workers to display their capability and it even becomes obstructive of an ever-lasting evolution of a company.

2.1.3 *Jidoka.* The term 'Jidoka' as used at Toyota means 'to make the equipment or operation stop whenever an abnormal or defective condition arises'. In short, its distinctive feature lies in the fact that when an equipment trouble or machining defect happens, the equipment or entire line stops, and any line with workers can be stopped by them.

The reasons for 'Jidoka' being so important are as follows:

(1) To prevent making too much. If the equipment is made to stop when the required amount is produced, making too much cannot arise. Consequently, the just-in-time production can be accurately carried out.

(2) Control of abnormality becomes easy. It will only be necessary to make improvements by directing attention to the stopped equipment and the worker who did the stopping. This is an important requirement when making up the system of 'full utilization of workers' capabilities' related next.

Toyota has made countless number of improvements to realize 'Jidoka'.

2.2 *Full utilization of workers' capabilities*

This is Toyota's second basic concept of making the best use of Japan's favoured labour environment and excellent workers. It has built up a system of respect for humans, putting emphasis on the points as follows: (1) elimination of waste movements by workers, (2) consideration for workers' safety, and (3) self display of workers' capabilities by entrusting them with greater responsibility and authority.

2.2.1 *Elimination of waste movement by workers.* Workers may realize their work worthy only if the labour of diligent workers is exclusively used to raise added value of products.

Then what are the waste movements that lower added value and which we must eliminate? The first of these is workers' movements accompanying the waste of making too much. The movements of material handling operations between the equipment and between the processes due to large inventory are all waste movements. It has become possible for Toyota to effect large reductions of this waste by making up a system that allows thorough just-in-time production.

However, even though the waste of making too much is reduced, it will be of no avail if the waste of workers' waiting time is created as a result. In the just-in-time production, even when there is surplus capacity in the equipment, only as much as the subsequent process has withdrawn is produced. Thus, if the equipment and workers are tied together, workers are subject to idleness. To prevent such waste of waiting time being created, various improvements have been made, such as (1) separating the workers from the equipment by assigning a worker to multiple equipment, (2) concentration of workers' zones at the automatic lines, and (3) making up lines that do not require supervisory operation.

The second waste is to have the workers perform operations that are by nature not suitable for men. Operations involving danger, operations injurious to health, operations requiring hard physical labour, and monotonous repetitive operations have been mechanized, automated, and unmanned.

The third waste is workers' movements as a result of troubles of defects. Thorough 'Jidoka' by Toyota has greatly reduced this kind of waste.

2.2.2 *Considerations to workers' safety.* Workers of Toyota are diligent and enthusiastic about attaining production. Thus, he may not stop operation if the trouble is not of a serious nature and will take non-standard methods just to keep the line running. If waiting time occurs, he will become impatient and eventually start doing something extra. However, such kinds of unusual operation or extra work are often accompanied by accidents, troubles, or defects.

The 'Jidoka' and elimination of waiting time now being advanced by Toyota is not only for reducing the production cost, but also effective as a measure for safety.

The results have been reflected in the fact that from an international standpoint the frequency rate of injury at Toyota is low.

> Note: Comparison with the frequency rate of injury in American automotive industry shows that against the 1.5 shown in the United States (ILO 1974 statistics), Toyota had 0.8 or about one-half lower.

2.2.3 *Self-display of workers' ability.* Nowadays, it has become an international interest to respect humanity of workers in production shops. Toyota firmly believes that making up a system where the capable Japanese workers can actively participate in running and improving their workshops and be able to fully display their capabilities would be foundation of human respect environment of the highest order.

As the first step in this method, all workers at Toyota have a right to stop the line on which they are working.

Even in a long line like the final assembly line, if any abnormality comes up such as the worker finding himself unable to keep up or discovering an incorrect or defective part, he can stop the entire line by pressing the stop button near at hand. It is not a conveyer that operates men, while it is men that operate a conveyer, which is the first step to respect for human independence.

As the second step, at all shops in Toyota, the workers are informed of the priority order of the parts to be processed and the state of production advancement. Therefore, the actual authority for decisions of job dispatching and overtime is delegated to the foreman, and this allows each shop to conduct production activities without orders from the control department.

As the third step, Toyota has a system whereby workers can take part in making improvements. Any employee at Toyota has a right to make an improvement on the waste he has found.

In the just-in-time production, all processes and all shops are kept in the state where they have no surplus so that if trouble is left unattended, the line will immediately stop running and will affect the entire plant. The necessity for improvement can be easily understood by anyone.

Therefore, Toyota is endeavoring to make up a working place where not only the managers and foremen but also all workers can detect trouble. This is called 'visible control'.

Through visible control, all workers are taking positive steps to improve a lot of waste they have found. And the authority and responsibility for running and improving the workshop have been delegated to the workers themselves, which is the most distinctive feature of Toyota's respect-for-human system.

3. Kanban System

3.1 *Aim of Kanban System*

A production control system for just-in-time production and making full use of workers' capabilities is the Kanban System. Utilizing Kanban System, workshops of Toyota have no longer relied upon an electronic computer. It is shown in Fig. 1.

The reasons to have employed Kanban System instead of computerized system are as follows:

(1) Reduction of cost processing information. It calls for huge cost to implement a system that provides production schedule to all the processes and suppliers as well as its alterations and adjustments by real time control.

(2) Rapid and precise acquisition of facts. Using Kanban itself, managers of workshops may perceive such continuously changing facts as production capacity, operating rate, and man power without help of a computer. Hence, data of schedules corresponding to the change are accurate, which urges workshops to found responsibility systems and to promote activities for spontaneous improvements.

(3) Limiting surplus capacity of preceding shops. Since an automotive industry consists of multistage processes, generally the demand for the item (the part) becomes progressively more erratic the further the process point is removed from the point of the original demand for finished goods.

Literal Reproduction of Original English-Language Document

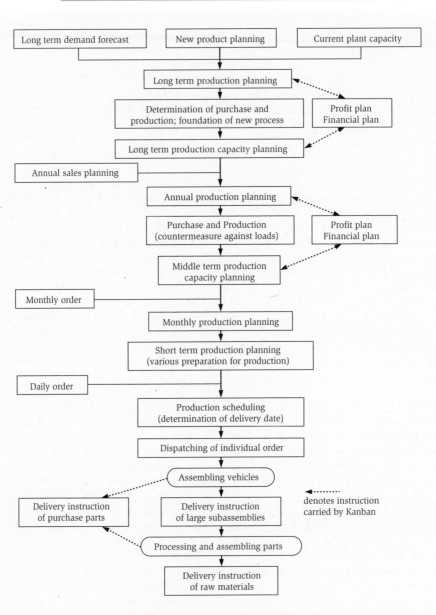

Figure 1. Structure of production planning

Preceding processes become required to have surplus capacity, and it is more liable to have waste of over-producing.

3.2 *Description of Kanban System*

(1) In the Kanban System, a form of order card called Kanban is used. These come in two kinds, one of which is called 'conveyance Kanban' that is carried when going from one process to the preceding process. The other is called 'production Kanban' and is used to order production of the portion withdrawn by the subsequent process.

These two kinds of Kanban are always attached to the containers holding parts.

(2) When content of a container begins to be used, conveyance Kanban is removed from the container. A worker takes this conveyance Kanban and goes to the stock point of the preceding process to pick up this part. He then attaches this conveyance Kanban to the container holding this part.

(3) Then, the 'Production Kanban' attached to the container is removed and becomes a dispatching information for the process. They produce the part to replenish what has been withdrawn as early as possible.

(4) Thus, the production activities of the final assembly line are connected in a manner like a chain to the preceding processes or to the subcontractors and materialize the just-in-time production of the entire processes.

The flow of parts and Kanban are as shown in Fig. 2.

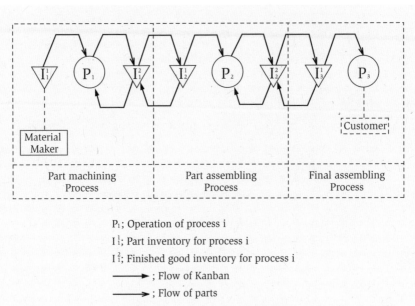

P$_i$; Operation of process i

I$_i^1$; Part inventory for process i

I$_i^2$; Finished good inventory for process i

———▶ ; Flow of Kanban

———▶ ; Flow of parts

Figure 2. Flow of parts and Kanban

The equation for calculating the number of Kanban that play the most important part in this system is as follows:

Let, y = Number of Kanban

D = Demand per unit time

T_w = Waiting time of Kanban

T_p = Processing time

a = Container capacity (not more than 10% of daily requirement)

α = Policy variable (not over 10%)

Then, $y = \dfrac{D\,(T_w + T_p)\,(1 + \alpha)}{a}$

Literal Reproduction of Original English-Language Document

3.3 *Notable points of operations of Kanban System*
—Meaning of the equation computing number of Kanban—

In order to materialize Toyota production system through Kanban System, we do not accept each factor as a given condition, but we attach importance to modify each by means of positive improvements.

(1) α is a policy variable which is determined according to a workshop's capability to manage external interference.

(2) D is determined with a smoothed demand.

(3) Value of y is rather fixed despite variation of D. Therefore, when D increases, it is required to reduce the value of $(T_p + T_w)$, that is, a lead time. At a workshop with insufficient capability of improvement, they cannot avoid overtime for a while. They might even cause line-stops. However, the ultimate objective of Toyota Production System is to visualize such wastes as overtime and line-stop, and to urge each workshop to become capable in improvement. Incapable shops might have to cope with the situation by means of increasing α, that is, number of Kanban for the time being. Hence, the top managers consider the value of α as an indicator of shop capability in improvement.

(4) In the case that demands decreases, the lead time becomes relatively larger. Consequently waste of increasing idleness becomes visible, which is an object of improvement called 'Syojinka'—to decrease the number of workers as demand (production) decreases.

(5) Work-in-process inventory could become much less by conducting an improvement to reduce the value of a, α, and $(T_p + T_w)$.

What Toyota considers as a goal through Kanban System related above is total conveyor line production system connecting all the external and internal processes with invisible conveyor lines. Because a set of values of a, α, and T_w is 0, 1, and 0, respectively, which means nothing but attributes of a conveyor line. All the parts that constitute a vehicle are processed and assembled on a conveyor line, raising its added value. Finally they come out as a completed vehicle one by one. On occurrence of troubles, the whole line may stop, but it begins to move again immediately. Toyota Production System is a scheme seeking realization of such an ideal conveyor line system, and Kanban is a conveyer connecting all the processes.

4. Expansion of just-in-time production by reduction of setup times of pressing dies

In applying the concept of just-in-time production for reduction of lead times and work-in-process inventory, we faced difficulty in press shops practising lot production. After discussing a solution of this difficulty in lot production, we concluded that lead time was proportional to setup times, using the following illustration.

Let, T = Operation time a day or 480 minutes

S = Total setup time for all products, assuming that S is independent of sequence of products

t_{mi} = Unit processing time for the ith product

d_i = Demand for the ith product per day

x = Lead time for all products (in number of days)

Q_i = Lot size for the ith product

Then, $T \cdot x = S + \sum_i t_{mi} \cdot d_i \cdot x$

Hence, x $= \dfrac{S}{T - \sum_i t_{mi} \cdot d_i}$

Literal Reproduction of Original English-Language Document

Lead time is proportional to setup times for a given set of t_{mi} and d_i for all i = 1, 2, ..., n. And lot size for each product Q_i is: $Q_i = d_i \cdot x$ for all i = 1, 2, ..., n.

Improvements in production engineering have been made so as to reduce setup times since 1971. We have succeeded in reducing setup time down to ten minutes at 800 ton line pressing hood, fender and others, while it used to take one hour. (Under the present condition of western countries, four to six hours as shown in Table 1).

Table 1. Press plant productivity characteristics (hood and fender).

	Toyota	A (U.S.A.)	B (Sweden)	C (W. Germany)
Setup time (hour)	0.2	6	4	4
Number of setups a day	3	1	—	0.5
Lot size	1 day-use*	10 days-use	1 month-use	—
Strokes per hour	500–550	300	—	—

*For less demanded products (below 1,000 units per month), as large as 7 days-use.

5. The result = the present condition of Toyota

As related above, Toyota has built up a unique production system through its history of more than 20 years. The results are as follows:

(1) Labour productivity is the highest among automotive industries of major countries. (Table 2)

(2) Turnover rate of working asset is also extremely high. (Table 3).

(3) Number of proposals and rate of acceptance in a proposal system shows the condition that workers positively participate in improvement. (Table 4).

Literal Reproduction of Original English-Language Document

Table 2. Man-hours for completion of a vehicle in automotive assembly plants of major countries.

	Takaoka Plant of Toyota	A (U.S.A.)	B (Sweden)	C (W. Germany)
Number of employees	4,300	3,800	4,700	9,200
Number of outputs a day	2,700	1,000	1,000	3,400
Man-hours for completion of vehicle	1.6	3.8	4.7	2.7

Table 3. Turnover ratio of working assets in automotive companies of major countries.

	Toyota	A (Japan)	B (U.S.A.)	C (U.S.A.)
1960	41	13	7	8
1965	66	13	5	5
1970	63	13	6	6

Table 4. Transition of number of annual proposals per capita and acceptance rate.

	Total number of proposals	Number of proposals per capita	Acceptance
1965	9,000	1.0	39%
1970	40,000	2.5	70
1973	247,000	12.2	76
1976	380,000	15.3	83

References

JAPAN INDUSTRIAL MANAGEMENT ASSOCIATION, 1975, *Handbook of Industrial Engineering* (in Japanese) (Tokyo: Maruzen).

MURAMATSU, R., 1977, *Production Planning and Production Control* (in Japanese) (Tokyo: Kigyo-shindan-Tsushin-Gakuin).

MURAMATSU, R., 1976, *Production Control* (in Japanese (Tokyo: Asakura-Shoten).

TOYOTA MOTOR CO., LTD., 1973, *Toyota Production System* (in Japanese) (unpublished).

Chapter V

Total Quality Control and the Toyota Production System

A Talk by **Masao Nemoto**

As recorded and edited by **Koichi Shimokawa** *and*
Takahiro Fujimoto *with* **Nobuya Orihashi**

The Talk

This is the first time that I have spoken publicly on the subject of total quality control (TQC) in connection with the Toyota Production System. I have been reluctant to stand before an audience and trumpet Toyota's

About the Text

This chapter presents a talk given in July 1997 by Masao Nemoto, a former Toyota executive. As with the talk by Michikazu Tanaka presented in chapter 2, the audience was a study group convened through the Japan Technology Transfer Association and chaired and cochaired by the editors of this volume. That study group, as explained elsewhere, comprises automotive production engineers and university researchers and has met regularly since 1991 to develop a vision for production systems in the automobile and automotive parts industries. The text presented here reflects subsequent editing by Nemoto.

Toyota's surging competitiveness in the late 1970s owed a lot to the Toyota Production System, as conceived and promoted by Taiichi Ohno. But it also owed a lot to TQC. The long-term contribution of TQC to Toyota's competitiveness was entirely comparable to that of the Toyota Production System.

accomplishments. I certainly don't want to give the impression that we did something fantastic at Toyota, something above and beyond what other companies accomplished with TQC. But the organizers of this gathering have insisted that I tell you about our experience. So I have done my best to prepare a talk that will fulfill their expectations.

Here are four things that are pertinent to our subject for today and that I have discussed previously in talks: supplier relations, dealer relations, labor-management relations, and management of the transition to mass production. As for supplier relations, I could easily talk to you off the cuff for an hour and a half about building long-term supplier relationships and about involving suppliers in product development, starting in the earliest stages.

As for dealer relations, Japanese dealers do not switch freely among automakers, like their American counterparts do. Toyota dealers provide valuable feedback to Toyota's product development divisions about customer trends. A dealership that handles a Toyota model has a sense of

Students of Toyota's competitiveness tend to devote more attention to the Toyota Production System than to TQC. The academic and business literatures abound with books and articles about the Toyota Production System. Little has appeared in print, however, about TQC at Toyota, a notable exception being a 1995 study compiled at Hosei University (Center for Business and Industrial Research [now the Research Institute for Information Management], Hosei University, *Nihon Kigyo no Hinshitsu Kanri* [Quality Control at Japanese Companies], Tokyo: Yuhikaku, 1995). That is presumably because the Toyota Production System was an original invention, albeit an extension of Ford's system, and thus rewards the researcher with a wealth of unique material. TQC, in contrast, was something that Toyota adopted from external sources.

What is more, Toyota was a relative latecomer to TQC. Companies in other industrial sectors adopted TQC well before Toyota. Even in the automotive

ownership in that model, and the dealer has a vested interest in helping Toyota increase the customer appeal of the next-generation model. All of Japan's automakers, however, have that kind of relationship with their dealers [so competition is intense].

As for labor-management relations, they are not adversarial. We had an adversarial relationship in 1950, and a labor dispute nearly brought down the company. Things were touch and go for the next 10 years. But by 1960, people had come to terms with each other sufficiently to issue a declaration of labor-management solidarity.

As for managing the transition to mass production, the term concurrent engineering has taken hold recently in the United States. Well, we were doing that 30 years ago. The guys in production engineering are waiting on the guys in product development. They finally get tired of waiting and go take a look at what's going on. What they find is some half-finished product diagrams. So they get some copies of the diagrams and take them back to the shop and set to work on new production processes.

---

sector, the Toyota affiliate and parts supplier Nippondenso (now Denso) was an earlier adopter, as was Toyota's rival Nissan. Toyota displayed a great deal of originality, however, in implementing TQC, and that originality reinforced the competitive benefits that it derived from the methodology. Innovative approaches were notably apparent in the ways that Toyota put in place a framework to ensure the lasting effectiveness of TQC measures; systematically encouraged its suppliers to adopt the methodology; elicited active participation at every level of the company, from senior executives to line workers; and promoted TQC through policy management (*hoshin kanri*)—the technique whereby Toyota famously translates overall goals into concrete targets for each organizational unit.

This record of Nemoto's talk addresses the unfortunate and long-standing dearth of commentary about TQC at Toyota. It is a trove of insight from

In the United States, the product development people apparently retain absolute control over the design specifications, and my understanding is that they don't release them to the production engineering people until the specs are final. That's too late to get things done on time in the factory, so the production engineering people in Japan do whatever is necessary to get hold of the design specs earlier. They can do that because of the generally good relations among product development, production engineering, and manufacturing. That's why the Americans came up with the term concurrent engineering to describe how we work. And even we in Japan have adopted the term in the interest of making things easier to understand.

Toyota's approach is a combination of TQC and the Toyota Production System. Our approach also addresses the four themes that I have just mentioned [supplier relations, dealer relations, labor-management relations, and management of the transition to mass production], along with human relations development and other things.

---

an individual who participated directly in implementing that methodology in the Toyota workplace. Nemoto's comments will prove hugely enlightening for anyone interested in quality control or in production technology.

About the Speaker

Masao Nemoto was a central figure in deploying TQC at Toyota in the 1960s. He joined Toyota Motor in 1943 and later served in a series of general manager positions as the head of the production control division, a machining division, and the purchasing control division.

Nemoto became the inaugural general manager of the purchasing control division when Toyota created that unit in 1965, and in that capacity he promoted and supervised the adoption of TQC at Toyota suppliers. He subsequently served as a managing director and as a senior managing director

That brings me to a book that came out of the United States a few years ago called *The Machine That Changed the World* (James Womack, Daniel Jones, and Daniel Roos [New York: HarperCollins, 1991]). That book presents the findings of a research consortium based at the Massachusetts Institute of Technology (MIT). It's a truly excellent book. Its one really disappointing flaw is that it fails to mention the role of TQC in lean manufacturing. It's a pretty thick book, but even where it mentions quality control, it leaves off the *T* [for total].

I have a theory about why *The Machine That Changed the World* omits TQC in its description of Toyota's approach. My theory is that the lead author at MIT wanted to issue a warning to U.S. manufacturing industries. I think he recognized that the United States faced a serious threat from Japan, that Japan was equipped with a superb production system, that American managers urgently needed to study that production system, and that stirring industry to action would depend on capturing the attention of senior management.

at Toyota before moving in 1982 to the Toyota affiliate Toyoda Gosei. There, Nemoto served as president and later as chairman. He was a member of the faculty of Aichi Gakuin University at the time he gave the talk presented here.

The several books that Nemoto wrote about TQC include one that is available in English as *Total Quality Control for Management: Strategies and Techniques from Toyota and Toyoda Gosei* (trans. David Lu [Upper Saddle River, New Jersey: Pearson Education, 1987]). Nemoto passed away in March 2002 at the age of 82.

Masao Nemoto as a Toyota senior managing director

The author presumably felt that writing about quality control would be an ineffective way to convey the necessary sense of urgency. After all, quality control was an American invention, and the Japanese version of TQC was merely a broader application of that invention. To attribute Japan's growing competitiveness to TQC would be unconvincing and even insulting to American executives. I assume that the author was fully aware of the importance of TQC to Japanese manufacturing but that he chose to omit TQC from the book's discussion of lean manufacturing for the reasons I've mentioned.

Japanese readers of *The Machine That Changed the World* need to keep in mind the book's crucial omission. Otherwise, they could come away with a serious misunderstanding: that simply using the Toyota Production System is all they need to do to achieve higher quality. To be sure, quality does improve with the Toyota Production System. But the system does not provide for improving all aspects of quality.

Here is what the Toyota Production System says about quality, as you can read in all the books and articles about the system: If you notice a defect, stop the line. That's a wonderful way to raise quality awareness, but it only works with problems that people can see. Workers can over-look problems that are not readily visible. And a lot of quality issues with automobiles are not apparent to the eye of the worker on the line. That includes things like high-speed performance, noise, vibration, durability, and reliability. So you can't make quality automobiles without using TQC activities.

1. The Reasons for Adopting TQC

TQC is, as its name suggests, about managing quality comprehensively. Americans seem to favor the term TQM, for total quality management, over TQC. That's because, in the United States, quality control implies something just for people in the workplace to do, something that doesn't require the attention of senior management. The term QC, as used in Japanese, refers to the same thing that people call QM in English. Using different terms for the same thing can be confusing, so people have started using the term QM in Japanese, too. But I'm here today to talk to you about history, so I'll use the old term.

Toyota announced in 1961 that it would adopt TQC. At that time, TQC was emerging as a potent force in Japanese manufacturing. Toyota [though a relative latecomer to TQC] was soon among the leading practitioners. And TQC helped Toyota become a pioneering winner of the Deming Application Prize [for company-wide quality management, in 1965].

Companies that adopt TQC usually do so for one of two reasons. At some companies, people are aware of serious problems with quality that they are eager to fix. At other companies, people are not necessarily certain where they stand in regard to quality, but they adopt TQC because everyone else is or because someone urges them to do so. We at Toyota came to TQC with the frank admission that we had problems with quality and with a determination to do something about those problems. We adopted TQC more enthusiastically than people did at companies that were less forthright about acknowledging problems with quality.

Eiji Toyoda was an executive vice president at our company at that time and was responsible for product technology, production engineering, and manufacturing. He took the initiative in declaring that we had problems with quality and in calling for us to tackle those problems with TQC. His commitment provided crucial momentum to our efforts.

One of the problems we had was a rising rate of defects detected in our factories. We had doubled the size of our workforce over the five years to 1961, and our production volume had increased fivefold. We were pouring people into the workplace without providing them with sufficient training. And quality suffered as a result.

Another problem we had was the failure of our Toyopet Crown in the U.S. market. We had begun producing that model in 1955, and I was a production manager on the Crown assembly line. Our product strategy centered on marketing the Crown in Japan to use as taxis and as chauffeured transport for corporate executives. Management decided after a couple of years to try exporting the Crown to the United States and shipped a few across the Pacific for trial marketing. The exports would earn dollars and thereby help Japan import food and other essentials. We'd be doing a service to our nation and to our fellow citizens. Unfortunately, the car was utterly unappealing to U.S. customers.

The biggest problem with the Crown was lousy high-speed performance. The car took forever to get up to speed after pulling onto a freeway, and the poor driver would soon hear angry honking from oncoming cars behind. When the car finally did get up to a speed of 100 kilometers per hour (about 60 miles per hour), it rattled and shook and became wholly unpleasant to be riding in. Japan didn't have any freeways yet, so Japanese customers didn't need a car that could cruise easily and comfortably at 100 kilometers per hour. But a car that couldn't do that would never sell in the United States.

Another problem with the Crown was that it broke down a lot. Driving one across the desert from Los Angeles to Las Vegas would be genuinely

risky. You'd face a real chance of breaking down somewhere along the way. Getting stuck in the desert can be a life-threatening experience. Nobody would want a car like that. So we gave up on the Crown in the U.S. market and brought home the unsold cars.

Toyota's Toyopet Crown, launched in 1955

The failure of the Crown in the United States was, of course, a big disappointment. Around that time, the people at our affiliate Nippondenso suggested that we give TQC a try. Nippondenso had been using TQC for two or three years [though they didn't call it TQC], and the people there reported that it was extremely effective. They said that TQC heightened quality awareness among employees; that everyone shared ideas about ways to solve problems; that TQC promoted cooperation among the people in product technology, production engineering, and manufacturing; and that it mobilized employees throughout the company in kaizen initiatives through team activities.

That's how we at Toyota ended up tackling TQC. We went to work on TQC in 1961, and we earned the Deming Application Prize in 1965 and the Japan Quality Medal [from the Union of Japanese Scientists and Engineers] in 1970. What is most important is that our quality really did improve dramatically over that time. And around 1970, our exports to the United States finally took off.

TQC was thus a success at Toyota. It succeeded because we acknowledged forthrightly that we had problems with quality and because someone in senior management [Eiji Toyoda] had a clear vision of what we were setting out to do.

2. Thorough Training

Starting at the top

When a company adopts TQC, senior management needs to take the lead in studying how the methodology works. I was once helping put TQC in place at a Toyota dealership. The president said to me, "We're doing TQC because that's what Toyota told us to do. Frankly, I don't think that TQC will do one bit of good for our company. I'm the president here, but I have no intention of taking part in the study sessions. I'll send one of our managing directors instead."

The president at that dealership was sure that TQC would pass by the wayside sooner or later. He figured that he simply needed to wait things out. That was despite the fact that presidents at other companies were taking part actively in learning and adopting the methodology. The lack of direct participation of the president would mean that TQC would never take hold at that dealership. And TQC did indeed get off to a poor start there.

I was a senior managing director at Toyota by then, and I announced that I'd take part personally in overseeing the TQC preparations at the dealership. I gave instructions for all the managers and above at the dealership to gather for the next study session. The president could hardly skip the session if a senior executive from Toyota was going to be there. So he attended, and he finally began to see that his company would be missing out on something important by not adopting TQC.

At a dinner gathering after the study session, the president said to me, "Nemoto-san, you said you were coming to hold a study session for our managers. The study session was really for me, wasn't it?" He was right, of course. I'd come myself because we needed to get the president to take part in the training. And no sooner did he begin to take part than he saw the light and got the spirit.

More than seminars

Lots of training programs begin and end with seminars. But just participating in a seminar doesn't give you real understanding of anything. To gain a real understanding, you need to take what you've heard in a seminar, put it into practice in your own workplace, and show your boss how it can generate results.

Hearing something in a seminar corresponds to the planning phase [of the plan-do-check-act cycle]. Learning depends on doing in the workplace, undergoing a follow-up check by your superiors, and determining what action is necessary to make things work better. Only then have you really learned what you heard or saw in the seminar.

I head up to Tokyo sometimes to give the closing lecture in a course for section and division managers at the Union of Japanese Scientists and Engineers. The participants will go back to their companies and thank their superiors for giving them the chance to undergo the training. And I ask them what their superiors are likely to say. No one has ever given me a convincing answer.

I wonder if any bosses out there will ask the managers who come back from the seminar something like this: "What did you hear that left an especially strong impression? What did you learn that you want to try out immediately in the workplace here? Let me know what you want to try. Then, have a go at it and report back to me in a couple of months about the results." A few bosses like that might exist, but they are few and far between, and we can only envy the companies where they work.

When my managers came back from seminars, I always reminded them that some things they'd learned would be useful immediately and that some would take time to jell. I'd note that things that might not seem useful at the moment might prove useful a few years down the line. I'd tell them to keep track of everything they'd learned and to start with the stuff that promises immediate results.

Monitoring managers' growth

As I've said, we'd start with the annual policy, and the section managers would go to work on their allotted targets under the policy. We'd hold review sessions where we'd ask the managers how they were doing.

Sometimes, the division managers would run the review sessions, and sometimes someone more senior would take charge.

The abilities of the section managers would be crystal clear. The good ones would say something like this: "We tried our idea for two months. Things didn't go very well, so we tried some new things. That seemed to do the trick, and we're looking for ways to iron out the remaining problems."

In contrast, some managers would simply say, "We tried an idea, but it didn't work out." You can't give a passing grade to people like that. A company that had a lot of managers like that would need to provide training to set things right.

Fostering the spirit of "quality first"

The need for this should be obvious.

Building quality into processes

Everybody naturally talks a lot about quality when a company starts using quality control. The folks in the workplace tend to assume at first that rigorous inspection is all that needs to happen. They'll rest easily as long as the company assigns a lot of people to the inspection processes. I remember thinking along those lines myself. The idea of building quality assurance into the production processes never came to mind.

Eiji Toyoda had the right idea when he said, "You can't rely on the inspections. You've got to take responsibility in your processes for providing output of the necessary quality." His words still resound in my ears. He was insistent about building quality assurance into every process.

3. Strengthening Interdivisional Cooperation

I'm concentrating on management issues in my remarks today. I've managed a whole plant, and I've been a production manager on the plant floor, but I don't want to bore anyone with technical explanations. So I'll try to focus on elements of my experience that are illuminating from the standpoint of management.

The following process as the customer

In TQC, we talk about the following process as the customer. That's different from the ordinary concept of customer. People usually think of the customer as someone outside the company—someone to whom a manufacturer delivers a finished product. At Toyota, that would be the vehicle dealerships, and their customers would be the people who buy cars and trucks.

We tell our people to treat the following process as the customer, even though it's inside the company. We train people to do everything possible to avoid causing problems for the following process. That put things in a whole new light for me when I first encountered the concept. After all, the people in different processes aren't actually exchanging goods and cash. The guys in the following process can't complain about paying a high price for shoddy work.

Another thing you hear at Toyota is that we should seek the causes of problems in upstream processes. When you get a complaint from the following process, you can't necessarily solve the problem in your process. You do everything possible in your process, and if that's not enough, you go to the production engineering people and ask them to take a look at the upstream processes. Everyone needs to understand their process in the context of the whole manufacturing sequence.

Here's an experience I had when I got back to the workplace after four months of seminar training in Tokyo. I was the general manager of the production control division at the time. That division has three functions: issue monthly production instructions, issue daily production instructions, and manage the inventories of parts and materials purchased from suppliers.

One time, we started having problems with cracking in stampings. The problem had never occurred before, and it only happened when we used sheet metal from a particular coil. It didn't happen with any other coil. We soon discovered that the problem coil was old. That was interesting. I had never thought that sheet metal had a "good until" useful life, like food products do. Although I had majored in mechanical engineering in college, I had never heard that sheet metal deteriorates. But it does.

So we figured out that an old coil was to blame for the cracking. The guys in the stamping shop said that we in production control weren't doing inventory management right, that we weren't handling stuff on a first-in, first-out basis. We had an old coil sitting in the back of the storage place, and problems occurred when we pulled it out to use.

I assumed that one of my people was failing to abide by first in, first out, and I went to take a look. When I got to the workplace, I found that the inventory management was taking place properly on a first-in, first-out basis. The design and layout of the process ensured that the first coils that came in would be the first ones taken out. Production control was not the source of the problem. It wasn't my fault!

In the United States, that would have been the end of the story on our end. "It's not our fault. Get out of here." But that's not how we operate in Japan. And responding like that would have run counter to everything we were trying to do with TQC. We had received some important information, for which we should be grateful. We had encountered an opportunity to do kaizen, so we should be happy.

We had determined that the problem was not with production control. So we needed to seek the cause of the problem in upstream processes. In this case, that meant the steelmaker. I went to the steelmaker's plant, and I found a mountain of inventory at the shipping dock. Anyone could see that new and old coils could easily get mixed up there. I talked with the steelmaker's production control manager and asked why they kept so much inventory sitting around like that.

Steelmaker: This is Toyota's fault. Toyota issues monthly production instructions, but we work with longer lead times than that in steelmaking. A month's notice doesn't give us enough time to respond, since we're working with two-month lead times in production planning. Toyota makes changes all the time in its purchasing volumes. We can't handle sudden increases in demand on a monthly basis. So we put aside a little when we have some extra output to have ready when needed.

Nemoto: I see. So the problem was with our production instructions. All right, we'll come up with some way to accommodate [the longer lead times in production planning in] steelmaking. But please get rid of this extra inventory.

Steelmaker: That'll be great. We'll be happy to get rid of the inventory. We'd prefer not to have this much on hand, but we needed it to keep Toyota happy.

So we came up with different scheduling in our purchasing of sheet metal to accommodate the steelmakers. That was necessary on account of the long lead times in steelmaking, and it didn't have any effect on our purchasing from other suppliers. And it solved the problem of cracking in stampings!

Managing things by function

Manufacturing proceeds through the sequence from design to preparations for mass production to factory production to sales. Interaction among different sectors of that sequence can become difficult in large-scale operations. People tend to lose a sense of involvement in the larger sequence and to focus entirely on their own territory. When problems occur, they're prone to say something like, "Don't ask me. That's a design problem."

In U.S. management science, organizing things by function in integrated, semiautonomous units is the standard formula for organizing large-scale operations. The companies assign performance targets to the units, and the heads of the units lose their jobs if they fail to meet the targets. That's not practical in automobile manufacturing because of the close interaction between design, preparations for mass production, factory production, and sales. Dividing those functions into highly autonomous units would make our work impossible. Close interaction is especially crucial in design, where people from manufacturing need to help fabricate prototypes, and in preparations for mass production, where the designers need to participate in things up to the last minute.

Here's how we tackled the challenge of addressing issues on a function-by-function basis while maintaining good cross-functional interaction. We focused people's attention on the issue of quality in every sector of operations. When we were getting a lot of customer complaints about something or if we had even a single really serious product defect, we'd get everyone together. Everyone was focusing on their own territory, and their natural first response was to make excuses. Each person at the meeting would insist that their division was doing things properly and that some other division was surely to blame for the problem.

Whatever problem we were gathered to discuss was a problem for the company as a whole. And simply exchanging denials for blame wasn't going to solve the problem. But getting people to see that was no easy matter.

Toyota strengthened quality assurance and other cross-divisional functions by putting senior executives in charge of those functions. Figure 1 shows some examples of divisional functions—the vertical columns—and of cross-divisional functions—the horizontal rows. The person in charge of a divisional function was usually a general manager, who was sometimes also a member of the board of directors. We assigned the cross-divisional functions to managing directors and even to senior managing directors. They had no direct connection with any division, and they were senior to the guys in charge of the divisions.

The section managers appear in the figure as circles. They answered to the general managers in charge of their divisions, but they also needed to pay heed to the even more senior executives who were in charge of cross-divisional functions, including quality assurance. That was a new approach in our industry.

U.S. management theory has emphasized the importance of clear lines of command. The idea is that each person should have one boss. That emphasis has a long tradition and European roots. The assumption is that

Fig. 1: Divisional and Cross-Divisional Functions

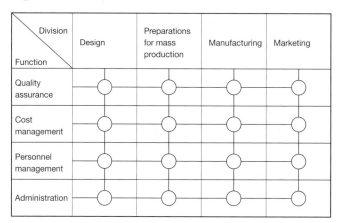

Function \ Division	Design	Preparations for mass production	Manufacturing	Marketing
Quality assurance	◯	◯	◯	◯
Cost management	◯	◯	◯	◯
Personnel management	◯	◯	◯	◯
Administration	◯	◯	◯	◯

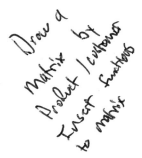

a company suffers from any lack of clarity in who people are supposed to report to. We all study the concept of one man, one boss in school, but we encounter the need for a different kind of command structure when we go to work in companies. We need divisional bosses, but we also need bosses for the cross-divisional functions.

The need for cross-divisional authority is especially pressing in regard to quality assurance. A company needs to pursue quality assurance vigorously, even if that entails sacrificing some efficiency at the divisional level. Focusing narrowly on optimizing things by division will prevent you from optimizing things at the company level. Optimizing things in parts does not add up to optimizing things as a whole.

Since we didn't operate on a one-man, one-boss basis, we didn't entrust personnel evaluations entirely to the divisional heads. The division general managers would tend to evaluate employee performance from the perspective of their own interests. That would reinforce the tendency to optimize in parts rather than optimizing as a whole. So we secured the participation of the heads of the cross-divisional functions in evaluating employee performance. An employee whose work spanned multiple cross-divisional functions would receive evaluations from multiple executives.

So we operated on a one-man, multiple-bosses basis, rather than a one-man, one-boss basis. Most of the companies in the automobile industry now use that approach in one way or another. But Toyota was already using it [in the 1960s].

Eiji Toyoda was a great believer in the importance of interdivisional cooperation. He was an executive vice president then and was in charge of product technology, production engineering, and manufacturing. Whenever we held a gathering of production managers, he'd show up and call for more cooperation among the divisions.

The U.S. practice of dividing operations by function into semiautonomous units was becoming popular in Japan. But as I have mentioned, that doesn't work in the automobile industry, and all of our senior executives were emphatic about the continuing need for interdivisional cooperation. The president would also emphasize that need to everyone at every opportunity. For example, he'd address all the managers at an annual gathering, and cooperation among divisions would always be one of the two or three priorities that he'd discuss. That continued for 10 years or so.

4. Emphasizing Kaizen Capabilities

Plan-do-check-act (PDCA) cycles are fundamental to TQC. They correspond to the traditional threesome of plan, do, and see. "See," in English-speaking environments, carries a broad meaning that easily encompasses the notion of monitoring results. Japanese, however, tend to regard "see" in the narrowest sense of mere visual perception. We therefore opted for the term "check" to denote seeing in a proactive sense. The addition of the fourth element, act, completes the cycle [of planning, implementing, monitoring results, and taking suitable follow-up measures].

Systematic planning and concrete targets

We adopted PDCA cycles as part of our TQC at Toyota. PDCA, as conventionally taught, was mainly a tool for maintaining quality and productivity. We were more interested in raising quality and productivity, and we made several adjustments in the PDCA methodology for that purpose.

An especially important adjustment was to establish a systematic approach in the planning stage, as well as establishing concrete targets. And we made sure that the checking stage included careful evaluation of how fully we had attained our targets and how well our approach had worked. That might sound obvious enough, but it was a big change from how we had operated at first.

Our initial approach had consisted of little more than establishing kaizen targets and then telling people to *"gambare!"* (just do it!). Japanese love to urge people on with that word in sports, in the workplace, in school, and in every setting imaginable. That's a wonderful way to cheer the home team on in athletic events, where each athlete knows his or her role and the cheering helps the team members summon a little extra energy and concentration. But "just do it!" is hardly sufficient as guidance for employees in tackling a complex kaizen project.

For example, a team of employees might be tackling the target of reducing defects 50% in a year. Saying "just do it!" doesn't tell any of them what they need to do to achieve that target. So we work out a crystal-clear approach that provides a solid framework for allocating individual responsibilities.

Attaining targets through effective and sustainable processes, rather than just attaining them by any means available, is the essence of TQC. Our emphasis on establishing a systematic approach in PDCA was largely responsible for the surge in kaizen that we achieved (fig. 2).

To be sure, simply trying harder can improve performance in some cases, even in the absence of a systematic approach. Brokerage firms and real estate agencies can increase their revenues sometimes by simply getting their salespeople to make more calls. Companies occasionally even reap windfall profits without doing anything, simply as a result of changes in the business environment. Even

Fig. 2: Targets and Policy in the Context of PDCA

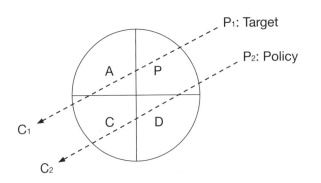

P_1: Target
P_2: Policy

in manufacturing, external events, like advantageous shifts in currency exchange rates, can raise profitability. But you can rarely achieve any lasting improvement in workplace performance, such as lower defect rates, without a systematic approach.

Value engineering

I was once responsible for overseeing Toyota's 10 production engineering divisions. In the first year, the budget requests from the divisions totaled more than ¥150 billion. I pared the total down to ¥150 billion and took our budgeting proposal to the executive vice president (EVP) in charge. Here's what ensued.

EVP: I can't sign off on ¥150 billion. Cut it 20%.

Nemoto: If we're going to cut our production engineering budget 20%, shall we also reduce the number of model changes 20%?

EVP: Don't be ridiculous. We do what we need to do. And you do your part with 20% less spending.

Nemoto: Do you seriously think that's possible? If that was possible, we would have been doing it a long time ago.

EVP: That's what your brain is for. That's why we put you in charge of production engineering.

Nemoto: So I'm supposed to come up with a way?

EVP: That's right.

So I went to work on coming up with a way to complete our assigned mission while trimming our budget. That budget was the result of a lot of careful planning and calculation and negotiation. So cutting it 20% would be no easy matter. When I was in charge of purchasing, we worked with suppliers in value engineering activities to lower parts costs while maintaining quality and performance. The idea occurred to me that we could use value engineering to reduce our investment expenditures. I gathered the division general managers to explain what I had in mind. They were predictably opposed to the idea. Here is an exchange that ensued with one of them.

General manager: You accomplished your value engineering results with vehicle parts. But production engineering is a completely different story. With parts, you start with drawings and put together prototypes. Next, you evaluate the prototypes and prepare revised drawings based on your findings. Only then do you move on to mass production. In production engineering, we only get one shot. We prepare the drawings and then make the equipment based on those drawings. If we get something wrong, we don't have the opportunity for trial and error like you do in developing parts.

Nemoto: I see what you mean. And I figured that's what you would say. But I'm determined to get the budget down 20%. That's our mandate from above, and I want you to work with me to see if we can't do something. I'm thinking that we ought to be able to use value engineering in some way to do that, and I want you all to go back to your divisions and give this some thought. Talk about it with your people and see what you can come up with.

We all got together a week later for another meeting. Here is an exchange that took place at that meeting.

Nemoto: So did you come up with anything?

General manager: Yes.

Nemoto: Well?

General manager: Take a look at this.

What the general manager then showed me was a metal plate of the kind that machinists use to check flatness. It was a standard tool, but it represented a large platform big enough to drive a car onto. We used big precision plates like that to check how much the height of cars shifted at different positions during endurance testing.

When we ordered the plates from specialized manufacturers, we specified the dimensions. But we were always too busy to bother checking the drawings carefully. The general manager and his people had taken a fresh look at the drawings. What they found was that the platforms sported beautifully finished surfaces on their sides and bottom, as well as on their top.

The plates in question were something that we never put on display. They sat in holes dug in the ground in product-testing shops. The purchasing inspector would glimpse at the sides and bottom of the plates when we took delivery. After that, no human eye would light on those surfaces for years or even decades.

All of this is to say that providing the bottom and sides of the plates with a lovely finish served no purpose whatsoever. And dispensing with that finishing would reduce the cost of the plates about 20%.

The example of the precision plates inspired a wave of value engineering activities. I established a set of procedures for those activities. Every Tuesday became a sounding day for value engineering proposals. I put a poster on the door to my office that urged everyone to participate in the value engineering activities, and we set aside time on Tuesdays to air ideas.

Each division prepared a growing set of case studies. That started when the people in one of the divisions set out to gather some examples of value engineering activities and ended up with a surprisingly large number. The general manager of that division told me that they'd be putting the case studies in a pamphlet, and I asked him to give me a copy when it was ready.

I told the other divisions about the pamphlet, and they all went to work on their own sets of case studies. I never told anyone to make such a thing, but the divisions ended up competing to prepare better compilations of case studies. A big reason that everyone liked making the pamphlets was that people's names appeared on the case studies. Appearing in a pamphlet was like winning an award.

We also secured the cooperation of the equipment manufacturers in our effort. That included holding a value engineering exposition in a gymnasium. We asked the manufacturers to exhibit equipment that they supplied to Toyota that provided good examples of value engineering. They could exhibit diagrams instead of equipment if the equipment was too big to put on display.

Just like the case study pamphlets, our exposition triggered a spirited competition to present the best examples. The most proactive companies took the opportunity to acquaint their engineering personnel with the principles of value engineering. The presidents at some of those companies took charge personally of the value engineering activities.

On the other hand, some companies were reluctant participants in the exposition. They took part only because we asked them to or only because other suppliers were participating. The difference in attitude was readily apparent in the exhibits. And the companies that displayed a half-hearted commitment lost the confidence of the production engineering people at Toyota. Our people became less inclined to order equipment from those companies.

The purchasing people at Toyota noted that the companies in question were established suppliers, and they sought to continue placing some of our orders with those companies. But people in production engineering and in other sectors demanded to know why we should buy equipment from such uncommitted suppliers. They reminded the purchasing people of those suppliers' miserable showing at the exposition. They argued that buying equipment from those suppliers would undercut our value engineering effort, and they called for shifting our purchasing to more-committed suppliers. Everyone in the sectors concerned at Toyota soon knew which suppliers were taking value engineering seriously.

Planning for the checking

You need to determine in the P (planning) stage of a PDCA cycle when you're going to do the C (checking). You can't just let things ride and decide toward the end of the year that maybe you should start checking on things pretty soon. It's all too easy to let things slip through the cracks. You might have five checks that you're supposed to do and end up deciding that two is enough. The review by the president is especially prone to omission.

Presidents tend to be extremely busy, and ones who aren't strongly committed to TQC frequently evade their responsibility in the check stage of the PDCA sequence. That has a horrible effect on the attitudes of their employees toward TQC. Establishing a clear schedule for the required checks in the planning stage of PDCA helps prevent that problem.

Here's something I did to ensure proper checking in PDCA when I served concurrently as the plant manager of Toyota's Motomachi Plant (which assembles passenger cars) and Miyoshi Plant (which produces drivetrain parts and other components). I prepared a form that required people to fill in information about the policy for conducting PDCA, the measures that we would undertake, the organizational unit responsible for each item, and the schedule for conducting the checks.

My form required descriptions of measures for addressing such issues as quality, cost, safety, pollution, and personnel. The name of the organizational unit responsible for the overall PDCA sequence appeared inside a double circle, and the names of the units responsible for individual parts appeared inside single circles.

We devoted special emphasis to the checking method, and the form required a calendar for doing the checks. I would do my checks as the plant manager in June and December. Those checks were for evaluating our progress in fulfilling our annual policy, and we'd reflect the findings of the December checks in our annual policy for the next year. Those were the most important checks, but we also did others. Some could be extremely troublesome, especially the ones for exhaust emissions.

The adverse effect of emissions on health had become an issue. Governments had adopted strict new regulations for emissions, and we needed to make sure that we complied with those regulations at each model change. As the plant manager, I was responsible for ensuring that our vehicles complied with Toyota's emissions guidelines. We did emissions testing for each vehicle produced at the Motomachi Plant and shipped only vehicles that passed the test.

Designing and developing vehicles to comply with the emissions guidelines was the responsibility of the project managers in the product development divisions. That work frequently came down to the wire. Two or three months before mass production was to begin, the product development people would still be trying to get things right. We'd come down to two or three days before the scheduled start of mass production, and the new model might still be out of line with the guidelines. That would necessitate a judgment call.

Toyota's guidelines were stricter than the government regulations. We had the option of going ahead with mass production as long as the model complied with the government regulations. Alternatively, we might decide to delay the start of mass production. The product project manager, the engineer responsible for the engine, and I would get together to decide what to do. Our decision also went onto the PDCA form. Things like that necessitated lots of checks apart from the June and December checking. I'd make it clear to everyone at the beginning of the year which checks I would handle as the plant manager.

The PDCA form thus presented clearly what we would tackle in cooperation with the product development people, how we would coordinate our efforts with annual policy, how we would monitor activity in the

workplace, how we would obtain reports from the teams about their progress, and other crucial procedures and methods. It also presented a clear
schedule for every activity.

I once gave a talk about this subject at the Japan Society of Business
Administration. People were amazed at the amount of checking that our
approach obliged the plant manager to do. My position is that a plant
manager is inherently responsible for overseeing the activity that I've
described. And my PDCA form helped me fulfill that responsibility by
clarifying what needed to be done and when. Without the form, we'd be
sure to let a lot of things slip by.

5. Kaizen Activities by Group Leaders and Team Leaders

Range of activities

Our group leaders and team leaders tackled kaizen activities across a lot
broader range than their counterparts at other companies. That includes
the range of work covered and the time span covered.

Kaizen presentations by group leaders

I once served as the general manager of a machining division at the
Motomachi Plant. While I was in that position, the group leaders tackled
the task of improving some key processes. The goal that I had assigned
was to build quality assurance into the processes. I used histograms to
illustrate the process capabilities. We used the histograms to take a look
at dimensional variation in the items that came out of the processes.

In the example shown in figure 3, the items were running a little large,
so we needed to shift things a little toward the small side of the acceptable
size range. Some processes were exceeding the tolerances on both ends of

the size spectrum, and we therefore needed to narrow the range of dimensional disparity. In every case, we needed to analyze the reasons for the dimensional variation and undertake kaizen to resolve the problems.

We made this undertaking a job for everyone. Monthly kaizen presentations in the [six sections in my division] became study sessions for the group leaders and for the chief leaders above them. The chief leaders were nearing retirement age, so expecting them to absorb a lot of new ideas was unrealistic. Instead, we focused on the group leaders. And they really took things seriously. Each group leader would make a presentation once every four months. As soon as a group leader had made a presentation, he'd need to get started on kaizen for the next presentation. That got the group leaders thinking about kaizen every day.

Our program for promoting kaizen activities by the group leaders had three main emphases: (1) get the group leaders to understand a new approach, (2) make each participant's progress apparent to the participant and to his superiors, and (3) let everyone know when we had achieved a target. As general manager, I attended all the kaizen presentations for the six sections without fail. My giving top priority to the kaizen presentations underlined the importance of the presentations. It reminded everyone that the boss was taking an active interest in the activities, and that had a motivational effect. And the presentations were inspiring for me.

Here were group leaders whose formal education had ended after elementary school, and they were each

Fig. 3: A Sample Histogram of Process Capacity

giving their all to the kaizen projects. No sooner had they finished one project than they threw themselves wholeheartedly into a new project. Their enthusiasm extended the range of the kaizen activities dramatically.

Distinguishing the group leaders' activities from the QC circle activities

The group leaders were responsible for overseeing QC circle activities, as well as for initiating kaizen projects. I once saw QC circle activities at a company in Shizuoka Prefecture that were comparable to our group leaders' kaizen projects. QC circles were a motivational change of pace for line workers, who performed tasks over and over, all day long. The circles were a chance for those workers to choose a leader and resolve issues that they encountered in their daily work. That said, let's recall that the workers were plenty busy with their daily work. Any effort that they devoted to kaizen was above and beyond the call of duty. On the other hand, kaizen was part of the job description for the group leaders.

I asked the president of that company in Shizuoka if the group leaders at his company did kaizen. The president expressed surprise at the notion of group leaders initiating kaizen. Entrusting all workplace kaizen to QC circles is one way of doing things. But that is to lose sight of the group leaders' crucial responsibility for initiating and supervising kaizen. Group leaders that can't fulfill that responsibility are basically useless.

For the record, QC circles convene two or three times a month at the initiative of the participating line workers. The participants discuss issues that they encounter in the workplace and consider ways of resolving those issues (fig. 4). That occasions progress by workers in honing their capabilities. It fosters a motivating and stimulating workplace. And it thereby contributes to growth for the company.

Honing capabilities and fostering a motivating and stimulating workplace are contributions to corporate vitality that accumulate gradually.

Calling on QC circles to offset a company's red ink in the present fiscal year would be ridiculous. I've seen managements make that mistake, and I always suggest that kaizen conducted by the group leaders is a more-effective way to proceed. The group leaders need to know that they can't just sit around and wait for the QC circles to come up with the necessary improvements. They need to know that they are responsible for taking the initiative.

6. Policy Management in Two Stages

When we at Toyota first went to work on TQC, we adopted it in the context of our annual policy. For example, we'd tried exporting some cars to the United States, and that hadn't worked out very well at all. So we sat down and identified what seemed to be the problem [and how to address that problem in the year ahead]. Our first two years with TQC centered on identifying annual policy for pertinent items, putting our plan in place, carrying out the plan, evaluating our progress, and taking countermeasures as necessary. The idea was to accustom everyone to running PDCA cycles at every level of our organization, from the president down.

We were proceeding like that [on a division-by-division basis] when people started to raise questions about our approach. The people in product development and in personnel would remind us that they were working on stuff to generate results two or maybe three years down the road, and they'd note that achieving

Fig. 4: The Positioning of QC Circles

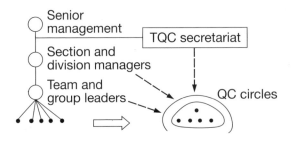

those results would depend on parallel efforts in other divisions. For example, the product development people would say, "We're working on future products, but we can't be sure that we'll have the people we need to make those products happen." Likewise, the people in personnel would say, "We're hiring people on the basis of some long-term assumptions, but we can't be sure that the company will really need the people we're hiring."

Everyone in the company was beginning to notice that we needed a longer-range planning framework than our annual policy provided. So we started preparing long-range policy.

Books about policy management usually start with a discussion of long-term planning. When they talk about adopting TQC, the assumption is that a company will begin by drawing up a long-term plan. But the business environment changes even while the company is preparing that plan, which requires adjustments. That paralyzes progress in adopting TQC at some companies. People feel like they need to wait for the long-term plan to get finalized before they can get started, so they end up doing nothing.

I noticed that waiting on the long-term plan could delay our work on TQC at Toyota, and I was determined not to let that happen. We needed enough flexibility to get started, so we handled things in two stages (fig. 5). The books about this kind of approach would talk about starting by drawing up a long-term plan, and that was only natural. But we actually started with annual policy. For the first couple of years, we simply determined an annual policy, put it in place, carried out the policy, evaluated our progress, and took the necessary countermeasures. The idea, as I've mentioned, was to get everyone used to running PDCA cycles.

People got a feel for the value of annual policy and began to sense the need for longer-term planning. Only then did we move on to stage two in policy management. You need to get moving and keep moving with the annual policy of stage one. You need to do that even if the longer-term stuff of stage two doesn't take shape right away. That's especially important to keep in mind if you learn TQC from a textbook. We at Toyota operated entirely on the basis of annual policy for the first two years.

7. Quality Assurance at Toyota Suppliers

Here is a comment from one of the evaluators when Toyota received the Deming Application Prize: "Toyota itself has improved immensely. But we had a look at some of your parts suppliers, and they still have a long way to go. You're making your vehicles with parts from those suppliers. You won't be able to make really good vehicles until you get your suppliers to raise their level of quality."

That comment was right on the mark. It touched on something that we had sensed, too. We needed to provide our suppliers with guidance and assistance and tackle quality assurance together. And that's exactly what we did. Toyota set up a new division, the purchasing control division, to coordinate guidance and assistance for suppliers. Whoever took charge of that division would have a clear mandate: to help the suppliers achieve TQC comparable to that at Toyota.

Management fretted over the choice of a general manager for the new division. The division would be furnishing technical support, so appointing an engineer seemed

Fig. 5: Two-Stage Policy Management

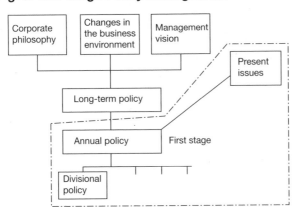

a good idea. But engineers are reluctant to render judgment until the results are all in, and that reluctance can hinder the work of providing necessary direction. Someone who knew that I was passionate about TQC came up with the idea of assigning the job to me. So I became the inaugural general manager of the purchasing control division and spent five years making the rounds of Toyota suppliers' plants.

The big suppliers had teams of college-educated engineers. Working with them was fairly simple. We'd explain that we wanted them to do TQC, and they'd say, "Understood." We'd promise to keep them supplied with useful information and then leave them to the task. As for smaller suppliers, I took personal charge of overseeing work on TQC at the ones in the Nagoya vicinity.

We established the Toyota Quality Prize to motivate the suppliers in their work on TQC. Even our dealers got involved in the effort. After all, our work depended to a large extent on getting prompt feedback from the dealers about customer complaints and on working out countermeasures through our product technology divisions. I should mention that the TQC that all our dealers in Japan tackled 15 years later was something else. That was a matter of adopting TQC in dealership management.

8. Special Training for Management Personnel

Overview

We introduced a special training program for section and division managers in 1979. The program spanned two years and covered 760 people. I coordinated the program, and every member of the board of directors participated as a supervisor. Most of our section and division managers didn't know much about TQC. The program was an effort to familiarize them with the methodology.

Approach

Each section manager and division manager registered a single item as his (Toyota didn't have any female managers yet) chief policy priority. Every six months, his boss's boss would evaluate his progress in tackling that priority (fig. 6). The managers' immediate superiors continued to evaluate their performance in regard to other policy priorities.

Evaluation Criteria

The first thing that the bosses' bosses looked at was progress in promoting collaboration with other organizational units. That cooperation is usually essential in tackling big problems. The second thing they looked at was progress in using PDCA cycles to prevent the recurrence of problems. And the third thing they looked at was progress in honing skills in persuasiveness. Those skills were especially important in promoting cooperation among organizational units.

9. Genchi Gembutsu

Statistical quality control included the principle of fact-based management. That was a matter of taking data samples and measuring the amount of discrepancy in the data. When we started doing TQC, some people reported omitting problems from the policy because they couldn't secure pertinent data. That was a serious concern, since problems were problems, regardless of data availability.

We couldn't afford to have people ignoring important problems. So I told everyone to use data samples for things where data was available and to do *genchi gembutsu* checks in the workplace when data was unavailable. Data for the rate of occurrence might not be immediately available, for example, when defects occurred, but we could learn a lot by taking a look at the situation in the workplace.

Fig. 6: Evaluation by the Bosses' Bosses

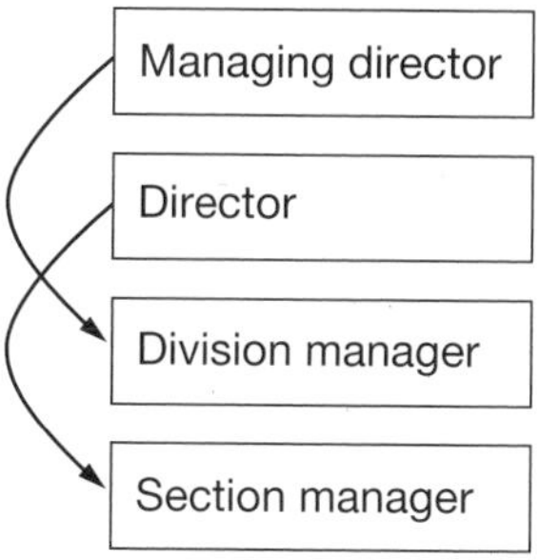

Managing director

Director

Division manager

Section manager

Genchi gembutsu became part of our TQC methodology, along with data sampling. I don't know if the term originated at Toyota, but we ended up using it a lot. The principle of *genchi gembutsu* took hold in our fact-based management, and it appears in books that came out later about TQC.

10. Synergies with the Toyota Production System

As you all know, the Toyota Production System consists of just-in-time management and *jidoka*. We use the kanban and other tools to operate the system, and the ultimate goal of the system is to lower costs or, in other words, raise productivity (fig. 7).

Ways that the Toyota Production System amplifies the benefits of TQC

Highlighting quality problems

The effectiveness of the Toyota Production System in highlighting problems has raised quality awareness dramatically. The principle of stopping the line when you notice a problem has had a huge effect on manufacturing. In the United States, only the plant manager had the authority to stop the line. And here was Toyota giving every ordinary worker the right to stop the line, just by pulling on a cord. Stopping the line let everyone know that a problem had occurred. It was a truly revolutionary innovation. The line-stop system calls attention to things like delays and mechanical malfunctions, as well as to quality defects.

Fig. 7: Schematic Diagram of the Toyota Production System

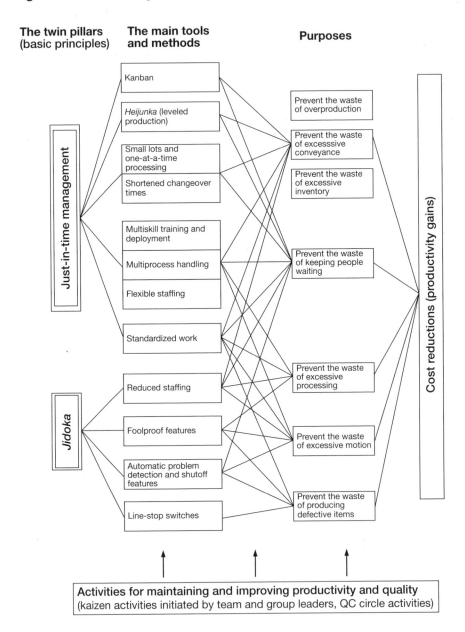

Workers tend to want to keep inventory on hand to allow for covering up problems that occur. Toyota took away the inventory buffers to expose problems immediately. Shining a light on problems in that way has been crucial to everything that we have done.

Speeding countermeasures for defects

Another benefit of the Toyota Production System for TQC was the way it speeded our response to problems. That includes moving faster and more effectively to prevent the problems from recurring.

Simplifying retroactive investigation

When we hear from a customer about a serious problem, we need to work back through the manufacturing sequence to determine what happened and why. Keeping our inventory volume small makes that easier, and it minimizes the range of parts we need to replace when problems occur.

Reducing deterioration in storage and damage in conveyance

Maintaining minimal inventory reduces the problem of rust and other kinds of deterioration. And reducing the frequency of conveyance [by arranging the processes in a single flow] helps prevent the scratching and other damage that can occur in handling.

Ways that TQC amplifies the benefits of the Toyota Production System

Reinforcing quality assurance and reducing quality defects

TQC gave us a tool for improving quality in regard to invisible things, like reliability and performance. Without TQC, Toyota could never have achieved the high level of quality that it maintains today. No amount of effort with the Toyota Production System alone could have achieved comparable results.

Fortifying policy management

All of the plant managers and division managers worked on policy management. We stepped up the monitoring of progress in fulfilling the plant managers' policies, and that helped strengthen the leadership capabilities of the section managers and division managers in regard to administering the Toyota Production System. That system was the brainchild of Taiichi Ohno.

Ohno-san first put his ideas to work in a shop for making power train components, and he later extended them to an entire manufacturing division. His system was a counterintuitive approach to managing production. It could only have taken hold in a top-down management structure.

I was lucky to be the production manager on an assembly line where I ended up working directly under Ohno-san. That gave me the chance to participate in putting his system into practice. By the time that we earned the Deming Application Prize, cost cutting had become a big part of our TQC activities. We were working hard on finding ways to reduce the amount of work required to get things done.

I was at the Motomachi Plant at that time. We had heard about what they were doing with the Toyota Production System under Ohno-san at the Honsha Plant, and we agreed that we ought to give the system a try. Our plant manager and the division managers at the plant all got behind the idea. We adopted the system as a tool for tackling our targets in connection with policy management. Our version of the system left a lot to be desired, but policy management had become the vehicle for spreading the Toyota Production System.

Strengthening the kaizen capabilities of workplace leaders

Adopting TQC and earning the Deming Application Prize contributed visibly to strengthening the kaizen capabilities and other capabilities of our group leaders and other workplace leaders.

Invigorating QC circle activities

Our QC circles also benefited greatly from adopting TQC. In 1964, we added cost cutting to the menu of themes that the QC circles could tackle. That combined a core element of the Toyota Production System with the QC circle activities. The QC circles started working on things like reducing the number of people required for work and making automation work more efficiently.

Ohno-san didn't expect the QC circles to generate much in the way of results. He concentrated on the group leaders and above and didn't expect the line workers to come up with much on their own. In fact, the QC circles contributed a lot toward putting the Toyota Production System in place throughout our operations.

Questions and Answers

Q: How did the Toyota Production System begin?

Nemoto: The history of the system begins with the principle of the supermarket [where shoppers could pick and choose freely from among different merchandise]. Eiji Toyoda and Shoichi Saito [later chairman of Toyota, went to the United States in 1950 and] studied Ford's operations for three months. They brought back the understanding that Ford's way of doing things wouldn't work in Japan [without modification]. It was simply too expensive.

For example, Ford had separate stamping lines for different body parts: fenders, roofs, hoods, and so on. That meant having several stamping lines for each model. Ford had maybe 200 or 300 lines altogether. Toyota couldn't possibly afford that kind of investment. Our challenge was to adopt the same basic principles of automobile manufacturing [that Ford was using] without spending much money.

When people who don't have much money set out to make automobiles, they've got to think of new ways of getting things done. One way was to make different items, such as fenders, roofs, and hoods, on the same stamping line. That meant finding ways to shorten the changeover time for the stamping dies, and that's what we did. And it was all because we didn't have any money.

Q: When did the Toyota Production System begin? And when did TQC get started at Toyota?

Nemoto: The Toyota Production System really got started around 1950. Of course, people had tried a couple of things before then. But that was when the system really started to take shape. We adopted TQC formally in 1961. We had quality control of a sort before that, but it was statistical quality control. So we date the history of quality control at Toyota from 1961.

Statistical quality control was something that we used for inspection and for process control during the Korean War. [That was when we were racing to keep up with surging demand for trucks from the U.S. military.] They told us to monitor our performance and prepare graphs based on statistical quality control, so that's what we did. Japan's Self-Defense Forces ordered vehicles of similar specifications after the end of the Korean War and demanded similar statistical documentation. So we had more or less continuous experience with statistical quality control, starting around 1950.

[Other companies got started with TQC before we did. But] TQC started getting a lot of attention in Japan around 1961. And that's when we adopted the methodology formally.

That brings us to the question of what Ohno-san was doing at that time. Eiji Toyoda was leading the effort to adopt TQC on a company-wide basis. And Shoichiro Toyoda (the son of Toyota founder Kiichiro

Toyoda and later a Toyota president) was also solidly behind the effort. Ohno-san was not directly involved in coordinating the TQC activities, and he simply stood by and listened quietly when TQC study sessions were under way. But that wasn't because he felt that speaking up for the Toyota Production System would interfere with our efforts to promote TQC. Ohno-san understood as well as anyone the importance of improving quality. And he was more than ready to cooperate in any measures for accomplishing that purpose.

We succeeded in earning the Deming Application Prize in 1965, and quality awareness at our company was high. The next step was to promote TQC at our suppliers. That was also a time when we were thinking of promoting the Toyota Production System at suppliers. I was the general manager of Toyota's purchasing control division, and I broached the subject with Ohno-san.

"I've done pretty much as I liked up to now," confided Ohno-san. "But the time has come to do things differently. You're in charge of purchasing control. So you do whatever you need to do to get the quality that we need. And if you ever need any guidance in regard to the Toyota Production System, just let me know."

We were in total agreement about the basic issues. I would visit our suppliers and provide guidance in regard to quality control. When we needed to provide guidance in regard to the Toyota Production System, Ohno-san would lend a hand. That's how we proceeded up to the 1970s, when the Toyota Production System had become a phenomenon. By then, people were talking about sharing the system with companies throughout Japan. Here was something that Ohno-san had built in obscurity inside the Toyota circle of companies. And suddenly, it was famous.

As for TQC, Japan might have never moved beyond statistical quality control if someone hadn't pushed for something more. That said, the need for something better had become clear by the late 1950s. We were beginning to see that simply inspecting things wasn't making our cars any better. The people in the inspection units of the quality control divisions were about the only ones who participated in statistical quality control. To come up with better cars, people in other divisions would need to get involved. People in design, in manufacturing, in divisions throughout the company would need to contribute. Senior management would need to lead the effort.

Nippondenso got started with TQC a little before we did, and it also earned the Deming Application Prize before we did. But people were still speaking in terms of statistical quality control. Nippondenso created really strong processes by promoting statistical quality control throughout the company, not just in the inspection units. The slogan there was that quality control was a job for everyone. Senior management provided leadership, and the products got better.

Q: What is the origin of the name TQC?

Nemoto: The name TQC originated in the United States [where it first appeared as the title of a chapter in Armand Feigenbaum's *Quality Control: Principles, Practice, and Administration* (New York: McGraw-Hill, 1951)]. But TQC in the United States meant something different from what we call TQC today in Japan.

Feigenbaum argued that the engineers in different sectors of an organization need to study together to achieve high quality. Some people in Japan studied his teachings, and some Japanese companies adopted American-style TQC. But that approach is inadequate to achieve its purpose at most Japanese companies.

Things won't go right at a typical Japanese company unless you get the general managers and even the president directly involved. And that's what we mean by TQC. Although they didn't use the term TQC at Nippondenso, what they were doing was extremely close to what it's about.

Policy in TQC focuses entirely on what your quality policy is in every phase of work. But we at Toyota broadened the policy aspect to encompass more elements.

Q: How did you promote cooperation between divisions?

Nemoto: One way was to reward people for being cooperative. In introducing a new compensation scheme, we broadened our criteria for employee evaluations. We included new criteria for evaluating employees' contributions to their teams and divisions with criteria for evaluating contributions that extend beyond their organizational units.

Divisions naturally tend to focus on their own interests. You need to overcome that focus to achieve effective cooperation and to secure solutions that serve the company's larger interests.

Q: How did you promote TQC at Toyota operations outside Japan?

Nemoto: Toyota's first vehicle plant in the United States [and its first large vehicle plant outside Japan] was New United Motor Manufacturing, Inc. (NUMMI). That plant is a joint venture with General Motors near San Francisco, and we launched it at an old plant that GM had closed.

Imports from Toyota and other Japanese automakers had led to the closure of some U.S. vehicle plants. Some of the people who got laid off at those plants complained that their jobs had gotten exported to Japan. So we decided to go to the United States and make some of our cars there. As long as a plant was available, that seemed like a good place to set up shop. And if some of the people who had gotten laid off there were still out of work, we might as well provide them with some jobs.

GM provided the plant. Toyota provided the production methodology. The ownership was 50:50, but Toyota was in charge of day-to-day operations. In dealing with the [United Auto Workers] labor union, we agreed to hire back people who had been laid off from the plant, but we insisted on eliminating the detailed job categories that the plant formerly had. We would have only two job categories—direct production work and preparatory work [to give us the freedom to use Toyota-style multiprocess handling]. We let it be known that only people who accepted that condition need apply. So everyone there when we started out had accepted a basic premise of Toyota manufacturing.

One thing that didn't go very well at first was the QC circles. In Japan, QC circles motivate people by giving them the chance to discuss workplace issues with their colleagues. The Japanese approach didn't sit well initially with our American employees because of the ambiguous positioning of the circle activities. "Is this part of our job," people would ask, "or not?" No one ever asked that kind of question in Japan. I should mention that deciding not to participate in QC circle activities at a Toyota plant in Japan has no bearing on an employee's wages or on his or her other benefits. On the other hand, it will affect the group leader's evaluation of that employee adversely.

Q: How does TQC differ from total productivity management?

Nemoto: Everything in TQC begins with an awareness of the customer. Our ultimate goal in TQC is to earn customer satisfaction. In contrast, total productivity management has an internal focus. It's a means of doing things like reducing defects detected in the factory and eliminating line stoppages. Total productivity management is also about customer satisfaction in the sense that it reduces costs. But it lacks the direct customer focus that is fundamental to TQC.

Q: What kinds of problems can occur with QC circles?

Nemoto: The biggest problem with QC circles is that the presentations are too showy. I can understand that people naturally want to make the most of the chance to show what they've accomplished. People are bound to get a little carried away. But I worry about the danger of conveying the wrong impression of what TQC is really all about. So I always cautioned people to focus on the essence of what we're doing, even in their presentations.

I knew that Eiji Toyoda didn't have spending money when he went to the United States to observe Ford's operations. So I was curious when he mentioned a souvenir. What I found was a thick booklet titled *Suggestion Plan.* We translated it into Japanese and changed all the places that said "Ford" to "Toyota." That became our employee suggestion system.

Ford's system resulted in a lot of suggestions that had nothing to do with the workplace where the suggestions arose. In any case, Ford gave the employees half of any savings or profit that resulted from their suggestions.

The system we put in place was the same as Ford's, but the results were completely different. Nearly all of the suggestions were for improvements in the employees' own workplaces. And we got suggestions that would have been unthinkable in the United States. For example, people would suggest ways to reduce the staffing in their workplace. In the United States, that would mean laying people off, so no one would suggest something like that there. But our employees felt secure enough about their jobs to propose ways to streamline work.

Chapter VI

The Guiding Management Perspective

Two Interviews with **Eiji Toyoda**

As recorded and edited by **Koichi Shimokawa** *and* **Takahiro Fujimoto** *with* **Nobuya Orihashi**

The 1987 Interview

Moderator: We are preparing to celebrate the 50th anniversary of the founding of our company. So we have decided to devote the New Year's edition of *Toyota Management* to the subject of Toyota's origins. Our basic idea is that huge growth lies ahead for Toyota in the 1990s and that fulfilling that potential depends on reconfirming our roots, reaffirming our

---

About the Text

This chapter presents two interviews with Eiji Toyoda, the revered former chairman of Toyota Motor Corporation. Eiji was the most influential figure in Toyota's growth and development during its first six decades in the automotive business, and he oversaw the development of the Toyota Production System from the standpoint of management.

Surprisingly little remains in the way of a written record of spoken commentary by Eiji Toyoda about his years at Toyota. Japan's business literature abounds, for example, with volumes rich in piquant quotations from Kiichiro Toyoda and from Honda founder Soichiro Honda. The few notable sources of first-person insight from Eiji include *Ketsudan* (Decision), a 1985 compilation of autobiographical articles that originally appeared in the popular "Watashi no Rirekisho" (My C.V.) feature in Japan's leading business newspaper, the *Nihon*

---

identity, and thinking anew about the kind of company that we want to be. Today, we have the opportunity to hear from Chairman Toyoda about Toyota's origins, and that is a subject of immense interest for the readers of *Toyota Management* at Toyota and at our dealers and our suppliers. This interview will be in the format of a dialogue with Professor Koichi Shimokawa, a leading expert on the automobile industry.

Shimokawa (Q): You have worked with Toyota for a half century. You have been instrumental in laying the foundation for Toyota's present prosperity, and I know it has not always been easy. Today, I want to take this opportunity to hear about your experiences at Toyota and your impressions of the company, and I also look forward to hearing about what your successors need to do to preserve the Toyota spirit and maintain the company's momentum into future generations. Toyota evinces a highly unique management culture, and I am especially eager to hear about the different facets of the philosophy that underlies that culture.

Keizai Shimbun (*Nikkei*); *Toyota: Fifty Years in Motion*, an English-language autobiography published by Kodansha International in 1987 based on *Ketsudan*; and several episodes recorded in official Toyota histories.

Eiji Toyoda on becoming president of Toyota in 1967

These interviews, therefore, offer rare and valuable perspective on the evolution of the Toyota Production System. The first one took place in January 1987. Koichi Shimokawa interviewed Eiji Toyoda at the request of the editors of the in-house, Japanese-only magazine *Toyota Manejimento* (*Toyota Management;* cited in the text as *Toyota Management* in the interest of familiarity), and the text of the

1. Troubleshooting Everything

Q: On joining Toyota, you participated immediately in setting up the Shibaura research unit in Tokyo, and you then moved to the Auditing and Improvement Department. Please describe your earliest memories of Toyota and the role of that department.

Toyoda: Joining the company back then wasn't what it is today. There was no ceremony and no formal appointment to your first job. I don't remember what my salary was at first. I joined [Toyoda Automatic Loom Works] right out of college and spent my first year in Tokyo. In May 1937, I moved to the company's headquarters, in Kariya.

Kiichiro Toyoda had set up the Auditing and Improvement Department. That was a place where you could do pretty much whatever you wanted to do, and he assigned me to that division. They had just started making cars, and there were problems and issues everywhere. My job was to

interview appeared in the January 1987 issue of that magazine. Shimokawa and Takahiro Fujimoto reproduced that text in the original, Japanese edition of this book with the permission of the editors of *Toyota Management*.

Toyoda fielded wide-ranging questions from Shimokawa, starting with his work in supervising improvements in manufacturing shortly after joining Toyota. The questions and answers also touched on the beginnings of quality control at Toyota; on the creation of an employee suggestion system; on the basic concepts that underlay technological strategy at the company; on the origins of the Toyota Production System; on the close, three-way coordination among Toyota and its parts suppliers and its vehicle dealers; on Toyota's and the automobile industry's response to the drastic tightening of emissions regulations in the early 1970s; on Toyota's decision to globalize production and the attendant concerns about the "hollowing" of the Japanese manufacturing

fix them one by one. When defects turned up in the vehicles they were making, I was supposed to figure out why the problem had occurred and which process was responsible. I was also supposed to do kaizen to prevent the defects from popping up again.

Q: Was the Auditing and Improvement Department mainly for automobile manufacturing?

Toyoda: It wasn't just for automobiles. I was responsible for inspecting and fixing things everywhere. People would come and complain to me if there was a pothole in the road out front. I even got involved in improving meals in the cafeteria. The [automobile operations were] just getting started, and we hadn't even finished putting our team together. So I got to deal with all the problems that occurred. Thanks to that experience, I became familiar with nearly all the work that the company was doing.

industry; and on Toyoda's hopes and expectations of the company. Especially valuable are Toyoda's references to insights gleaned from his three-month residency at Ford in 1950.

The second interview that appears here was by Fujimoto, who is grateful to Akira Kawahara, a former managing director at Toyota Motor Sales, for making the arrangements. It took place in May 1998. Fujimoto was eager to hear directly from Toyoda about several crucial issues from a production-system perspective. Toyoda fielded the questions off the cuff, and a discrepancy is occasionally evident between his answers and the questioner's intent. The raw text of the interview—as reproduced by Fujimoto and by Nobuya Orihashi from a tape recording—furnishes a revealing and highly personal portrait of Eiji Toyoda and of his exceedingly frank manner and practical approach. For that reason, the editors have elected to present Toyoda's comments unedited.

When I later went to Ford to study, the people there were amazed at my questions about this and that. They said there weren't five people there who were familiar with as broad a range of stuff as I was.

Q: Is the spirit of that original Auditing and Improvement Department still alive at Toyota today?

Toyoda: The basic function is still in action, though it has evolved over the years. Every company has an accounting division and an administration division. But the Auditing and Improvement Department was unique to Toyota, both in name and in concept. The basic idea was to take the initiative in finding problems that needed solving and to summon the wisdom to make the necessary improvements. That's as important today as it was then.

Here, then, is a glimpse at the thinking of a man who shepherded the development of the Toyota Production System. Here is a first-person account of how Eiji Toyoda understood what Taiichi Ohno and others were doing on the shop floor and how he supported their efforts from the standpoint of senior management.

About the Speaker

Eiji Toyoda, born in Nagoya in 1913, is a nephew of Sakichi Toyoda, the founder of the Toyota Group. He is thus a cousin of Kiichiro Toyoda, Sakichi's son and the founder of the group's automotive operations. Eiji earned a degree in mechanical engineering from what is now the University of Tokyo in 1936. On graduation, he accepted an invitation from Kiichiro to join Toyoda Automatic Loom Works (now Toyota Industries).

2. Shifting the Focus from Individuals to Teams

Q: Toyota has a long history of promoting quality control activities and encouraging employee suggestions for improvements. Does that tradition date from the beginning of the company? I know that you spent time at Ford. Did Toyota's quality control activities and suggestion system incorporate a lot of elements that you learned there?

Toyoda: [Systematic] quality control was an approach that Japan imported from the United States after the war. When I went to Ford, they were using the term quality control. I asked them to teach me what it was about, and they gave me a lecture. I might've gotten something out of it if they'd've explained stuff in the workplace while showing me actual things. But just listening to someone blabbering away in English wasn't any way for me to learn something. So quality control wasn't something that we got from Ford.

Kiichiro promptly assigned his cousin to his automotive skunk works, first at a posting in Tokyo and then at headquarters in Kariya, near what is now Toyota City. Eiji moved to Toyota Motor Co., Ltd., on its establishment in 1937 and became a director there in 1945, a managing director in 1950, a senior managing director in 1953, an executive vice president in 1960, and the president in 1967. Toyota Motor merged with its marketing counterpart, Toyota Motor Sales Co., Ltd., in 1982 to form Toyota Motor Corporation. Eiji became the chairman of the new organization, and Kiichiro's elder son, Shoichiro, became the president.

As for the suggestion system, I saw the word *Quality* written all over the place when I got to Ford. I asked what it was all about, and they explained to me that it had been an employee's suggestion. I received a pamphlet about the suggestion system, and when I got back to Japan I could see it was something we could do without spending any money, so we started our own suggestion system.

Q: I just got back from the United States the other day. Lots of companies there are using quality control activities and suggestion systems in the name of worker involvement. The U.S. approach seems to focus in the suggestion systems on recognizing individuals. At Toyota, your focus in your suggestion system and in your quality control activities seems to be more on promoting group participation.

Toyoda: Our suggestion system also started out with an emphasis on individuals. When we later introduced total quality control, we started having a lot of group activities, and suggestions started coming in from teams. We didn't go out of our way to promote team suggestions. That's just how things happened. And when people started to work on suggestions in teams, the suggestions gradually became more substantive. The slogan Good Thinking, Good Products [which appears prominently at all Toyota plants in Japan] came out of the suggestion system.

Q: Toyota earned the Deming Application Prize [for quality control management] in 1965. You were an executive vice president then. Were you counting on [the systematic effort that went into] earning the Deming Prize to foster a total quality control atmosphere at Toyota?

Toyoda: We had the conceptual beginnings of total quality control even before we went to work on the Deming Prize. But we weren't applying the concepts systematically. The ideas gradually developed on their own, and we organized them into a system. Our company had gotten big. We had a lot of new people. Simply letting them watch the veteran employees work was not enough to pass on our way of doing things. I wanted to organize stuff in a way that would keep us going.

3. Developing Things In-house

Q: Toyota learned a lot, technologically, from General Motors and from Ford, but your company has also worked hard from the beginning on creating original technology. An excellent example is the Crown, which debuted as a full-fledged passenger car in 1955. The Crown was an impressive achievement of original development. Other Japanese automakers have relied heavily on technological tie-ups with foreign automakers. Why has Toyota focused continuously on developing things in-house?

Toyoda: We at Toyota have the principle expressed by [Toyota Group founder] Sakichi Toyoda like this: "You can only master technology by working through the technology yourself." People at Toyota have always believed that technology accumulates through hands-on effort. You try things yourself. If you fail, you learn why you failed. If you succeed, you learn how you succeeded. That [learning] only happens if you do things yourself.

In the old days, someone once stole some diagrams of our automatic looms. I thought that would be a big deal, but the people in charge didn't seem very worried. I asked why they weren't more concerned, and they answered me like this:

"Competition is intense in our industry. So creating new products is just part of the story. You've got to keep refining them, or you won't survive. Someone can make a loom just like the ones we're producing today by building it in accordance with our diagrams. But fixing the problems and improving the design are all but impossible for someone who hasn't been through the trial and error of creating and evaluating the original. By the time someone makes a loom based on the stolen diagrams, we'll be making a better one, so this isn't anything to worry about."

The theft, therefore, didn't become much of a problem for our company. But it was a valuable lesson for me about the importance of doing development in-house.

Q: [Toyota was basically a truck manufacturer in the prewar years.] Did you not even consider an alliance with a foreign automaker when you started making passenger cars [after the war]?

Toyoda: Some of Japan's vehicle manufacturers were making preparations to make passenger cars, and some weren't. The [U.S. occupation authorities] prohibited the production of passenger cars in the early postwar years. For whatever reason, an opportunity arose for us at Toyota to ask about preliminary development work. They said that doing basic research and making prototypes would be all right.

So we got a little bit of a jump on the other Japanese vehicle manufacturers. That gave us the momentum to develop [passenger cars] independently while the others were rushing off to find foreign partners.

4. Breakthroughs

Q: Let's turn now to the subject of manufacturing. The consultancy Arthur D. Little recently published a book called *Breakthroughs*. That book discusses 13 commercial and industrial breakthroughs of the past 20 years. And the authors chose the Toyota Production System as one of those breakthroughs.

The Toyota Production System is now famous around the world. But I'd like to hear what you thought about Kiichiro Toyoda's just-in-time concepts and methods when the company was just starting out. I'd also like to hear about your role in developing the Toyota Production System.

Toyoda: The Toyota Production System began with Kiichiro. He really devoted himself to getting things right. He put down his ideas in writing, and they filled up this much paper (holds his hands up to show a thickness of about four inches). Kiichiro was always teaching those ideas to the section managers and to the assistant managers and the supervisors. He was calling for a switch from batch production to flow-based production, and the supervisors out on the plant floor required some convincing.

We moved [in 1938] from [the Toyoda Automatic Loom Works plant in] Kariya to the new plant [now known as the Honsha (Headquarters) Plant in what is now Toyota City]. Kiichiro laid out the plant to accommodate the new production system. That took some conviction.

With our new system, making too much of anything was against the rules, and so was making too little of anything. But it was a flexible system. If you had done everything you were supposed to do, you could go home. We put the new system into operation in autumn 1938 and used it for about two years. But Japan was shifting to a war footing, and government planners took control of the economy. That put an end to our system for the time being. We resurrected the system after the war. Then, it was Taiichi Ohno and his group that did the trial and error that went into refining the system.

Q: Later, you built the Motomachi Plant, which opened in 1959. Wasn't that a huge decision to make?

Toyoda: We had been making everything at the Honsha (Headquarters) Plant, and we needed to add capacity somehow. An incremental increase in capacity at the Honsha Plant was an option, but we decided that building a new plant was the best way to go.

Q: What was your outlook [for Japan's automobile market] at that time?

Toyoda: First of all, we figured that demand for passenger cars would take off sooner or later. Second, we figured that we'd find

Vehicle production at Toyota's Koromo Plant (now the Honsha [Headquarters] Plant) in the late 1930s

ourselves competing someday with overseas automakers. And if we were going to compete, we wanted to compete to win. So scale would be important. That weighed in favor of building a new plant. But we had no idea how many cars we could actually sell, and we were naturally worried about the danger of overinvestment. President [Taizo] Ishida had a great feel for business, and he called for us to be bold. In the end, the project turned out successful.

5. Three-Way Collaboration in Building the Toyota Organization

Q: People frequently cite the close interaction between Toyota and its suppliers and its dealers as a contributing factor to Toyota's competitiveness. That interaction appears to have been a driving force in Toyota's growth from the beginning. How did the thinking behind that interaction originate?

Toyoda: As for our relationships with suppliers, we had limited resources, so we never had the option of making everything ourselves. So our vehicles contained a combination of parts that we made ourselves and parts that we obtained from suppliers. Of course, all the parts that went into the finished vehicle needed to work right, or the vehicle wouldn't amount to anything. We needed to make sure that every part was what we wanted, and we provided guidance to our suppliers from the very beginning in regard to quality, technology, and management. When I was in the Auditing and Improvement Department, I spent a lot of time at parts makers overseeing kaizen activities.

As for dealers, Kiichiro was an engineer, and he always said that he found selling things more difficult than making things. He left the marketing to [Shotaro] Kamiya [who built Toyota's sales organization and became known as "the god of Japanese marketing"].

Kamiya had been at [the Japanese operations of] General Motors, and he knew the dealers' weaknesses from his own experience. He was determined to eliminate those shortcomings and to build a national network of Toyota dealers that conformed to his ideal. He was like a guy raising a potted plant, watering and fertilizing it carefully. That made a big impression on dealers who had been part of GM's or Ford's sales networks in Japan. They trusted Toyota and switched over to our network.

6. Coping with Emissions Regulations

Q: You coordinated cooperation in Japan's automobile industry as the chairman of the Japan Automobile Manufacturers Association (JAMA) from 1972 to 1980. That was a period when the industry faced huge issues in regard to safety and air pollution. What are your recollections of that era? What issues do you remember as being especially challenging?

Toyoda: Safety and pollution are completely separate issues. Pollution was especially difficult. People had been aware of the importance of safety ever since the invention of the automobile. But the demand for reducing emissions was a completely new challenge. It was an issue that we had never confronted before, so we didn't know what would work until we tried something.

We at Toyota were making several models. Something might work with one model. Something else might not work with another model. In a given time frame, we weren't going to succeed with everything. Some automakers had only one or two models. The ones that got things right the first time around were shouting for joy. Those that didn't were sulking quietly. That being the case, I worked hard as the JAMA chairman to help make sure that everyone got things right.

Q: You were struggling to cope at that time with the rapid growth in vehicle ownership in Japan. Reducing emissions came as a social mandate and was therefore unavoidable, but it certainly must have made things awfully difficult.

Toyoda: It was a social mandate, and the target was more arbitrary than scientific. The government essentially told us to cut emissions 90% in the interest of health. That was an extremely difficult thing to do.

In the United States, they passed the Muskie Act [formally the Clean Air Act Extension of 1970, an amendment of an act originally passed in 1963. Introduced and promoted by Senator Edmund Muskie, it established a new benchmark for air-quality regulations]. A lot of people said that helped the Japanese automakers penetrate the U.S. market. And they were right.

Our Japanese employees did a great job of coping with the emissions regulations. We ran into a lot of obstacles, and we sometimes got things

did it on our own, and the reward for that was we gained
ow.

7. The Surge in Overseas Manufacturing Projects

Q: One Japanese automaker after another is building and expanding production platforms overseas. You at Toyota have your joint venture with General Motors [New United Motor Manufacturing, Inc. (NUMMI), in California], and you have announced plans to build wholly owned vehicle plants in Kentucky and in [Ontario] Canada. What is behind the surging investment in overseas manufacturing?

Toyoda: Toyota was just about the last Japanese automaker to set up its own plant in the United States, so I don't want to overstate what we've done there so far. People have naturally been wondering what was taking us so long, but we have our own perspective on things. And from our perspective, the [other Japanese automakers] were being a little hasty. You can't rush into something like overseas manufacturing projects with insufficient preparation. Projects like that require a serious commitment.

It's still too early to give out any report cards [in regard to the Japanese automakers' new overseas projects]. We'll need to wait and see how things turn out.

NUMMI employees celebrate the completion of their first GM Nova in 1984

Q: You reinforced your U.S. presence by asserting a decisive edge over the Big 3 in productivity, quality, and cost. You saw Ford firsthand during its golden age. How did the Ford of that era differ from the Ford of today?

Toyoda: When I first visited Ford [in 1950], Americans still worked hard, even though they were rich [in comparison with Japanese]. I sensed a lot of energy in the *gemba* [production workplace]. Japanese were poor [in comparison with Americans], but they didn't work very hard. The Americans ate as much as they wanted, whereas the Japanese were going hungry [which might have figured in the different energy levels]. In any case, the rich folks were working hard, and the poor folks were slacking. "At this rate," I figured, "we'll never catch up." The Americans finally got lazy, and that gave us the chance to catch up.

Q: When you were [first] at Ford, did the people from design and development go out into the *gemba* a lot?

Toyoda: A lot of foremen who had worked under Henry Ford I were still on the job. They complained that the young guys those days just stayed in the office and didn't come out into the *gemba* [like their predecessors had]. Looking back, I guess that might've been a sign of the laziness that was beginning.

In the days of the elder Henry Ford, everyone at Ford participated in making production manuals, and they put them together to create the Ford system. Gradually, making manuals became the work of specialists, and those specialists imposed their manuals on the people in the *gemba* from a distance. At least, that's my understanding. The people who write the manuals need to go out into the *gemba* and show people what to do.

Q: Recently, Japan's autoparts manufacturers have followed the lead of the vehicle manufacturers in building plants overseas. Are you worried about a hollowing of Japanese manufacturing?

Toyoda: We see a serious hollowing [of the manufacturing industry] in the United States. But from my perspective, hollowing hasn't been a problem for the United States because that nation is [rich in natural resources and in other resources]. In Japan, industrial companies are getting by somehow despite the general lack of natural resources. Japan wouldn't survive if something happened here like what has happened in the United States.

I read the Maekawa Report [formally the first report of the Study Group on Economic Structural Adjustment for International Harmony. That group, chaired by former Bank of Japan governor Haruo Maekawa, was an advisory body set up by Japanese prime minister Yasuhiro Nakasone. The group's initial report, issued in 1986, called for reducing Japan's current account surpluses by promoting domestic demand and by integrating the nation more harmoniously into the global economy.] It talks about "reforming" Japan's industrial structure and makes everything sound easy. But any changes [in regard to Japan's industrial structure] need to take into account some basic realities.

I'm especially concerned about the way the report basically avoids the question of employment. We in Japan will need to be increasingly careful about securing enough jobs. We need to be careful to prevent the hollowing of our industry.

Q: I agree. Some hollowing is bound to occur, and employment adjustments will be a pressing issue. Training employees to handle multiple processes is a definitive feature of Toyota's approach [and that maximizes flexibility in employment. In the same sense] training employees to handle knowledge-based processes will become increasingly important.

Fortunately, Japanese managements are less inclined than their American counterparts to uproot their manufacturing and shift it overseas. I think that they will keep their [core manufacturing resources] in

Japan. So I don't think that the hollowing of Japanese industry will be as drastic as some people are suggesting.

8. Learning from Mistakes

Q: The readers of *Toyota Management* include a lot of young managers, and the future of Toyota is in their hands. What advice do you have for those readers?

Toyoda: An awful lot of people these days are always thinking up excuses for whatever goes wrong. That's no way to make any progress. I always tell people to give their all to their work and not worry about mistakes. I also tell people to write up reports about what goes wrong, though not many actually do it. If we don't write down what went wrong, and we only store the experience in memory, we won't be sharing what we learned with the next generation, and that's no good. You occasionally see someone new on the job going around telling people how to do things and leading them into the same mistakes we went through 10 years ago.

Another thing has to do with the knowledge-based processes that you mentioned a moment ago. A lot will depend in the future on how people use their time away from work. I tell our new employees every year that they'll be working about 8 hours a day and doing something else for 16 hours. How they use that 16 hours will determine their futures. So I tell them to use their free time well. People can't afford to just sit around looking at the weekly magazines.

9. The Masters of Our Destiny

Q: Let me conclude with a question about your long-term perspective. The 1990s are sure to be a time of profound change for the world automobile industry in regard to technology and competition. How will Toyota approach the years ahead as Japan's leading automaker and as an increasingly prominent global corporation. Please leave us with some forward-looking thoughts suitable to the New Year's edition [of *Toyota Management*].

Toyoda: As for the automobile, let us recall that exactly 100 years have passed since its invention. A lot of people believe that after 100 years the automobile must be nearing the end of its lifespan, but the automobile still has a lot of life remaining. Humankind will continue to use the automobile.

Owners are certain to replace about 10% of the world's cars and trucks [each year], so we definitely need to make at least that many vehicles. That ensures a basic balance [for our industry]. In addition, a lot of people out there would love to [own vehicles] but can't. When the time comes that they can afford to buy vehicles, that will mean further growth in demand.

So it's way too early to write off the automobile. But competition will escalate, and if we come out on the short end we'll end up looking like stragglers from a beaten army. We need to compete, and we need to win. But competing too aggressively would be counterproductive. We need to demonstrate a commitment to international cooperation.

As a forward-looking thought for the New Year, let me assure you that our future is in our hands. No matter how things change, we need to respond flexibly. Organizations tend to become bureaucratic when they get big. Even if we get big like the battleship *Yamato*, we still need to be able to turn hard starboard immediately if necessary. We need to make sure that our organization can turn easily. I guess we need power steering.

Moderator: We still have lots that we could ask about, but we will conclude on that note. The questions and answers have provided a wealth of valuable hints. We Toyota employees need to take those hints as guidelines as we strive to achieve further growth for the company. Thank you.

The 1998 Interview

The editors owe this interview, as noted, to the good offices of Akira Kawahara, a former managing director at Toyota Motor Sales (which merged with Toyota Motor in 1982 to form Toyota Motor Corporation). Kawahara is the author of an important history of Toyota, *Kyosoryoku no Honshitsu* [The Essence of Competitiveness] Tokyo: Diamond, Inc., 1995), published in English by Springer Publishing Company in 1998 as *The Origin of Competitive Strength*.

Eiji Toyoda talked with the interviewer, Takahiro Fujimoto, for about an hour. In the interest of conveying Toyoda's engaging persona, the editors have made only minimal changes in the text and only in the interest of improving understandability. Fujimoto's questions focused narrowly, given the limited time available, on nine subjects: (1) the employee suggestion system; (2) the *genchi gembutsu* principle of commitment to the workplace; (3) labor-management relations; (4) the relationship with Ford; (5) the construction of the Motomachi Plant and other vehicle assembly plants; (6) total quality control (TQC); (7) asserting international competitiveness; (8) the challenge of environmental protection; (9) the process of deciding when and where to invest in new production capacity.

The basic content of Toyoda's responses is consistent with earlier accounts of his words and thoughts. Some of his comments, however, offer fresh grist for the mills of students of the Toyota Production System. He cites the employee suggestion system, for instance, as the best example of a truly Toyota-like initiative in organization. Toyoda refuses credit, meanwhile, for supervising the adoption of TQC. And he characterizes—in a definitive example of his character—the construction of the Motomachi and Takaoka vehicle assembly plants as "gambles."

Alfred D. Chandler, the prominent management historian, argues in *Scale and Scope* (Cambridge, Massachusetts: Belknap Press, 1990) that the timing of investment decisions is the key to corporate growth. Toyoda personified that timing and decisiveness as the central figure in launching the Motomachi and Takaoka projects. Those projects highlighted him as a leader of special note, even in the pedigree of renowned leaders.

1. The Employee Suggestion System

Fujimoto (Q): Toyota employees and the Toyota organization are always searching for problems and are always working to identify and resolve the root causes of those problems. We rarely see that kind of effort in the same degree of thoroughness at other companies. When and how did that problem-solving culture arise at Toyota? And how has Toyota conveyed that culture to each new generation of employees?

Toyoda: Things really got started with the employee suggestion system. We solicit employee suggestions for improvements [*soikufu* (so-ee-koo-foo); literally, "innovations"]. And we've been doing that for several decades—since around 1950. That's what's produced the results that you've mentioned in your question.

Q: We read about blue-collar workers participating in the suggestion system since around 1950. But what about white-collar employees and engineers? Do they really tackle problems in the same way as the blue-collar employee? Do they really go after the root causes?

Toyoda: We don't make any distinctions among employees in encouraging people to come forward with ideas for improvements. With white-collar employees and with blue-collar employees, it's all the same. Everyone works as team members toward the same goals. Japanese seem to have a strong inherent sense of curiosity. Give them the chance to display that curiosity, and they produce the kind of results that we're talking about.

The suggestion system is something that I saw at Ford and simply copied back home at Toyota. But the results were different. I guess that a strong sense of curiosity is less common in Americans.

You start with a lot of curiosity, you put a system in place, and you let your people take it from there. Each new generation has carried on the activities. Of course, not everyone participates actively. Some people do a lot with the system, and some don't do much at all.

Q: Do you teach the spirit of innovation and improvement in your classroom training for new employees when they join the company in April and during their first two or three years on the job?

Toyoda: Our initial training is the usual stuff. As for what's "usual," well … it's just the usual stuff. In any case, people tackle the *soikufu* improvements in teams. So the team leaders provide a lot of guidance. New employees receive that guidance. Everyone does. And when people do something really well, they get cash prizes.

Q: Are the prizes usually for teams?

Toyoda: Yes, they tend to go to teams. But it doesn't really matter whether the prizes go to teams [or to individuals]. We get a lot of suggestions. Simply evaluating the suggestions is a big job. Naturally, we need to distinguish between the good ideas and the dumb ideas.

Q: Do you handle the evaluations in each division?

Toyoda: I really don't know how they're doing things these days. Anyway, we get so many suggestions that we need to start with rough sorting at the division level and then make the final selections at the company level. I'm pretty sure that's how they're still doing it. I'm not involved in the process anymore, and I haven't really heard lately.

I can tell you that we tried the system outside Japan and that it worked. Even in the United States. I was doubtful at first, but people gradually warmed to the system and made it work. It's also starting to work for us in other nations.

When you visit one of our U.S. plants, they tell you all about the suggestion system. The explanation is in English, however, so I don't get much of what I'm hearing [laughs]. At our Turkish plant, they explained the system to me in Japanese!

Q: What is the basic stance that your people bring to problem solving?

Toyoda: You need to start by deciding which problem to tackle. All sorts of problems pop up before our eyes in our daily work. Whether or not people recognize those problems as problems and go to work on solving them is a matter of instinct. When you've acquired that instinct, you begin to notice all kinds of things. You don't need to go looking for problems. You simply latch onto the problems that pop up in front of you. And since you see so many problems, you face the issue of deciding which ones to solve.

Q: And the way that people learn how to choose which problems to tackle is by watching their more-senior colleagues?

Toyoda: Exactly. They see how things work at the hands of experienced employees. In a word, that's all there is to it. At the beginning, we wrote down the rules for suggesting improvements and gave them out to everyone in pamphlets. But I don't think we have any pamphlets like that anymore. The system has taken hold [so thoroughly that everyone knows how it works].

Q: So you put things down in writing at first?

Toyoda: Yes.

Q: Was that basically a description of what you had seen at Ford in 1950?

Toyoda: I got a copy of the pamphlet that they were using at Ford, and we put that into Japanese to imitate the system at Toyota. But when I visited Ford later, they told me that they had stopped using the suggestion system, that it didn't work [laughs].

Q: But Ford was still using the suggestion system when you were there in 1950?

Toyoda: Yes, they were still using it. That was in 1950, and the young Ford [Henry Ford II] was running the show. He was enthusiastic, and I guess he was trying all kinds of new things. I suppose that the old guard saw him as a young upstart and probably wasn't very cooperative. The young Ford had become president [in 1945, after the death of his father, Edsel] and his grandfather, Henry Ford, who started the company, had died [in 1947]. Lots of guys were still on the job who had worked with the grandfather, and they weren't much inclined to listen to his grandson.

Q: So the system wasn't something that Ford had been using for a long time but was something that Henry Ford II had started recently?

Toyoda: My understanding is that it was something that the young Ford started. And it apparently didn't take hold.

Q: But it took hold in Japan.

Toyoda: [That's right.]

2. The *Genchi Gembutsu* Principle of Commitment to the Workplace

Q: Toyota's commitment to the workplace, to the *gemba*, strikes me as different from the workplace commitment at other companies. How would you characterize Toyota's focus on the *gemba?*

Toyoda: What do you mean by commitment to the *gemba?* Are you talking about *gemba gembutsu* [also *genchi gembutsu*, literally, "the actual place and the actual thing," a commitment to seeing things (*gembutsu*) firsthand as they really are in the workplace (*gemba* or *genchi*)]?

Q: A strong production workplace that has the power and the authority to get things done is a big advantage. The group leaders and team leaders on the floor in our plants make decision after decision on their own. That vitality and initiative are what I meant by *gemba* focus.

Toyoda: We're in the business of making things, so we have a production workplace, and we have the things that we make. It's only natural for us to view our work in regard to the workplace and the things we make. But we don't just talk about the *gemba* in regard to the production workplace.

Our white-collar people—everyone—focus on the actual work at hand. We'd never get anything done otherwise.

Q: Your people in the production workplace are making things, so they naturally focus on the *gembutsu*, the things that they're handling. But your white-collar people adopt the same basic stance in their work?

Toyoda: Gembutsu is simply the actual thing [whatever kind of work we happen to be doing]. The *gemba* functions in the context of factory systems and [other kinds of] organization.

Q: So you have a marketing *gemba* in your marketing operations and an R&D *gemba* in your R&D operations?

Toyoda: Yes, that's how we operate.

Q: We frequently hear about the profound trust that you inspired in people in the production workplace. How do you build that kind of trusting relationship?

Toyoda: In a word, you work hand in hand with the people in the *gemba*. That way, the people in the workplace view you as someone who comes around a lot, as someone who understands what's going on. You can't lie to someone who knows what's going on. He'd see right through you.

Q: Does that stance go all the way back to the prewar years?

Toyoda: I guess it does. Of course, people come and go, so it's not as simple as it sounds.

3. Labor-Management Relations

Q: Please tell us about the labor dispute of 1950.

Toyoda: Well, if you get rid of a bunch of people, you're going to end up with a strike on your hands.

Q: You had laid off something like 2,000 people before the strike, hadn't you? But demand picked up soon after that in connection with [vehicle orders from the U.S. military for] the Korean War. Was there a big difference in people's attitudes in the workplace before and after that sequence of events? Or was the only difference the number of people?

Toyoda: First, the number of people dropped on account of layoffs. And we operated for a while with the reduced workforce. Then, sales grew, and we started to bring on more people again. Nothing much changed, I guess, for the people who were there all along. For the young people who came aboard, we provided training.

Q: We read in Toyota's official histories and elsewhere about the strong sense of craftsmanship at your plant before the war [and about the skilled workers' jealous territoriality in regard to the processes under their care].

Negotiations to resolve the labor dispute of 1950

The number of people who view themselves as craftsmen seems to have declined.

Toyoda: I guess you could say the number declined. But that depends a lot on how you define "craftsman." At a factory, people above a certain rank are managers, and they have a sense of pride as managers. The number of people who pride themselves on craftsmanship in the sense of owning a process, such as lathing, has declined, but the number who pride themselves on their job skills as managers will not decline.

Q: By taking pride in "job skills as managers," you mean a sense of professionalism as managers?

Toyoda: That's exactly what I mean: professionalism.

Q: In the 1960s, labor and management at Toyota issued a declaration of solidarity. That declaration proclaimed a mutual commitment to building a cooperative relationship based on trust. That declaration came several years after the labor dispute, and it presumably followed a lot of determined and patient work on building a solid foundation for cooperation. At what time did you begin to feel that Toyota had succeeded in building a sound foundation for close and lasting cooperation between labor and management?

Toyoda: Our labor-management relations weren't especially bad before the dispute. We had come through the war together. Then, the fall off in demand after the war obliged us to lay off people. No matter how good your relationship is, things can get so bad that you can't keep everyone.

That said, let me note that the union was something that the workers organized after the war. It came at a time when extremism was in the air. And the union at Toyota was not exactly free of external influence.

Anyway, when people say that I adopted a cooperative stance toward the union that doesn't mean that I had been uncooperative. It simply means that we formalized our commitment to cooperative relations in the labor-management declaration. And we etched that commitment in a stone memorial on some anniversary of the declaration. That's about all there is to say. We put it all in writing on a stone monument in front of the entrance to our headquarters building. I went by there the other day, and I can assure you that the monument is still standing [laughs].

4. The Relationship with Ford

Q: You traveled to the United States for three months right after the labor dispute in 1950 and visited Ford and other companies. What was the main purpose of your U.S. trip? Did you gain anything more than you had expected? You had held talks with Ford before the war about possible collaboration. Why were you closer to Ford than to General Motors? And what were your aims in visiting Ford?

Toyoda: I was interested in setting up some kind of technical collaboration. I was thinking in terms of establishing a technical collaboration with Ford. My idea was that Ford would dispatch some engineers to work with us at Toyota. Our group from Toyota held talks with the people at Ford, and we even came up with a rough draft of an agreement. Ultimately, Ford said that it couldn't dispatch the engineers we wanted, and that killed the agreement. The people there offered to show us as much as we wanted to see in their factories, though. They said we might as well have a look, seeing as how we'd come all the way from Japan. So we ended up spending three months there.

Q: Did you have free run of the plants?

Toyoda: Pretty much. The Ford people asked me what I wanted to see, and I said, "Everything." They said that we wouldn't understand what we were seeing even if we saw everything, that only a handful of people at Ford really understood everything. I said, "That's probably true, but our plants are small, so I've got to know everything."

We ended up getting a look at this and that. But when I asked to see quality control, they sent us to a classroom where someone was giving a lecture on quality control. We spent a couple of hours there, but I didn't understand a word that was being said, so we gave up on quality control. Something similar happened when I asked to see bud-

An article by Eiji Toyoda in Toyota's employee newspaper about his experiences in the United States

get control or something like that. They sent us to a classroom where new employees were hearing a lecture. We sat through the lecture, but I didn't understand a bit of it.

Q: When you say quality control, you're talking about statistical quality control?

Toyoda: I guess so.

Q: Where they would design inspection procedures and stuff like that?

Toyoda: I suppose so. And inspection organizations. But I already knew about the inspection organizations. I didn't get anything new about that from Ford.

Q: What about things that you found that you hadn't expected, like the suggestion system?

Toyoda: The biggest thing was the training for new employees. A company like Ford, which basically grew up from a factory shed, wouldn't ordinarily teach quality control and other management subjects to new employees. But the young Henry Ford [II] insisted that Ford couldn't afford to be just a factory shed grown large. He argued that the future of Ford would depend on management. And he decided that the company would teach new employees about management, including quality control. So Ford started holding classes, and that's what we sat in on, though I didn't understand anything.

Ford really had grown up from a factory shed. People said that Henry Ford himself had written the checks to pay the bills, just like at a tiny machining shop. But they sure had a lot of people. When the young Henry Ford [II] became the president, he recognized that the company couldn't operate like that anymore. So he set about making changes. When I was there in 1950, that was right in the middle of the changes that he was making.

Q: Would you say that the changes that Henry Ford II intended didn't take hold? Or do you think that they caused problems by going too far?

Toyoda: That's a good question. I wouldn't say that they didn't take hold at all. I really couldn't say.

Q: You talked with Ford about a possible collaboration on different occasions, dating back to before the war. Why did you talk with Ford and not with General Motors?

Toyoda: I guess that's just the way things happened. We talked with Ford once before the war. At that time, we and Nissan got together to talk with Ford. At least I think that was with Ford.

Q: Yes, it was with Ford.

Toyoda: And that came to nothing. I really don't remember why it was we chose Ford at that time. The next time we talked with Ford was when I went after the war, in 1950. We'd talked with a guy from Ford, who was in Yokohama.

Q: Had Ford sent people back to Japan?

Toyoda: Yes. Someone was here. Ford had owned a plant in the Koyasu district of Yokohama, and Nissan had been using that plant. Japan lost the war, and Ford took back the plant and had some people there, I think.

Of course, our [Shotaro] Kamiya came to us from General Motors. So we could just as well have ended up talking with General Motors. But for whatever reason, we ended up talking to Ford.

That [Ford guy who was in Yokohama] went together with us to the United States. We visited GM, as well as visiting Ford. And Kamiya knew people at GM. The more I think about it, the more I wonder why we talked to Ford.

The next time we talked to Ford, it was about setting up a joint venture in Japan. That was in the late 1950s.

Q: Was that when you were thinking about joint production of the Publica?

Toyoda: That's right. Once again, the talks got fairly serious, but the people at Ford finally decided that the project wasn't all that appealing, and they walked away. I'm not sure when the next time was. I just remember that I went to Ford's headquarters for the 1950 thing and for the Publica thing.

Q: It sounds like a tie-up with Ford just wasn't in the cards. But you seem to have retained a sense of affinity for Ford throughout.

Toyoda: Yes, I guess you could say so. I just remembered when the next time was. It was before we set up [the New United Motor Manufacturing, Inc. (NUMMI), joint venture with General Motors in California in the 1980s]. Before we went ahead with NUMMI, we were talking with Ford about a similar joint venture. Ford walked away from that one, too, and we turned to GM.

Q: So GM wasn't your first choice as a partner for a U.S. joint venture.

Toyoda: We wanted to produce the Camry at the joint venture, but Ford was against that idea. I proposed to Ford that we do the Camry together in the United States. Ford turned me down because they were making a model similar to the Camry. So we teamed up with GM to make the Corolla.

Q: Had you made a decision that a joint venture was the best way to begin producing vehicles in the United States—better than building a plant on your own?

Toyoda: Here's where we were at. The [U.S. government and automobile industry] were moving to restrict vehicle imports from Japan. Their main target was finished vehicles. We needed to find a way around the growing resistance to imports of vehicles.

Some people naturally think that we should've just gone in on our own from the start. But I had a different view of things. We could do it on our own, [in which case we would surely end up] bringing all the parts and assembling them there. That's what Japan's electrical appliance manufacturers were doing back then. The U.S. government wouldn't let them bring their products. So they brought the parts and assembled things locally at screwdriver plants [a disparaging term for Japanese plants in the United States that simply assembled products from parts imported from Japan and imparted minimal value-added]. For us [to assemble cars like that] would not amount to really making them in the United States.

The whole point of all this was to achieve a local content of more than some percentage. And we'd tend to end up like a screwdriver plant if we did things on our own. The temptation to bring nearly all the parts from Japan would be irresistible. Our critics in the United States were on guard for exactly that sort of approach. And we needed to do things in a way that would avoid triggering resistance.

Our best bet for avoiding restrictions was to tie up with the biggest player on the U.S. side. So we persuaded the biggest U.S. automaker to work with us in a 50:50 joint venture. No one would care about the local content of the cars that GM sold. No one would make an issue of whether the parts came from Japan or wherever. If we achieved a high local content in the cars that we sold, we ought to be able to accomplish something with the joint venture. That's how I pitched the joint venture when we set it up. In the end, we didn't have to go as far as I thought we would to make it work.

5. The Construction of the Motomachi Plant and Other Vehicle Assembly Plants

Q: The construction of the Motomachi Plant [which began operation in 1959] was a turning point for Toyota. You have written that building the Motomachi Plant enabled Toyota to leapfrog its competitors in Japan and establish the leadership that it enjoys there today. How did you reach the decision to build the Motomachi Plant?

Toyoda: We were making all our vehicles at the plant that we now call the Honsha (Headquarters) Plant. Our production volume kept growing, and the production capacity of the Honsha Plant was becoming insufficient. So we decided to build a new plant, and that was the Motomachi Plant. We could see that demand for passenger cars would grow. So as long as we were going to build a plant, we decided that it ought to be a passenger car plant. And we would move our passenger car production from the Honsha Plant to the new plant.

Thing was, the Honsha Plant was turning out only about 3,000 vehicles a month, but the Motomachi Plant would be able to produce 10,000 a month. In other words, we were setting out to build a plant whose production capacity would be three times bigger than what we had before. If the cars didn't sell, we'd be in trouble. But in the end, things turned out well.

Q: Had you decided from the start that simply expanding the Honsha Plant would be insufficient?

Toyoda: There wasn't enough space for the necessary expansion. The place where we built the Motomachi Plant was a site we'd bought during the war to build a factory for making airplane engines. So we already had the land. Several things had happened, including the nationalization of the ownership during the war. But we got the ownership back and built [the Motomachi Plant].

Q: Did you actually produce aircraft engines?

Toyoda: The answer to that question gets complicated [laughs]. In short, we didn't make the engine that we were planning to make on the site where we built the Motomachi Plant. It became impossible. Mitsubishi relocated production from its Nagoya Plant to our site just before the Nagoya Plant got bombed. That was one thing. Then came the national-ization and other issues. So we didn't produce airplane engines there, but we produced them at another place—a nine-cylinder model.

The 1959 line-off ceremony for the first car pro-duced at the Motomachi Plant

Q: Was making aircraft engines different from making truck and passen-ger car engines?

Toyoda: No connection at all. Our experience with truck and passenger car engines was completely irrelevant. Airplane engines are completely different from automobile engines. The engine that we were preparing to make at the Motomachi site was a Mercedes-Benz inverted-V liquid-cooled engine. It came over on a submarine or something. We got hold of the engine and reverse-engineered it.

Q: So you constructed the Motomachi Plant as a new passenger car plant on [what was then] an empty field, right?

Toyoda: We built a 10,000-vehicle plant when we were only selling about 3,000 cars and trucks a year.

Q: You went on to build the Takaoka and Tsutsumi vehicle plants. Had you decided that building new plants on new sites was the best way to make large increases in production capacity?

Toyoda: It's not like we're making the same model everywhere. If you doubled or tripled your output of one model—say, the Crown—you could never sell all that output. So you increase your output of Crowns this much, and you increase your output of the Corona [and other models] this much. You don't need to do everything at the same plant. It's not necessarily even efficient. For example, distributing production among different plants helps avoid traffic jams when your people are commuting to and from work. Concentrating everything at one site would create horrible congestion. So we arranged our plants in a ring.

Q: What was your rule of thumb for deciding when to build a new plant? Did you have an upper limit in mind for production volume at each plant?

Toyoda: With our present production volume [in 1998], our basic unit of production capacity is about 20,000 vehicles a month. For example, our Kentucky plant [Toyota Motor Manufacturing Kentucky, Inc.] makes two times 20,000 a month. NUMMI turns out about 20,000 a month at full capacity. Twenty thousand seems to be some sort of natural economic unit. Whether you're talking about one model or a number of models, you're not dealing with a very large number of [20,000-vehicle] units. And you can only sell 20,000 vehicles a month with each model if you have just a few models.

Q: Conversely, is a monthly sales volume of 20,000 units—including exports—a target for you with a new model?

Toyoda: You can have a sales plan that calls for selling 20,000 a month, but you don't really know until the car hits the market whether it'll really sell that well. It isn't that easy. Our biggest gamble was when we built the

Takaoka Plant [which began operation in 1966] to produce the Corolla. We built a new plant to produce a new model. So if the model didn't sell, the plant would be useless. We're still around today because things worked out all right there.

6. Total Quality Control

Q: Please describe how you at Toyota ended up deciding to adopt TQC and how you went about introducing the system. People say that TQC and the Toyota Production System are the twin pillars of manufacturing at Toyota. Please describe how you view the interaction of the two. How do you combine the two in your training for employees?

Toyoda: I'm not in a position to answer that question. I wasn't involved [in adopting TQC]. Other people handled that work.

Q: Toyota's official history contains comments from you about TQC.

Toyoda: I guess I said, "Do it." TQC rolls off everyone's tongue easily these days, but it wasn't TQC from the beginning. It started out as just QC. It took a long time to get the T. That was something that the professors added while they were studying the system. TQC was the work of the professors. We didn't have much to do with things.

Q: Who inside Toyota pushed for the adoption of TQC?

Toyoda: That's a good question. I don't remember clearly if it was the technology guys, the inspection guys, or who.

Q: We've heard about the introduction of TQC from Masao Nemoto [Toyota's first general manager of purchasing planning, later a senior managing director (page 171)].

Toyoda: Oh, Nemoto. He came along a little later. He was a big believer in TQC, wasn't he? [Hanji] Umehara was one of the guys hollering "QC! QC!" at first.

Q: I assume that people like Taiichi Ohno and Masao Nemoto were working at times with both TQC and the Toyota Production System. And we hear that TQC and the Toyota Production System were the twin pillars of manufacturing at Toyota. How did people inside Toyota view the two? Should we regard them as two aspects of the same basic system? Or should we regard them as separate systems?

Toyoda: You can look at them either way. If you'd've asked Ohno, he'd've told you they were different systems: TQC and the Ohno System.

Q: Your TQC people also say that they're two different systems.

Toyoda: So people think of the two as separate systems. I see no special reason to think of them as one system. In short, QC is about quality issues, and [the Toyota Production System] is about management issues.

Q: From an external perspective, they appear to have taken hold at Toyota in different ways: TQC was transplanted into the company all at once from outside sources, and the Toyota Production System was developed internally by Taiichi Ohno.

Toyoda: Ohno did a good job. He did a good job, and the things he started are still going on. They are moving right along without losing any steam. They've also spread more widely than anyone would have expected. I'll go to someone's plant where I've never been before, and everyone's saying, "Ohno! Ohno!" I'll ask what they're talking about, and I learn that they're talking about Taiichi Ohno. The people there explain that they're running Ohno lines.

Q: You're talking about overseas plants?

Toyoda: Yes, exactly. I went to Detroit Diesel, where they make diesel engines. They asked me to come see the plant, so I went. Everyone there was bragging about doing the "Ohno System." They don't even know that I outranked Ohno.

Anyway, it really has spread all over the world. At least the name has spread all over the place. Whether or not people are really using the system properly is something else again. They insisted that I come take a look, so I did. But I didn't see enough to know how well they're really doing.

Q: The QC circles and related activities in TQC would seem to have a lot in common with the suggestion system that we discussed earlier. Did the two approaches merge naturally? Or would we better think of them as completely separate?

Toyoda: QC is essentially a top-down approach. The [suggestion system] is a bottom-up thing. The suggestion system is a matter of people getting together on their own and thinking of better ways to do things, so it's essentially a bottom-up approach. QC is something the Americans came up with during the war to get more production out of people. But when it became TQC, it was no longer an American thing. It had become a Japanese thing.

Q: And when TQC came to Toyota, you already had the suggestion system, so TQC became a Toyota thing, right?

Toyoda: That's part of what happened.

Q: TQC originated in capital goods industries well removed from automobile manufacturing, didn't it? And when it reached Toyota, it underwent further change, right?

Toyoda: I guess so. But you'd really need to talk with the QC experts to get a proper answer to that question.

7. Asserting International Competitiveness

Q: Around 1950, you were still learning from Ford. By the time you set up NUMMI in the 1980s, a role reversal had occurred, and you had become the teacher to a U.S. automaker [General Motors]. You presumably began to sense at some point that you had overtaken Ford, GM, and the other U.S. automakers in overall international competitiveness. But I don't think that the U.S. automakers noticed until well into the 1980s. When did you become convinced that you had established a clear advantage over the U.S. automakers?

Toyoda: It must have been at the beginning of the 1980s. After all, they had decided that they couldn't compete with our cars and had started restricting imports under the name of voluntary restraints. That's a pretty good indication that we had gained the upper hand.

Q: That was after they really began to feel threatened. But didn't you begin to see hints sometime earlier?

Toyoda: Americans resort to stuff like that a long time before they think the threat is really serious. They start with claims of dumping. They try to block you on the grounds of dumping, no matter what you're bringing in. Dumping is an excuse to call for high tariffs or for import restrictions. In our case, we managed to avoid that kind of trouble for the most part [laughs].

Then came the so-called voluntary restraints. Adopting voluntary restraints is a pretty clear sign of problems on the other side. We still had doubts about whether we had really built such a big competitive edge. But they seemed to be convinced that we had [laughs].

8. The Challenge of Environmental Protection

Q: Automakers face a lot of future technological challenges in addressing environmental issues and other issues. The automobile itself is bound to change in the years ahead. What are your greatest expectations of Toyota in that regard as we approach the 21st century? And what do the people at Toyota need to be most careful about?

Toyoda: To tell you the truth, I don't think much about those things. Even if I did, I don't have any answers for anyone [laughs]. Seriously, it really is impossible to tell right now how [cars] will change in regard to any single environmental issue. I'm trying to recall when it was that we first encountered environmental issues as a major challenge in our business, when it was that people started howling about emissions.

Q: Wouldn't that have been around the mid-1970s?

Toyoda: That was the first time we had encountered a problem like that. None of us had thought that something like that would ever be a big issue for our industry. Suddenly, people were talking about regulations. The regulations got tougher and tougher, and you hear that the exhaust from cars is now cleaner than the air outside. It's like we're manufacturing air filters [laughs].

You really have to wonder how things will turn out. People say that the increase in carbon dioxide is a concern, and so they held the conference in Kyoto [in December 1997: the 3rd Conference of the Parties to the United Nations Framework Convention on Climate Change. The participants adopted the so-called Kyoto Protocol]. But the first question is whether or not an increase in CO_2 really causes a rise in temperature. We don't really know.

Nor do we really know whether [the atmospheric concentration of] CO_2 is actually increasing. We don't know either if a rise in temperature is really a bad thing. You can't go to work on something on the basis of a bunch of stuff that you're not sure about.

Turning back the clock is no answer. Turning back the clock would mean giving up cars and getting around in horse-drawn cars. That would be the simplest solution. But people don't want to do that.

So we start with the problem that the population won't go back to the size it used to be. So we use more and more energy. So it might be only natural for temperatures to rise, regardless of what's happening with CO_2. Even in the U.S. Congress, some members don't think that [ratifying the Kyoto Protocol] is necessary. And the U.S. manufacturers are putting all the pressure they can on Congress [to reject the protocol].

In any case, the Japanese automakers gained the upper hand through the fury over cleaning up emissions and through the oil crisis [of 1973].

And the U.S. automakers ended up the losers. So Japan came out on top, but it wasn't like we won on the basis of an edge in fundamental competitiveness. Concerns about the environment worked to our advantage.

Q: Looking ahead, do you think that power-train technologies besides the gasoline engine will become common in the 21st century? My understanding is that Toyota and Mercedes-Benz lead the industry in alternative-energy technologies.

Toyoda: I don't really know. People say that fuel cells are the most promising technology right now in regard to protecting the environment. But fuel cells are still a long way from becoming practical. The U.S. government is subsidizing research on fuel cells. Chrysler's getting a lot of that support, and that raises the question of what happens after Chrysler gets together with Daimler-Benz [through the two companies' 1998 merger (dissolved in 2007)].

The subsidized research in the United States is just for the Big 3. They won't let us take part. They say that foreign automakers aren't eligible. But a Chrysler owned by Daimler-Benz is a foreign company, isn't it? I look at the newspaper, and I read that Chrysler says that it will still take part. The whole stingy unfairness of the United States begins with that kind of limiting participation [in joint initiatives] to U.S. companies.

Q: Things don't seem to be going very well with the U.S. supercar project [a partnership between the government and the Big 3. Then vice president Al Gore said the partnership was for developing a car that would travel "80 miles on a gallon of gasoline with no loss in performance, safety, or carrying capacity."] You and Mercedes-Benz appear to have grabbed something of a lead in fuel cells. We don't hear much of anything coming out of the U.S. industry in the way of exciting breakthroughs.

Toyoda: Nobody's come up with that kind of breakthrough yet.

Q: The United States enacted the Muskie Act. But I can't think of any example of the U.S. automakers pioneering an important new technology for environmental quality.

Toyoda: I don't think they have. Senator Muskie came to me and asked me to declare that we could meet the requirements of the Muskie Act. I told him that saying something like that wouldn't change what was [technologically] possible. He asked me to testify at a Senate hearing. I noted that I was Japanese and said that I hated the idea of appearing at a hearing like that. That persuaded him, I guess, and he let me off the hook [laughs].

The U.S. automakers fought the act down to the last minute, and I think they won some concessions. In any case, it was the Japanese automakers that complied with the new regulations first. One reason for that was the generally smaller body size of our cars. That made things easier for us. The American cars were bigger, which complicated the task for the U.S. automakers. It's only natural that we were able to comply with the new regulations faster. We were starting with lower emission levels.

9. The Process of Deciding When and Where to Invest

Q: You've been directly involved in managing Toyota since the company's beginning. What was your most difficult decision?

Toyoda: I don't remember any [decisions] as being especially difficult. On the other hand, maybe they were all difficult [laughs].

Akira Kawahara: I remember hearing from you that you agonized over the decision to build the Takaoka Plant. Toyota had begun production of the

Publica, and sales were still only about 7,000 vehicles a month. Takaoka was to produce 30,000 Corollas a month, and Toyota built it while the Corolla was still in the design stage. That was a huge gamble.

The Takaoka Plant in 1966

Toyoda: It was a leap of faith. We can brag about it now because things worked out well. If things hadn't worked out, that would've been the end of Toyota.

Kawahara: It was a historic decision. That's when Toyota pulled away from Nissan.

Toyoda: It was an incredible gamble.

Q: You took a calculated risk in building the Motomachi Plant, and then you took a similar risk in building the Takaoka Plant. And you were successful both times.

Toyoda: [Plant-construction projects] are gambles. You think through everything before you make your decision, but you forget all that after things work out all right. That's why I say I don't remember any tough decisions. If they'd've turned out badly, I'd remember.

Q: Thank you. You have provided us with some extremely valuable insights and information.

Afterword

Adapted from the Afterword to the Japanese Edition
Takahiro Fujimoto

Inspiring this volume has been the editors' interest in (1) highlighting a definitive Japanese contribution to the world and (2) examining the characteristically Japanese creativity that gave rise to that contribution. Japanese assembly manufacturing—epitomized by the Toyota Production System—pointed the way to historic gains in productivity and quality worldwide in the latter half of the 20th century. Numerous books have described in detail the strengths of Japanese manufacturing from the standpoint of managing people, systems, and processes. Little has appeared in print, however, about the creative and evolutionary capabilities that enabled Japanese to bring forth new and valuable systems of manufacturing.

Toyota manufacturing, like Ford manufacturing, evolved in the manner of a river that gains momentum through the repeated confluence of tributary streams. Taiichi Ohno was unquestionably the central current, but several other currents also figured prominently. And no single individual was ever in overall or total control of the complexity of riverine dynamics that became Toyota manufacturing.

We should also note that excellent manufacturing systems took shape at other Japanese automakers. Honda, for instance, is famous for innovative product development, but it also boasts a production system fully comparable to Toyota's in quality and efficiency, and Honda's production system differs from Toyota's in important respects. Nissan, Mitsubishi, and Mazda, along with several leading manufacturers of automotive parts, also built excellent and original production systems. The editors of this

263

volume have verified the impressive performance of all of those manufacturers' production systems through field surveys. Any one of those systems would reward the prospective researcher with fascinating and valuable discoveries.

Having noted the excellent production systems at other Japanese companies, let us acknowledge Toyota's preeminence. Toyota has conspicuously outperformed its rivals in continuously strengthening its competitiveness. That capacity for amassing competitiveness is Toyota's core competence, and it warrants careful, continuing study. Two books by the present writer that address that subject are *Competing to Be Really, Really Good* (Tokyo: I-House Press, 2007) and *The Evolution of a Manufacturing System at Toyota* (New York: Oxford University Press, 1999).

This volume complements the excellent descriptions and analyses of Toyota manufacturing by such authors as Eiji Ogawa, Hiroaki Satake, and Shigeo Shingo, not to mention Taiichi Ohno himself and Toyota's official histories. Those other accounts present Toyota manufacturing in a systematic context and thus gloss over the trial and error, the personal tribulations, and the diversity of inputs that shaped the Toyota Production System and Toyota's version of total quality control (TQC). The editors of this volume have addressed that omission by gathering personal recollections of the early days of automobile manufacturing at Toyota. These descriptions are by six pivotal figures in the history of Toyota manufacturing.

Chapter 1 presents an interview conducted with Taiichi Ohno in 1984. That was before the editors had any notion of producing the present volume, and they did not tape-record the interview. The resultant text, based entirely on handwritten notes, is therefore less complete than the other texts. It succeeds nonetheless in bringing the man to life in an ever-so human dimension. The interview took place on a sunny afternoon, and Ohno was in fine spirits. He spent about three hours with the interviewers, recounting early episodes in the creation of the Toyota Production System.

First-person accounts by Ohno of the origins of the Toyota Production System are available in several books, so the interview was largely a matter of clarifying details of those accounts. Ohno's recollections of the prewar benchmarking at Toyoda Boshoku (Toyoda Spinning and Weaving) afford fresh perspective, however, on his later exploits in Toyota's automotive operations.

The subsequent chapters surely rectify the common misconception of the progenitors of the Toyota Production System as automatons subservient to Taiichi Ohno. Each individual who appears in this volume evinces a forceful personality and a singularly personal sense of purpose.

Michikazu Tanaka, of Daihatsu Motor, reveals highly personal glimpses of himself in offering invaluable insight into the human side of Ohno. He helps us see beyond the caricature of Ohno as an impersonal strategist and presents his mentor as a sometimes terrifying but ultimately appealing figure. Based outside Toyota, Tanaka had nothing to gain in the way of career advancement or factional politics through serving Ohno. He is therefore a supremely objective commentator, and that very objectivity reinforces his message of admiration for the father of the Toyota Production System. Tanaka's commentary reminds us that Ohno's ever-so human appeal was an indispensable factor in propagating the Toyota Production System.

Kikuo Suzumura, more than any other person, led the practical application of Ohno's ideas in the workplace. The record of Suzumura's talks presented in this volume is the work of Hiroaki Satake and Takashi Matsuo, both of Fukui Prefectural University. They were acquainted with Suzumura through their participation in the New Production System seminars, in which he also took part. The story they convey is a rare, first-person account of overcoming indifference and even resistance in implementing the Toyota Production System in the workplace. Suzumura's colorful metaphors, such as the Tokaido Line, lend an especially personal touch to his descriptions.

Suzumura describes graphically how empty parts containers of known capacity became production instructions in Toyota's kanban-based pull system. He highlights the importance of delivering parts to the assembly line in synchrony with the order of product assembly. Suzumura is notably determined in describing how he synchronized the delivery of parts with the order of product assembly and how he coped with the ever-changing order of processing in the paint shop. The synchronous delivery described by Suzumura is the aspect of just-in-time management that proved most difficult to emulate outside Japan, so his insights are pertinent and timely as companies worldwide move to adopt elements of the Toyota Production System.

Kaneyoshi Kusunoki came out of Toyota's production engineering operations. His system-oriented, conceptual approach was something of a contrast with the trial-and-error, get-your-hands-dirty practicality of Suzumura. As described in the text, the editors interviewed him while he was serving as chairman of Hino Motors and, for the reasons cited, confined their questions narrowly to the subjects of body flow and buffer-inventory management.

Kusunoki responded in the manner of a mathematician solving simultaneous equations. He astounded the interviewers with a step-by-step historical account, utterly logical and thoroughly precise. He definitely ranks among the theoreticians of the Toyota Production System. Kusunoki was a leading force in formalizing the system and, with present Toyota chairman Fujio Cho and others, in articulating it for audiences beyond Japan.

The talk by Masao Nemoto, who led the initial adoption of TQC at Toyota, lends additional depth to the narrative. TQC was and is, as we have seen, an indispensable counterpart to the Toyota Production System.

It was possibly even more influential than the latter in shaping the corporate culture that we identify with Toyota. Of special note here is that TQC and the Toyota Production System did not meld into a single, integrated system but, rather, remained distinct, albeit complementary, entities. Nemoto was a convincing theorist who, appropriately enough, became a university professor after retiring from Toyota.

Rounding out the talks and interviews are two conversations with Eiji Toyoda. The Toyota Production System and Toyota's TQC were born of a rollicking interplay among charismatic figures, represented by the first five speakers in this series. That interplay took place under Toyoda's watchful eye and skillful guidance. Acknowledgments of his role in steering the development of manufacturing at Toyota appear throughout the remarks of the different speakers, including Ohno.

Toyoda rarely spoke out publicly about corporate or other matters [and that has resulted in underappreciation, outside the company, of his role in fostering Toyota-style manufacturing]. That role should be of great interest to anyone interested in Toyota or, for that matter, in modern manufacturing.

For more than half a century, Toyoda participated in every important decision that shaped his company's course. He was the central decision maker, for example, behind Toyota's bold and prescient investment in building the Motomachi Plant. That plant, as noted in the text, was Japan's first factory built expressly to mass-produce passenger cars. All too rare, however, have been the opportunities to hear directly from the man about his thoughts on management. The two interviews contained in this volume are therefore of tremendous value for contemporary students of Toyota and for posterity.

About the Editors and the Translators

The Editors

Koichi Shimokawa is a leading authority on the automobile industry. He is a professor in the Faculty of Business Administration at Tokai Gakuen University and a professor emeritus at Hosei University. Shimokawa was a member of Hosei University's Faculty of Business Administration from 1969 to 1999, and he previously taught at the University of Toyama. He holds a doctorate in economics from Kyushu University and studied at the Harvard Business School for two years in the late 1970s.

Shimokawa's research on the automobile industry centers on supply-chain management in a global context, on e-business models, on cross-border alliances and mergers, and on issues and opportunities in emerging markets. Shimokawa has authored and coauthored numerous books, including *Ushinawareta Junen* [Japan's Lost Decade] (Tokyo: Chuko Shinsho, 2006); *Joho Kakumei to Jidosha Ryutsu Inobeshon* [The Information Revolution and Innovation in Automobile Distribution] (Tokyo: Bunshindo, 2000), with Takao Iwasawa; *The Japanese Automobile Industry: A Business History* (London: Athlone Press, 1994); and *Transforming Automobile Assembly* (Berlin: Springer-Verlag, 1997), with Takahiro Fujimoto and Ulrich Juergens.

Takahiro Fujimoto has been a professor in the University of Tokyo's Graduate School of Economics since 1998 and has headed the university's Manufacturing Management Research Center since 2003. A 1979 graduate of the University of Tokyo, Fujimoto earned a doctorate in economics from the Harvard Business School in 1989 and subsequently worked at Harvard as a researcher, as a visiting professor (1996–97), and as a senior research associate (1997). He has served as a visiting professor at the University of Lyon and as a visiting researcher at INSEAD.

Fujimoto's research centers on technology and operations management and on business administration. Among the books by Fujimoto are *Product Development Performance: Strategy, Organization, and Management in the World Auto Industry* (Boston: Harvard Business School Press, 1991), with Kim Clark; *The Evolution of a Manufacturing System at Toyota* (New York: Oxford University Press, 1999); and *Competing to Be Really, Really Good* (Tokyo: I-House Press, 2007).

The Translators

Brian Miller works as a writer and translator in Japan, where he has lived for 30 years. He has handled the Japanese-to-English translation of several books, including Takahiro Fujimoto's *Competing to Be Really, Really Good*. Brian is translating selections from the Buddhist monk Eihei Dogen's *Shobogenzo* [Insight] and is writing a biography of the Bizen potter Anjin Abe.

John Shook worked for Toyota for 11 years, starting in 1983, and became the first non-Asian to work his way up through the company's ranks to a management position in Japan. His work at Toyota included creating training materials for the company's first vehicle-manufacturing operation in North America. John has authored the lean classic *Learning to See* (Cambridge: Lean Enterprise Institute, 1999), with Mike Rother; *Managing to Learn* (Cambridge: Lean Enterprise Institute, 2008); and *Kaizen Express* (Cambridge: Lean Enterprise Institute, 2009), with Toshiko Narusawa.

Index

Page numbers in italics refer to figures and tables.

a Manufacturing System at Toyota,
264

G

gemba (workplace) , xvi, 231, 240,
241; preparation integrated into, 97.
See also workplace
gemba gembutsu (*genchi gembutsu*),
26, 36–37, 59–60, 204–205;
as fundamental to Ohno, 37;
development people and, 67; spirit
of, 40
gembutsu, as actual thing, 241
General Motors, 13, 224, 228, 244,
246, 247, 256; joint venture with,
146, 213, 230, 248; local content
and, 249
GM. *See* General Motors
goals, perceptions of, 63
Gore, Al, 259
grinding process, 89; withdrawal
kanban and, 90
group leaders: kaizen activities and,
83, 198–199, 200; standardized
work and, 78

H

handcarts, 123
hangers, 95, 106; kanban on, 93
heat treatment, 87, 88, 89, 90, 92
Hino Motors, 133, 141, 266
histograms, 197, *198*
Honda, 59, 62, 217
Honda production system, 263
Honda, Soichiro, 59, 61, 62, 217
Honsha Plant, 5, 6, 17, 98, 101, 103,
208, 226, 227, 250; kanban and,
122; vehicle assembly and frame
lines at, 98–99
human resources, xiii, 12, 61, 62

I

Ikebuchi, Kosuke, 140
import restrictions, 248, 256, 257;
joint venture and, 249
information, 68, 84, 99, 103
in-house development, 224–225
in-process stock, 64; kaizen and, 57
innovations. *See soikufu*
installation, order of, 101
intelligent automation, 51–52
intercoms, 102
interdivisional cooperation, 188–189
International Motor Vehicle program,
xv
Interwriter, 99, 100, 101, 106
inventory, 18; accumulation and
excess of, 7, 97, 185; as buffer, 129;
just-in-time manufacturing and,
xiv; minimizing, 134; no system
for, 147; Ohno's four-day limit for,
147–148; rule of thumb for, 149;
taking of, 104–105; traditional
manufacturing and, xiv; wary of,
145
"iron computer," 109
Ishida, Taizo, 227

J

JAMA, 228, 229
Japan Automobile Manufacturers
Association (JAMA). *See* JAMA
Japan Industrial Management
Association, 141, 142
Japan National Railways, 102
Japan Quality Medal, 179
Japan Society of Business
Administration, 197
Japan Technology Transfer
Association, 21, 171
jidoka, 3, 4, 19–20, *127*, 205;
definitions of, 51
joint venture, U.S. production and,
248

Y